Networking Home PCs For Dummies®

Networking Jargon at a Glance

Tear out this handy list of frequently used networking terms and stick it to a wall, the dog, or anything else that doesn't move much. If you encounter terms that don't appear in this brief list (or if you're just looking for something to do until dinner's ready), turn to the Glossary at the back of this book.

10BaseT cable: Network cable that looks like telephone wire. Also called *twisted pair cable.*

Administrator: The person in charge of maintaining the network.

Backup: A copy of the files on your computer that can be used to restore data in case your computer meets with disaster.

BNC: A connector used with coaxial cable.

Bus: Frequently used as a synonym for a slot, it's actually the data transmission path from a slot.

Client: A computer that uses hardware and services on another computer (called the *server*).

Client/server network: A network model in which one computer (the *server*) provides services for the other computers (the *clients*).

Coaxial cable: Network cable that looks like cable television cable. Also called *10Base2 cable.*

Concentrator: The home base of a 10BaseT network to which all lengths of cable from the network computers are attached. Also called a *hub.*

Dial-Up Networking: A feature in Windows 98 and Windows 95 that enables your modem to connect to the Internet through an Internet Service Provider.

Drivers: Software that enables your operating system to communicate with hardware.

IP Address: A number that identifies a computer's location on the Internet.

IRQ (Interrupt Request): A communication channel assigned to a device so that it can communicate with the PC's processor.

ISP (Internet Service Provider): A company that provides Internet access to individuals and businesses.

Kbps: Thousands of bits per second (kilobits per second). A measurement of speed for data transmission through a modem.

LAN (Local Area Network): Multiple computers connected by cable.

NetBIOS (Network Basic Input/Output System): A program that permits applications on different computers to communicate within a network.

Network: Two or more computers connected to one another using network interface cards, cable, and networking software to communicate and exchange data.

NIC (Network Interface Card): A hardware device that enables networking by providing the features necessary for cable (or wireless) communication.

Peer-to-peer network: A network model in which each computer has the same capabilities and each computer can communicate with all the other computers.

Protocol: A set of rules (some people define it as a language) that computers use to communicate.

Proxy server: A server that acts as an intermediary between a workstation and the Internet. It provides security as well as efficient retrieval of Internet data.

RJ-45: The connector at the end of 10BaseT cable. Looks like the connector at the end of telephone cable.

Server: A computer that provides services for other computers (called *workstations* or *clients*) on a network. Also called a *host.*

Shared resources: Resources such as files, folders, printers, and other peripherals attached to a network computer that are configured for access by users on other network computers.

TCP/IP (Transmission Control Protocol/Internet Protocol): The basic communication language (protocol) of the Internet. It also can be used as a protocol for networks.

Workstation: A network computer that uses the resources of one or more servers. Also called a *client.*

...For Dummies: Bestselling Book Series for Beginners

Networking Home PCs For Dummies®

Cheat Sheet

Stuff I Need to Know About My Network Computers

If you have to replace a hard drive or a computer, it's easier to rebuild your network settings if you don't have to start from scratch (you probably won't be able to find the original documentation easily). To find this information, double-click the Network icon in the Control Panel. Then select each item and click Properties to see that item's settings.

Computer 1

Computer name: _____

NIC brand: _____

NIC IRQ: _____

NIC I/O address: _____

Network components installed: _____

_____

Computer 2

Computer name: _____

NIC brand: _____

NIC IRQ: _____

NIC I/O address: _____

Network components installed: _____

_____

Computer 3

Computer name: _____

NIC brand: _____

NIC IRQ: _____

NIC I/O address: _____

Network components installed: _____

_____

Stuff I Need to Know about My Network Printers

Printer 1

Printer manufacturer and model: _____

Ink or toner cartridge part number: _____

Attached to Computer #: _____

Shared as (share name): _____

_____

Printer 2

Printer manufacturer and model: _____

Ink or toner cartridge part number: _____

Attached to Computer #: _____

Shared as (share name): _____

_____

...For Dummies: Bestselling Book Series for Beginners

NETWORKING HOME PCs
FOR
DUMMIES®

NETWORKING HOME PCs FOR DUMMIES®

by Kathy Ivens

IDG Books Worldwide, Inc.
An International Data Group Company

Foster City, CA ♦ Chicago, IL ♦ Indianapolis, IN ♦ New York, NY

Networking Home PCs For Dummies®

Published by
IDG Books Worldwide, Inc.
An International Data Group Company
919 E. Hillsdale Blvd.
Suite 400
Foster City, CA 94404
www.idgbooks.com (IDG Books Worldwide Web site)
www.dummies.com (Dummies Press Web site)

Library of Congress Catalog Card No.: 98-89668

ISBN: 0-7645-0491-6

Printed in the United States of America

10 9 8 7 6 5 4 3 2 1

1B/RX/RS/ZY/IN

Distributed in the United States by IDG Books Worldwide, Inc.

Distributed by Macmillan Canada for Canada; by Transworld Publishers Limited in the United Kingdom; by IDG Norge Books for Norway; by IDG Sweden Books for Sweden; by Woodslane Pty. Ltd. for Australia; by Woodslane (NZ) Ltd. for New Zealand; by Addison Wesley Longman Singapore Pte Ltd. for Singapore, Malaysia, Thailand, and Indonesia; by Norma Comunicaciones S.A. for Colombia; by Intersoft for South Africa; by International Thomson Publishing for Germany, Austria and Switzerland; by Distribuidora Cuspide for Argentina; by Livraria Cultura for Brazil; by Ediciencia S.A. for Ecuador; by Ediciones ZETA S.C.R. Ltda. for Peru; by WS Computer Publishing Corporation, Inc., for the Philippines; by Contemporanea de Ediciones for Venezuela; by Express Computer Distributors for the Caribbean and West Indies; by Micronesia Media Distributor, Inc. for Micronesia; by Grupo Editorial Norma S.A. for Guatemala; by Chips Computadoras S.A. de C.V. for Mexico; by Editorial Norma de Panama S.A. for Panama; by Wouters Import for Belgium; by American Bookshops for Finland. Authorized Sales Agent: Anthony Rudkin Associates for the Middle East and North Africa.

For general information on IDG Books Worldwide's books in the U.S., please call our Consumer Customer Service department at 800-762-2974. For reseller information, including discounts and premium sales, please call our Reseller Customer Service department at 800-434-3422.

For information on where to purchase IDG Books Worldwide's books outside the U.S., please contact our International Sales department at 317-596-5530 or fax 317-596-5692.

For information on foreign language translations, please contact our Foreign & Subsidiary Rights department at 650-655-3021 or fax 650-655-3281.

For sales inquiries and special prices for bulk quantities, please contact our Sales department at 650-655-3200 or write to the address above.

For information on using IDG Books Worldwide's books in the classroom or for ordering examination copies, please contact our Educational Sales department at 800-434-2086 or fax 317-596-5499.

For press review copies, author interviews, or other publicity information, please contact our Public Relations department at 650-655-3000 or fax 650-655-3299.

For authorization to photocopy items for corporate, personal, or educational use, please contact Copyright Clearance Center, 222 Rosewood Drive, Danvers, MA 01923, or fax 978-750-4470.

 is a trademark under exclusive license to IDG Books Worldwide, Inc., from International Data Group, Inc.

About the Author

Kathy Ivens has written more than three dozen books about computers and has spent lots of years installing networks. Now a columnist for *Windows NT Magazine*, she had a variety of interesting careers — as well as a variety of boring careers — before becoming a computer nerd. She's still trying to decide what she wants to be when she grows up. She has three perfect daughters and one perfect granddaughter.

ABOUT IDG BOOKS WORLDWIDE

Welcome to the world of IDG Books Worldwide.

IDG Books Worldwide, Inc., is a subsidiary of International Data Group, the world's largest publisher of computer-related information and the leading global provider of information services on information technology. IDG was founded more than 30 years ago by Patrick J. McGovern and now employs more than 9,000 people worldwide. IDG publishes more than 290 computer publications in over 75 countries. More than 90 million people read one or more IDG publications each month.

Launched in 1990, IDG Books Worldwide is today the #1 publisher of best-selling computer books in the United States. We are proud to have received eight awards from the Computer Press Association in recognition of editorial excellence and three from Computer Currents' First Annual Readers' Choice Awards. Our best-selling ...For Dummies® series has more than 50 million copies in print with translations in 31 languages. IDG Books Worldwide, through a joint venture with IDG's Hi-Tech Beijing, became the first U.S. publisher to publish a computer book in the People's Republic of China. In record time, IDG Books Worldwide has become the first choice for millions of readers around the world who want to learn how to better manage their businesses.

Our mission is simple: Every one of our books is designed to bring extra value and skill-building instructions to the reader. Our books are written by experts who understand and care about our readers. The knowledge base of our editorial staff comes from years of experience in publishing, education, and journalism — experience we use to produce books to carry us into the new millennium. In short, we care about books, so we attract the best people. We devote special attention to details such as audience, interior design, use of icons, and illustrations. And because we use an efficient process of authoring, editing, and desktop publishing our books electronically, we can spend more time ensuring superior content and less time on the technicalities of making books.

You can count on our commitment to deliver high-quality books at competitive prices on topics you want to read about. At IDG Books Worldwide, we continue in the IDG tradition of delivering quality for more than 30 years. You'll find no better book on a subject than one from IDG Books Worldwide.

John J. Kilcullen
John Kilcullen
Chairman and CEO
IDG Books Worldwide, Inc.

Steven Berkowitz
Steven Berkowitz
President and Publisher
IDG Books Worldwide, Inc.

IDG is the world's leading IT media, research and exposition company. Founded, in 1964, IDG had 1997 revenues of $2.05 billion and has more than 9,000 employees worldwide. IDG offers the widest range of media options that reach IT buyers in 75 countries representing 95% of worldwide IT spending. IDG's diverse product and services portfolio spans six key areas including print publishing, online publishing, expositions and conferences, market research, education and training, and global marketing services. More than 90 million people read one or more of IDG's 290 magazines and newspapers, including IDG's leading global brands — Computerworld, PC World, Network World, Macworld and the Channel World family of publications. IDG Books Worldwide is one of the fastest-growing computer book publishers in the world, with more than 700 titles in 36 languages. The "...For Dummies®" series alone has more than 50 million copies in print. IDG offers online users the largest network of technology-specific Web sites around the world through IDG.net (http://www.idg.net), which comprises more than 225 targeted Web sites in 55 countries worldwide. International Data Corporation (IDC) is the world's largest provider of information technology data, analysis and consulting, with research centers in over 41 countries and more than 400 research analysts worldwide. IDG World Expo is a leading producer of more than 168 globally branded conferences and expositions in 35 countries including E3 (Electronic Entertainment Expo), Macworld Expo, ComNet, Windows World Expo, ICE (Internet Commerce Expo), Agenda, DEMO, and Spotlight. IDG's training subsidiary, ExecuTrain, is the world's largest computer training company, with more than 230 locations worldwide and 785 training courses. IDG Marketing Services helps industry-leading IT companies build international brand recognition by developing global integrated marketing programs via IDG's print, online and exposition products worldwide. Further information about the company can be found at www.idg.com. 10/8/98

Dedication

This book is dedicated to David Rogelberg, with a warning that in a couple of months I hope to be able to call him and say "nyah nyah."

Acknowledgments

This book is filled with information about technology that didn't exist a short time ago. Some of the technology was being developed as I was writing this book. The fun and challenge of learning about it added to the enjoyment of authoring, but because the hardware and software were so new (and changing so rapidly), I needed to bother a whole lot of people for information, all of whom were nice enough to put up with my conversations that started with "wait, I have another question" and "yeah, but what if this happens?"

I give grateful thanks to the following people who provided assistance about emerging technologies through their affiliation with the Home Phoneline Networking Alliance: Rick Roesler, Doug Walrath, Rachel Marler, Cyrus Namazi, Cheryl Murphy, and Lisa Lawler. I also want to thank Shawn Denton of Deerfield.Com and Drew Dowd at Miramar Systems for providing technical information that made it easier to explain complicated technology.

At IDG Books, a team of extremely talented people did a great deal of hard work to get this book to you. Joyce Pepple is a dream of an acquisitions editor who is fun to work with in addition to being extremely good at her job. Associate project editor Wendy Hatch oversaw the production of this book with efficiency, common sense, friendliness, humor, and all-around niceness — especially difficult because I kept changing things to throw obstacles in her path. Copy editors Ted Cains, Gwenette Gaddis, Rowena Rappaport, and Linda Stark did a marvelous job of making me seem literate, and technical editor Jim McCarter made sure I didn't make any embarrassing mistakes in the technical discussions.

Publisher's Acknowledgments

We're proud of this book; please register your comments through our IDG Books Worldwide Online Registration Form located at http://my2cents.dummies.com.

Some of the people who helped bring this book to market include the following:

Acquisitions, Editorial, and Media Development

Associate Project Editor: Wendy Hatch

Acquisitions Editor: Joyce Pepple

Copy Editors: Ted Cains, Gwenette Gaddis, Rowena Rappaport, Linda Stark

Technical Editor: Jim McCarter

Associate Media Development Editor: Joell Smith

Media Development Coordinator: Megan Roney

Associate Permissions Editor: Carmen Krikorian

Editorial Manager: Rev Mengle

Media Development Manager: Heather Heath Dismore

Editorial Assistant: Paul Kuzmic

Production

Project Coordinator: Valery Bourke

Layout and Graphics: Daniel Alexander, Lou Boudreau, Linda M. Boyer, J. Tyler Connor, Angela F. Hunckler, Todd Klemme, Jane E. Martin, Tom Missler, Brent Savage, Jacque Schneider, Kate Snell, Michael Sullivan, Brian Torwelle

Proofreaders: Christine Berman, Michelle Croninger, Nancy Price, Mildred Rosenzweig, Janet M. Withers

Indexer: Sherry Massey

Special Help

Bill Helling; Debbie Stailey; Publication Services, Inc.

General and Administrative

IDG Books Worldwide, Inc.: John Kilcullen, CEO; Steven Berkowitz, President and Publisher

IDG Books Technology Publishing: Brenda McLaughlin, Senior Vice President and Group Publisher

Dummies Technology Press and Dummies Editorial: Diane Graves Steele, Vice President and Associate Publisher; Mary Bednarek, Director of Acquisitions and Product Development; Kristin A. Cocks, Editorial Director

Dummies Trade Press: Kathleen A. Welton, Vice President and Publisher; Kevin Thornton, Acquisitions Manager

IDG Books Production for Dummies Press: Michael R. Britton, Vice President of Production and Creative Services; Cindy L. Phipps, Manager of Project Coordination, Production Proofreading, and Indexing; Kathie S. Schutte, Supervisor of Page Layout; Shelley Lea, Supervisor of Graphics and Design; Debbie J. Gates, Production Systems Specialist; Robert Springer, Supervisor of Proofreading; Debbie Stailey, Special Projects Coordinator; Tony Augsburger, Supervisor of Reprints and Bluelines

Dummies Packaging and Book Design: Robin Seaman, Creative Director; Kavish + Kavish, Cover Design

◆

The publisher would like to give special thanks to Patrick J. McGovern, without whom this book would not have been possible.

◆

Contents at a Glance

Cartoons at a Glance

By Rich Tennant

Table of Contents

Introduction

I think that if you have more than one computer in your home, you should have a network. That belief has its roots in the fact that I'm generally lazy, and I believe everyone should do everything in the easiest possible manner.

Using multiple computers is just easier if you have a network. You don't have to remember which computer you were using when you started that letter to Uncle Harry — you just reach across the network to get the letter if you want to finish it using another computer. And if you're sitting in bed at 2 a.m. working on that important 8 a.m. presentation on your laptop and realize that one of the files you need is on the computer in the kitchen, you don't have to leave your cozy bed and stumble downstairs — just grab the file from the kitchen computer across the network.

Home networks also reduce the number of things kids argue about. It doesn't matter if Bobby has his homework assignment on the computer in the den. Sally doesn't have to stop using that computer so that Bobby can get to work. Bobby can go to the computer in the basement and grab the file from the computer in the den across the network. And because you can set up network software that lets everyone use the Internet at the same time, those arguments about whose turn it is to surf the Net are also a thing of the past.

One of the best reasons to set up a home network is that when you install it, you become a network administrator (that's what the people who installed the network at your office or school are called). That makes you a computer geek. Because I think that being called a computer geek is a compliment, I offer my congratulations to you.

About This Book

This book isn't a novel or a mystery, so you don't have to start at page one and read every chapter in order — you can't spoil the ending. This book is meant to be digested on a subject-by-subject, not a chapter-by-chapter, basis.

However, because the process of creating the network requires that tasks be performed in a certain order, I recommend that you check out the chapters in either Part I or Part II before you go to any of the other chapters. Read

Part I if you're planning to connect your computers using standard cable (10BaseT or coaxial cable), or read Part II if you're planning to connect your computers using the telephone lines in your house. Of course, if you don't know which type of network you'd like to install or are just plain curious, feel free to read both of these parts, and check out Appendix A for some alternative networking techniques, including wireless networking technology.

After you get up to speed on the basics, you can decide which chapters you want to look at next as you figure out which network features you want to add to your home network. Each chapter is self-contained, covering a specific subject.

How to Use This Book

The best way to use this book is to find the subject you want to explore in the Table of Contents or the Index and then turn to the appropriate page.

If the book covers any additional information or preliminary steps for the subject of interest, you can use the cross-references that direct you to the appropriate chapter. It's not necessary to turn to the cross-referenced chapter immediately (although sometimes it's helpful). You can continue reading and then move to the other chapter to find more information when you want to.

Some conventions used throughout the book make it easier to follow specific instructions. Commands for menus appear with arrows between each selection (for example, the command Start⇨Settings⇨Control Panel tells you to click the Start button, choose Settings, and then choose Control Panel).

If you need to type something in a text box or a wizard window, the explanation uses **bold type** to indicate what you need to type.

If you're running Windows 95 without Internet Explorer 4.0 or Windows 98 without the Web interface, click the mouse button twice when you see the words "double-click" in numbered steps. If you took advantage of the Web interface available in Windows 98 (or Windows 95 with Internet Explorer 4.0), a single click is all that's required to open an object.

What You Don't Need to Read

I've learned that some people are really curious about why some computer functions work the way they do. Other people don't care why; they just want to find out how to perform those functions.

I put technical explanations that you don't need to read, but may be of interest to the little computer geek in your head, in sidebars or passages of text marked with a Technical Stuff icon. You can safely skip this information if you don't care about those details. (I'll never know.)

Foolish Assumptions

I am making several assumptions:

- ✓ You use PCs that run either Windows 98 or Windows 95.
- ✓ You want to share computers on a network, whether they're desktop computers or laptops.
- ✓ You have more people in the household than computers, so more than one person might use any single computer.

Regarding the differences between Windows 98 and Windows 95, I discuss the operating systems separately when a difference exists in the way they work. Otherwise, I just use the term Windows.

Although I don't cover Windows NT specifically (it's used mainly in business settings and by more advanced users), all the content in this book can be applied to the NT operating system.

I also don't mention laptops specifically in this book, except for in Appendix A, where I explain the easy process of adding a laptop to your network. Rest assured, though, that all the cool stuff I show you how to do in Parts III through VIII can be done on your laptop — you just do it on a computer with a smaller screen and a much smaller keyboard.

How This Book Is Organized

This book is divided into eight parts to make it easier to find what you need. Each part has a number of chapters (some have more than others).

Part I: Networking with Standard Cable

Setting up a home PC network doesn't have to be a chore. With a little twisted pair or coaxial cable, some network interface cards, the right software, and my expert advice in this part, you'll have your network up and running in no time.

Part II: Networking with Telephone Lines

Telephone lines aren't just useful for ordering pizzas and talking to Grandma. Take advantage of the latest technology and use your household telephone lines to connect your home PCs in a network. In this part, I tell you how to install telephone line networking hardware and software in standard computers, and I also tell you how to use the new network-ready computers.

Part III: Getting Personal

Don't worry — I don't ask you questions about your weight or tell you what I think about that sweater you're wearing. This part explains how users can log onto the network, protect their settings against changes by other users, and create passwords to keep stuff private.

Part IV: Communicating Across the Network

This part covers all the ways one computer can peek into other computers to find files, copy files, and generally share the contents of all the computers on your network. (If this doesn't sound terribly exciting to you, note that sharing includes playing games across the network.)

Part V: Sharing Hardware

This part explains how to share hardware that's connected to an individual computer, saving you time and money and helping you to make the most of your printers, peripherals, and modem. Every user can print from the single color printer in the household or share a single Zip drive. When you bring your laptop home from work, you can connect it to the network and share one of your network printers so you don't have to figure out how to squeeze the office laser printer into the back seat of your car.

Part VI: Keeping Your Network Working

Check out this part to find out how to keep your network running smoothly. I bug you about backing up (a good thing for me to nag you about), tell you how to check your hard drive for bad things that usually only get worse, and explain how you can protect your valuable computer equipment against surges and other dangers.

Part VII: The Part of Tens

The chapters in this part mention ten (or pretty close to ten) things that can motivate you to set up a network or make the most of the one you've got.

Part VIII: Appendixes

This is a computer book, so I definitely include appendixes (I think it's a rule — I've never seen a computer book without an appendix). Appendix A covers some network features that aren't yet commonly used, but that may be of interest to you. Appendix B tells you how to use the CD that's included with this book.

Icons Used in This Book

You can find several icons throughout the pages of this book. Each icon marks a particular type of information. Some icons mean, "Read this; I'm serious about it;" and other icons mean, "Hey, you can read this or not; it's not vitally important."

Here's what each icon means:

This icon points out technical stuff that computer nerds or highly curious people may find interesting. You can accomplish all the important tasks in this book without reading any of the material next to these icons.

This icon means, "Read this or suffer the consequences." You find it wherever problems may arise if you don't pay attention.

Pay attention to the text this icon flags if you want to make setting up and using your network easier (and who wouldn't want that?). Think of this cute little target as a gift from one network administrator (me) to another (you).

This icon marks information that could be useful down the line, so don't forget it.

Here's another non-urgent icon. It points out stuff that's cool, but not necessarily vital to the success of your network.

Where to Go from Here

Go ahead — check out the Table of Contents to see which neat networking feature you want to install first. But I do suggest that you check out Parts I and II for some networking basics.

It's quite possible that other members of the family will have opinions about the order in which you should install networking features — especially the kids, who seem to be born with an advanced knowledge of computing.

Creating a home network is satisfying, fun, and incredibly useful. Have a good time. You're on the cutting edge of computer technology. By reading this book, you prove that you're a networking nerd — and that's a compliment.

Part I
Networking with
Standard Cable

The 5th Wave   By Rich Tennant

OH, WAIT, WAIT, WAIT! I WAS READING YOU THE ANSWER FROM THE GARDENING COLUMN, WHICH IS RIGHT NEXT TO "ASK MR. COMPUTER".

In this part . . .

This part tells you everything you need to know to set up your home PC network with 10BaseT or coaxial cable. (If you want to use the new home telephone line networking technology, you can skip this part and read Part II instead.) I show you how to install network interface cards, run the cable through your house, and install the software your computers need so they can talk to one another.

Chapter 1

Installing Standard Cable Networking Hardware

In This Chapter

▶ Understanding network connections

▶ Buying the right hardware

▶ Installing network interface cards

A *network* is nothing more than two or more computers that are connected so that each computer has access to files or peripherals on another computer. To create a network, you must first install the hardware that creates the connections.

The primary hardware device is a *network interface card* (called a NIC). A NIC must be installed in each computer on the network. NICs are traditionally connected via cable. I say "traditionally" because some new wireless solutions are just coming to market (see Appendix A if you'd like to go that route). Additionally, new technology allows you to set up a network using your household telephone lines. (If you plan to set up a telephone line network, see Chapters 4 and 5 and feel free to skip the first three chapters in this book — I'll never know that you did.)

In this chapter, I tell you about different types of networks and the way in which you physically connect computers using standard cable (10BaseT and coaxial cable). See Chapter 2 for more detailed information about running cable through your house.

Understanding Network Types

You form a network by combining several elements that connect one or more computers. These elements are:

✔ Hardware that permits the computers to communicate

✔ A cable or a wireless technology that sends data between the computers

> ✔ Software (called *drivers*) that operates the hardware
>
> ✔ A network operating system that understands the hardware and the drivers

After you install and configure all the elements, you have a network. But the way in which you configure the network and the network operating system that you use both play a role in the way your network operates.

Client/server networks

Networking schemes that operate in *client/server* mode are common in businesses. These schemes include a main computer (called a *server*) that supplies the files and peripherals shared by all the other computers (called *clients* or *workstations*).

Large client/server networks frequently have multiple servers. Each server has a specific job — perhaps one server is used for e-mail, another server holds the accounting software, and another has the word processor.

All the computers are connected in such a way to give them physical access to the server. Each user who works at a client computer can use files and peripherals that are on his or her individual computer (the local computer) or on the server. Figure 1-1 illustrates the communication between computers in a client/server environment.

Even though all the computers are connected to each other, the communication is between each client and the server. The clients aren't usually configured to talk directly to each other.

The common network operating systems used for client/server networks are Novell NetWare, Windows NT, and UNIX.

Peer-to-peer networks

Peer-to-peer networks permit all the computers on the network to communicate with each other. Communication isn't limited to client/server. Figure 1-2 displays a typical peer-to-peer network communication structure.

If you have computers running Windows 98 or Windows 95, you can have a peer-to-peer network because the support for this type of networking is built into the operating system.

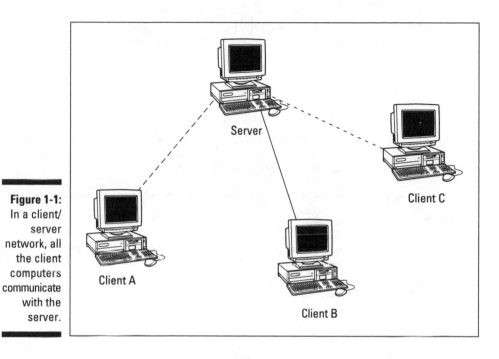

Figure 1-1:
In a client/
server
network, all
the client
computers
communicate
with the
server.

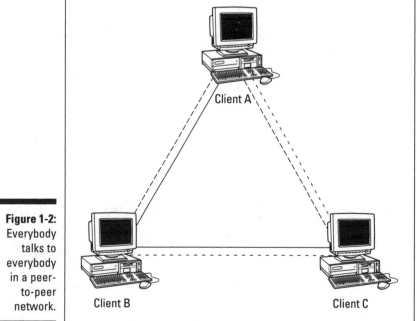

Figure 1-2:
Everybody
talks to
everybody
in a peer-
to-peer
network.

In fact, this book is about creating a peer-to-peer network in your home, so I'm assuming that you have one of those Windows operating systems on every computer you own.

Mixed networks

Just so you don't think that the computer world is rigid, I'll point out that some networks are both client/server and peer-to-peer at the same time. These business scenarios accomplish this feat:

- ✔ Networks that use Windows clients to reach NetWare servers
- ✔ Networks that use Windows clients to reach Windows NT servers

Users log onto the server and then use the server to access software and store the documents they create. Because the peer-to-peer networking is easily configured, users can transfer files from other clients. Users can also access printers connected to other clients.

Making Hardware Decisions

The only rule for creating a network is that you must install a NIC in each computer. Beyond that, you have enough choices to make your head spin. I'll try to slow down the spin rate by explaining the options before I drag you into the actual installation process.

NICs come in lots of flavors, and you must match the NICs you buy to two important elements:

- ✔ The type of card that each computer's motherboard accepts
- ✔ The type of network cabling that you want to use (see the section "Choosing a cable type," later in this chapter, as well as Chapter 2)

Matching the NIC to the motherboard bus

Forget public transportation. *Bus* means something else in computer jargon. A bus is a slot on your motherboard into which you insert cards. Technically, the name of the slot is *expansion slot,* and the bus is the data path along which information flows to the card. However, the common computer jargon is *bus*.

Each network interface card (sometimes simply called *card*) that you insert in a bus has a specific use. Your computers may have video cards, sound cards, hard drive controller cards, or other assorted cards.

Some computers have one or more of these devices built right into a chip on the motherboard instead of using cards. These built-in devices are called *embedded cards* or *embedded controllers*.

The NIC you purchase must go in an empty bus, and you must make sure that the NIC is manufactured for the bus type that's available on your motherboard. The common bus types are

- ✔ **ISA (Industry Standard Architecture):** ISA is a standard bus that's been used for a number of years. It's a 16-bit card, which means that it sends 16 bits of data at a time between the motherboard and the card (and any device attached to the card).

- ✔ **PCI (Peripheral Component Interconnect):** The PCI bus is built for speed. PCI is found in most new computers, and it comes in two configurations: 32-bit and 64-bit. Its technology is far more advanced (and complicated) than the ISA bus.

- ✔ **EISA (Extended Industry Standard Architecture):** Much less common, the EISA bus was developed as a 32-bit version of the standard ISA bus. It's faster than ISA and was popular for several years. It's not used in today's computers, but you may have EISA in one of your older computers.

You can read the documentation that came with your computer to find out what kind of cards you must buy. However, if you have mixed bus types on the motherboard (most of today's computers contain both PCI and ISA slots), the documentation doesn't tell you which slots are already occupied. You have to open your computer to find out what type of NIC you need to buy.

Follow these safety tips when you open your computer:

- ✔ **Don't use a magnetic screwdriver.** Magnets and disk drives do not peacefully co-exist — magnetic attraction can delete data.

- ✔ **Make sure that the computer is unplugged.** Either pull the plug from the wall or pull the plug from the back of the computer.

- ✔ **Discharge any static electricity in your body before you touch anything inside the computer.** You can do this by touching something metal.

- ✔ **Remove any metal jewelry, especially rings.** Gold in particular conducts electricity, including static electricity.

You can tell at a glance what type of bus is available if you know what to look for.

An ISA bus is usually black. It has metal pins or teeth in the center and a small crossbar about two-thirds of the way down the slot. Figure 1-3 shows an ISA bus.

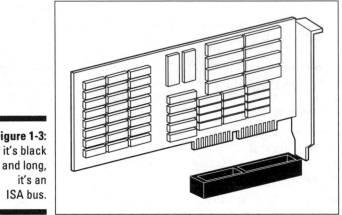

Figure 1-3:
If it's black and long, it's an ISA bus.

A PCI bus is usually white, and it's shorter than an ISA bus, as shown in Figure 1-4. It has a crossbar about three-quarters of the way down its length.

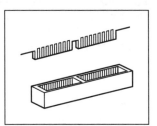

Figure 1-4:
If it's white and shorter than the black bus, it's a PCI bus.

An EISA bus is usually brown, which is almost the only way to differentiate it from an ISA bus. It's the same length as an ISA bus, so look at Figure 1-3 and pretend that the bus pictured there is brown, and you'll have a pretty good idea of what an EISA bus looks like.

Choosing a cable type

You have one more decision to make before you go shopping for your hardware — you have to choose a cabling system. The decision you make affects not only the type of cable you buy but also the NIC you buy. The NIC has a device that accepts the cable connector, so the NIC must be built specifically for the cable you choose.

You have two choices for cable: 10BaseT or coaxial. I go over the differences between them in this section, but before you make your decision, you may want to read Chapter 2, which covers the installation procedures for both types of cable. The differences in the way you run the cable through your house may influence your decision about the type of cable that you choose. (If you'd like to explore all your cabling options before making your decision, read Chapters 4 and 5, which discuss networking with home telephone lines; and Appendix A, which describes other networking techniques, including wireless networking technology.)

Both 10BaseT and coaxial cable are built for a cabling topology called *Ethernet.* I'd bore you to death if I were to go into all the details, but you can trust me when I tell you that Ethernet cable is today's cable of choice.

10BaseT cable

10BaseT cable is also called *twisted pair cable,* and it's today's standard. It looks like telephone wire, but it isn't the same thing — it's designed to transmit data rather than voice. Using 10BaseT requires the purchase of a *concentrator,* which is sometimes called a *hub.* All the network computers are connected to the concentrator, which disseminates the data, as shown in Figure 1-5.

The connector at the end of the cable looks like the connector at the end of your telephone cable, but it isn't the same thing. 10BaseT cable connectors are called *RJ-45 connectors* — telephone connectors are called RJ-11 connectors.

Each computer has its own direct connection to the concentrator. If something happens to the cable or connector for one computer, the other computers happily continue to operate as a network. Of course, if you have a two-computer network and one computer has a bad connection, you don't have much of a network.

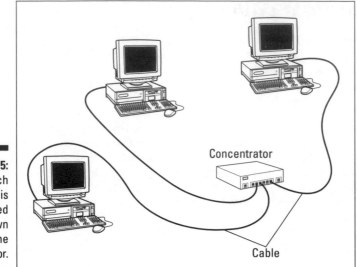

Figure 1-5:
Each
computer is
connected
to its own
port in the
concentrator.

Coaxial cable

Coaxial cable is also called *thinnet.* (Computer geeks usually shorten the name "coaxial" to "coax.") It looks like a thin version of the cable your cable television company uses, but it's fatter than 10BaseT. The connector used for coax is called a *BNC,* and it's a fat ring. Chapter 2 discusses attaching connectors to NICs.

Coax requires no concentrator. One long line of cable runs from one computer to the next computer, to the next computer, and so on, broken only to make the connection to each computer. The computers on the network are essentially attached to the same piece of cable. This means that if there's a break in the cable run, all the computers are victimized, and you have no network.

Today, coax is not as popular as 10BaseT, and it may be hard to find a coax cabling kit at your local computer or office supply store. However, you should be able to find the individual hardware elements that you need.

The best thing about coax is that you can frequently get it for free. Many companies are abandoning their coax network systems in favor of 10BaseT. I know people who asked for the coax NICs and the cable and were given the hardware free of charge.

Purchasing the Hardware

You're ready to shop. Grab your credit card, your checkbook, or some cash, and go shopping!

You can buy what you need at any computer store, most large office supply stores, or on the Internet. (Many computer supply companies now do business on the World Wide Web.)

Buying a kit

A number of manufacturers offer kits — a network-in-a-box, if you will. The kits are designed for a specific bus and cabling system. For example, a kit may be manufactured for PCI NICs with 10BaseT cable.

Kits come in a variety of sizes — in this case, *size* means the number of computers that you want to put on a network. The smallest kit is for two computers, and it contains two NICs and two pieces of cable. If it's a 10BaseT kit, it also has a concentrator, into which you connect each individual length of cable.

Kits also include floppy disks or CDs that contain the software your operating system needs to communicate with the NICs. These software files are called *drivers*. See Chapter 3 for the information you need to install the drivers.

You can only buy a kit if every computer on your network uses the same bus type. No kits contain one PCI NIC and one ISA NIC. If you have a mixed bus network, you need to buy individual hardware elements. (Read the next section.)

Buying individual hardware elements

If you have mixed bus types on your network, you can buy the individual hardware elements you need. You'll find what you need in the same sections of the stores that carry kits. The individual elements just come in individual packages.

You can mix NICs if you have different bus types in the computers that you want to connect. But don't mix cable types — you must decide to buy your NICs for 10BaseT or coax.

Remember that for each computer, you need one NIC and one length of cable with connectors attached. The NICs come with software drivers, usually on a floppy disk.

For 10BaseT, you need a concentrator with enough ports for all of your computers. You can buy concentrators that have from four to eight ports. If you need more than that, you can use one of the ports to connect another concentrator. Directions for linking concentrators come with the hardware.

Installing the NICs

You must physically install the NICs in your computers. You have to open your computer and remove the case. Please read the warnings earlier in this chapter in the section "Matching the NIC to the motherboard bus." You must take these precautions before opening the computer.

The following sections explain how to install NICS in your computers.

Making the end slot available

Locate the bus for the NIC that you're installing. At the end of the slot, at the back of the computer, you'll find a metal plate like the one shown in Figure 1-6. The plate is attached to the edge of the computer with a small machine screw (usually a Phillips-head screw).

A *machine screw* is a screw that doesn't come to a point at the end opposite the head. In case you drop the screw and lose it in the rug, or it bounces around the floor and gets lost, you have to know that it's a machine screw to replace it. Can you guess why this possible predicament occurred to me? Yep, I've dropped these screws a whole bunch of times!

Remove the screw and put it down — remember where you put it because you'll need it again. Remove the metal plate. You can discard it or put it away in case you think you'll remove the NIC someday and will want to close up that slot again.

Inserting the NIC

Now it's time to insert the NIC. Open the static-free bag that holds it, and remove the NIC. Touch something metal (not the computer) to discharge any static electricity in your body.

Follow these steps to insert the NIC in the bus. (You won't be confused about which way it fits into the bus because the metal edge of the NIC replaces the metal plate you removed from the back of the computer, as shown in Figure 1-7.)

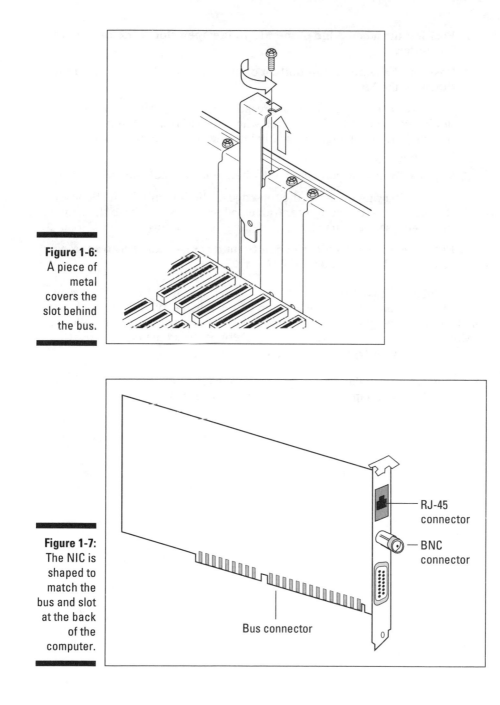

Figure 1-6:
A piece of metal covers the slot behind the bus.

Figure 1-7:
The NIC is shaped to match the bus and slot at the back of the computer.

RJ-45 connector

BNC connector

Bus connector

1. **Position the metal edge of the NIC in the open slot at the back of the computer.**

2. **Position the teeth on the bottom of the NIC in the bus, and then push down on the NIC.**

   You may have to apply a bit of pressure, which is perfectly okay — don't worry about it. You can tell when the NIC is inserted properly because the metal edge fits neatly into the slot at the back of the computer.

3. **Replace the screw you removed when you took out the metal plate.**

   The overhanging flange at the top edge of the NIC should nestle against the top edge of the computer frame. In fact, you should see the screw hole because the flange has an opening for the screw.

4. **Put the cover back on the computer and replace any screws that you removed when you opened it.**

You're finished! Wasn't that easy? Now, go do the same thing to the rest of the computers on your network. When you're finished, you'll notice that the back of every computer has a connection in the slot where you installed the NIC. (Figure 1-7 shows the RJ-45 and BNC connectors on a typical NIC.) That's where you attach the cable (see Chapter 2).

After the cable is hooked up, your next task is to install the software drivers for the NICs, and Chapter 3 helps you accomplish that.

Chapter 2

Cabling the House

• •

In This Chapter

▶ Working with cable — 10BaseT and coaxial

▶ Running with your cable plans

• •

*T*he network interface cards (NICs) that you install in your computers (see Chapter 1) provide the connections for computer-to-computer communication. When the computers "talk," all the software that enables that conversation travels through the NICs. The NICs communicate with each other via network cable.

Using network cable is the most common method of connecting NICs and usually provides the best speed when you're exchanging data. However, you can also connect NICs through your household telephone lines (see Chapters 4 and 5) or via infrared signals or your household electrical lines (see Appendix A).

In this chapter, I tell you everything you need to know to connect NICs using 10BaseT and coaxial cable, from planning your cable runs to making the connections.

Planning the Cable Runs

Cable is strung through a building in the form of a *run,* and your plan for running the cable depends on the type of cable (and matching NICs) that you choose for your network. In this section, I cover 10BaseT and coaxial cable. (See Chapter 1 for help deciding on the type of cable and NICs to use for your standard cable network.)

Working with 10BaseT cable

You can refer to 10BaseT cable as *twisted pair cable* because the cable's wires are twisted along the length of the cable (see Figure 2-1). Two types of twisted pair cable are available: unshielded twisted pair (UTP) and shielded twisted pair (STP). In shielded twisted pair cable, metal encases the wires, lessening the possibility of interference from other electrical devices, radar, radio waves, and so on. However, I haven't noticed a great difference in performance between UTP and STP. UTP is less expensive, and almost all the 10BaseT cable you purchase for computer networks is UTP.

Figure 2-1:
10BaseT cable is also called twisted pair cable because the wires are twisted along the length of the cable.

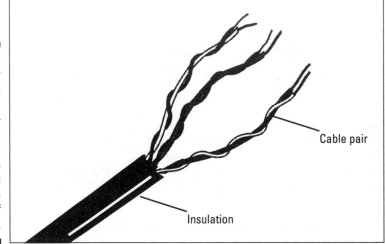

Cable pair

Insulation

When 10BaseT cable is used in a network, all the lengths of cable share the same home base, called a *concentrator* (also known as the *hub*). Each end of a cable length has a connector called *an RJ-45 connector.* One connector is attached to the concentrator, and the other connector is attached to the NIC in a computer. The computer jargon for this arrangement is *star topology,* although I'm not sure how that name developed. As you can see in Figure 2-2, the resemblance to a star is a little obscure. Perhaps "wheel spokes" is a more accurate description.

Positioning the concentrator

Because the concentrator is the core of the network, you should place the device in the most advantageous position. Here are some things to consider when you're deciding where to locate the concentrator:

> ✔ **Locate it near an electrical outlet.** The concentrator is an electrical device. Plug it into a surge protector (surges travel rapidly through cable, hitting all the connected computers), and then plug the surge protector into the wall outlet.

Figure 2-2:
A 10BaseT
network
has multiple
cable runs
from the
concentrator
to each
computer
on the
network,
creating
what's
called a
star
topology.

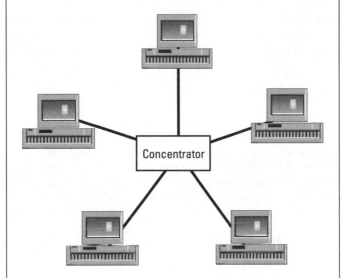

Concentrator

✔ **Position it near the cable run and make the most of your cable lengths.** Locate the concentrator near the place in the wall, ceiling, or floor that your cable run follows so that the cable can easily plug into the concentrator. If you purchased a kit or premanufactured cable, try to position the concentrator so that the cable lengths reach all the computers. However, if you can't accomplish this, you can always buy longer cable for any computer that's out of reach.

✔ **Air quality.** After you connect the cables, you don't have to play with the concentrator — no babysitting is required. You can tuck the concentrator away in a closet, but do try to give it a dry (not humid), dust-free environment. Don't cover it, place it in a drawer, or wrap it in plastic because it needs circulating air to prevent overheating.

✔ **Proximity to heat sources.** Keep the concentrator away from direct sunlight, radiators, heaters, and any other heat sources.

✔ **Proximity to other electrical devices.** Don't put the concentrator next to fluorescent lights, radios, or transmitting equipment.

Some concentrators come with devices that permit wall mounting so that the concentrator doesn't take up table or shelf space.

Adding more 10BaseT cable

If you purchased individual parts — NICs, assembled cable, and a concentrator — instead of a kit (usually because one computer requires a

PCI bus and the other computer offers only an ISA bus; see Chapter 1 for more information about determining the type of bus that's in each computer), you probably measured the distances between each of the computers and the concentrator and then purchased cable in the proper lengths. (See Chapter 1 for information about choosing the appropriate NICs for your computers' bus types.)

If, on the other hand, you purchased a networking kit (because all your computers have the same bus type and therefore require the same type of NIC), it probably included a concentrator, two or more NICs, and lengths of assembled cable (cable with the connectors already attached to each end of the cable). Buying kits can be convenient, but because the cable in kits usually comes in 20- or 25-foot lengths, you may find that the cable sometimes comes up short.

If you don't have enough cable to reach a computer, you have a couple of options for solving the problem.

Find assembled cable of the right length

Shop for a length of assembled cable that's long enough to reach the computer. Assembled cable comes in a variety of lengths, and you may find the distance you need at your local computer supply store. You can also order any size and length of cable from a cable company, a computer supply store, or any other retailer that distributes products for data communication.

Connect two lengths of assembled cable

You can connect two pieces of assembled cable with a coupler. A *coupler* is a small plastic device that features two receptacles that accept RJ-45 connectors, so you end a cable run in one receptacle and begin the next piece of cable in the other receptacle. The coupler works very much like an extension device for telephone lines. Do not, however, use a telephone coupler for your computer cable.

Couplers don't have a terrific history of reliability. Frequently, when you encounter problems with computer-to-computer communication, the blame falls on these connections. However, turning to a coupler isn't a bad temporary measure while you wait for delivery of cable lengths that are the right size.

Never put a coupler inside a wall or in any other location that's hard to get to. If you have to check or replace the connection made with the coupler, you need easy access to it.

Working with coaxial cable

Coaxial cable, shown in Figure 2-3, is also known as 10Base2 cable. (The specific coaxial cable you're using for your home network is RG-58 cable.) You may hear this cable called either *coax* or *thinnet*. I'm used to saying coax, so I use that term in this section.

Figure 2-3:
Coaxial cable looks a lot like the cable that connects your television set to your cable outlet, only it's thinner.

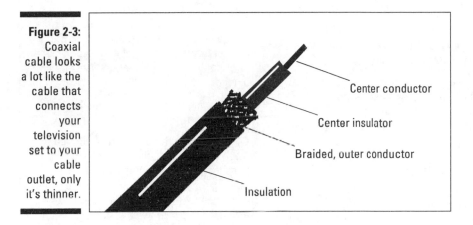

Center conductor

Center insulator

Braided, outer conductor

Insulation

Coax looks like the cable that connects your television set to your cable TV wall outlet, except that coax is thinner than TV cable. The coax cable connector is a round device called a *BNC*. (It's a smaller version of the BNC connector on your television cable system.) Installed at each end of a length of cable, the BNC features a center pin (connected to the center conductor inside the cable) and a metal tube (connected to the outer cable shielding). A rotating ring on the metal tube turns to lock the male connector ends to any female connectors.

BNC is short for Barrel Node Connector, British Naval Connector, or Bayonet Nut Connector — take your pick. I just call it a BNC.

When you use coax to cable your network, you essentially use one long piece of cable. Along the way, you connect each computer to the cable. You don't cable each computer separately back to a concentrator as with 10BaseT cable (see "Working with 10BaseT cable," earlier in this chapter) — there is no concentrator. You simply move from computer to computer in

Pros and cons of coax cable

Coax cable isn't all that easy to locate these days, but up until several years ago, it was the standard for cabling. Coax presents particular disadvantages and advantages that you should consider when choosing a cabling scheme.

Here are the two main disadvantages of networking with coax cable:

✔ Because coax cable is thicker than 10BaseT cable and because the BNC connectors on coax cable are much thicker than the RJ-45 connectors on a 10BaseT system, any holes you drill through walls, floors, or other obstacles have to be larger to accommodate coax cable.

✔ If a break occurs in the cabling of a coax network — for example, if you accidentally disconnect one of the BNC connectors from a T-connector — the entire network stops working. Even the computers that are still connected can't communicate. Just picture strings of old Christmas tree lights — if one bulb burned out, all the bulbs stopped working.

(You can, however, disconnect the T-connector from a NIC without disrupting the rest of the computers on the network, because doing so doesn't break the cable run — it only breaks the cable's connection to that particular computer. Only the connections at the crossbars of the T-connectors must remain intact. Need more information? See the section "Making co-axial connections.")

On the other hand, coax cable does have two big advantages:

✔ Coax cable is frequently free, or almost free. If you work for a company that's upgrading its computer system and replacing the coax cable with 10BaseT, see if you can take the used stuff home. I know a lot of people who have done this and built home networks without spending a penny.

✔ Less cable is needed because you just have to link the computers to one another; you don't have to run cable from each computer back to a concentrator.

one long line. At each computer, you break the cable to make the connection at that computer using a T-connector, discussed in the next section. Then the cable line moves on to the next computer. Make sure that the cable is long enough to reach from one computer to the next (and to the next if you have more than two computers on your network). A minimum of 1.64 feet of cable is required between computers.

Making coaxial connections

The BNC connector at each end of the cable doesn't connect directly to your NIC (even though you may notice a protuberance coming out of the NIC that looks like it's designed to accept a BNC connector). Instead, you need to place an additional connector on the NIC to provide a pass-through device so that the signal passes along to the next section of cable (which is connected to the next computer). Based on its shape, that additional connector is called a *T-connector*. Figure 2-4 shows this connection scheme.

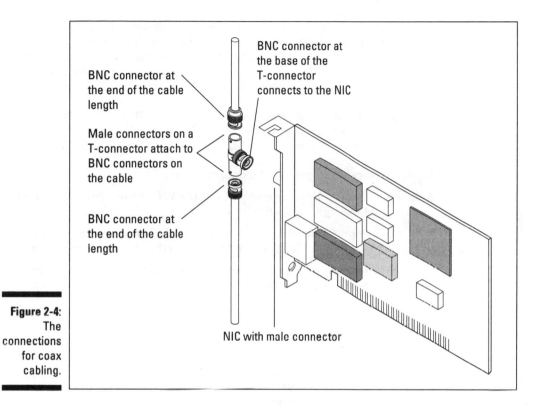

BNC connector at the base of the T-connector connects to the NIC

BNC connector at the end of the cable length

Male connectors on a T-connector attach to BNC connectors on the cable

BNC connector at the end of the cable length

NIC with male connector

Figure 2-4:
The connections for coax cabling.

Attach a T-connector to a cable run by inserting one of the T-connector's male connectors into a BNC at the end of a cable length and then turning the BNC clockwise until you feel the pin-lock mechanism click into place.

At the beginning and end of the cable run (the first and last computers), half of the T-connector is left unused. Each of these unused connections requires a special device called a *terminator*. Terminators have BNC connectors that let you attach them to the male connection on the empty crossbar of a T-connector.

Adding more coaxial cable

If the cable you have isn't long enough to reach from one computer to the next, you can easily add more cable. Because the computers on a coax network are essentially linked together by one long piece of cable joined by connectors, you just need to follow the same connecting principle you follow when connecting two computers when all you want to do is add another piece of cable — in fact, some people use a T-connector (which doesn't connect to any computer, of course). Barrel connectors, which are like T-connectors but with only a crossbar, are also available for this purpose.

Make sure that you don't use a connector on a section of cable that's in a wall, or otherwise hidden. If the connecting point isn't in full view, buy a longer piece of cable instead of connecting two shorter pieces. Many times, network communications problems are traced back to connectors, so you must be able to get to a connector to test it or replace it.

You can buy a roll of coax cable and make your own BNC connections, but don't expect the process to be a cakewalk. If you're still determined to give it the old college try, follow these steps:

1. **Strip the cable to expose the copper center.**

2. **Insert the cable into the small pin in the BNC connector. (You need excellent eyesight to do this.)**

3. **Put this connection into the small sleeve that comes with the BNC (used to cover the place where the connection is made) and crimp it.**

   You need a good BNC crimper (plan to spend at least $75) to do this. You can also buy BNC connectors that call for soldering rather than crimping.

Repositioning the computers

You may find that you need to alter the current placement of your computers to simplify cabling. Sometimes, you have to change computer placement to make cabling possible at all.

The cable that snakes its way to the NIC in your computer is going to come out of the wall (or the baseboard along the wall), down from the ceiling, or up from the floor.

If running cables through a ceiling or floor is necessary, plan to use a corner of the room, not the middle of the room. Nobody wants a piece of cable dangling from the middle of the ceiling or popping up in the middle of the floor.

So, if you currently have a computer in the middle of the den or bedroom, you need to move it closer to the point at which the cable enters the room. Otherwise, you'll have cable floating across the floor, which is not a terribly attractive interior design. Besides, it can be dangerous — don't say I didn't warn you when you trip over a cable on your way to the bathroom in the middle of the night.

Installing the Cable

After you plan the cabling arrangement according to your measurements — and perhaps change the placement of your computers — you're ready to install the cable.

Finding a clear run for the cable

If you're using 10BaseT cable, you have to run cable from the concentrator to each computer. For coax cable, you have to run cable from one computer to the next computer, and then on to any additional computers.

The ideal way is a clear run, just a straight line between the concentrator and each computer on the network, or a straight line from one computer to the next. If you're lucky, this is how it can work in your house. However, few home networks are cabled that easily. In this section, I discuss ways to cable your household if the task is more complicated than a straight-line path.

If your home network computers are in the same room, you have it made! In fact, you can probably skip this section.

Here are some general tips about running cable:

- ✔ When you drill holes to run cable between rooms or floors, make the holes slightly larger than the connector at the end of the cable. Connectors are delicate, so you don't want to force-feed them through openings.

- ✔ When you run cable from the entry point in the room (the entrance hole) to the computer, camouflage it by snaking it along the baseboard or the top of the quarter-round.

- ✔ Avoid bending cable at a sharp angle. If you have to run the cable around a corner, don't pull it taut.

- ✔ You can use U-shaped nails that act like staples to attach cable to the wall surface. Use staples large enough to surround the cable — do not staple into the cable.

- ✔ You can paint the cable to match your baseboard, quarter-round, or wall, but don't paint the connector.

Cabling between adjacent rooms

Cabling your network is easy when your computers are located in adjacent rooms on the same floor — and because you only have to drill one hole between the rooms, you don't wreck your house in the process. The following two sections discuss how to connect computers in adjacent rooms using 10BaseT and coax cable. (Note that I use two computers as an example in each of these scenarios, but these approaches also can be applied to a network of three or more computers. You just need to drill extra holes for the additional computers' cables and fish a few more cables through the walls or floors.)

Running 10BaseT between adjacent rooms

If your computers are on the same floor and in adjacent rooms, cabling is a snap. Put the concentrator in one of the rooms with a computer and run one section of cable to the computer in that room. Run another section of cable through the wall to the computer in the other room. You need to drill only one hole, as shown in Figure 2-5.

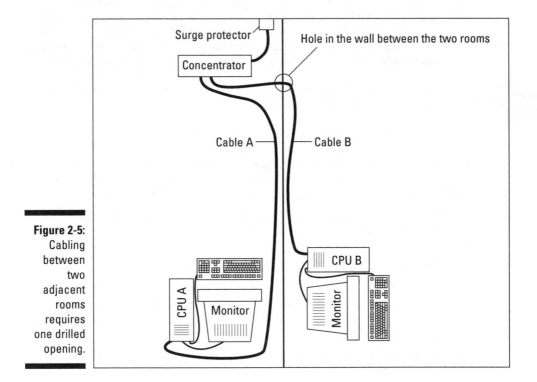

Figure 2-5: Cabling between two adjacent rooms requires one drilled opening.

Running coax between adjacent rooms

Cabling coax between adjacent rooms is a cinch. Drill a hole in an inconspicuous place. (Make sure that it's large enough to pass the BNC through.) Then attach the cable to the T-connectors, put terminators on the unused ends, and put the T-connectors on the NICs.

Cabling between non-adjacent rooms

If your computers are on the same floor but aren't in adjacent rooms, you have a bit more work to do. The most direct and efficient cabling route is along your home's beams. Most houses have beams that run straight through the house, either from front to back, side to side, or both. You usually can expect a clear run from one end to the other, and the jargon for this is a *chase*. Electricians who rewire homes head for the chase when they're planning the wiring.

The trick is to get to the chase, and the logical way to access it is to drill a hole in the ceiling or floor (depending on whether the chase is above or below the level you're working on).

I hate drilling holes in the ceiling because, to say the least, the blemish looks plain crummy, and even if I paint the cable to match the wall, I know it's there. Instead, I use closets. Here are the steps to wiring a chase through closets:

1. **Drill a hole in the closet ceiling or floor to get to the chase.**

2. **Drill a hole in the ceiling or floor of the closet of each room that contains a computer.**

3. **Fish the cable through the chase to each computer.**

   You can use a *fish* (a tool specially designed for fishing cable and sold in hardware stores) or a coat hanger you've untwisted (the hook at the end grabs the cable).

4. **If you have enough clearance under the closet door, run the cable under the door and then attach it to the quarter-round or baseboard with U-shaped staples as it moves toward the computers.**

   If there's no clearance under the closet door, drill a hole in the bottom of the door jamb to bring the cable into the room.

If one or both of the rooms lacks a closet, bring the cable into the room from the chase at a corner. If the cable enters the room through the ceiling from the chase above, bring the cable down the seam of the walls that create the corner (and paint it to match the wall). Then run the cable along the baseboard or quarter-round to the computer.

Here are a couple of other schemes to consider if all of your computers are all on the same floor:

✔ If your computers are on the second floor, run the cable across the attic floor (or crawl space above the second floor) and bring it down to each computer.

✔ If your computers are on the first floor, run the cable across the basement ceiling (or crawl space) and bring it up to each computer.

Here's a clever trick a friend and I used when we were wiring an enormous factory and warehouse. We decided to run our cable in the crawl space above the warehouse and drop each connection down to the computers. Rather than crawl through the crawl space (yuck, dirty!), my friend suggested something really nifty. She borrowed her son's toy remote control tractor and attached a length of cable to it. I stood on a ladder below each opening we'd drilled, shining a flashlight up. She stood at the end of the building peering down the crawl space and steered the tractor to the light beam. I reached up with a fish (a tool electricians use to grab and drag a piece of cable) and grabbed the cable. She brought the tractor back to her and connected another cable length, while I moved the ladder and beamed up into the next opening. We repeated this 50 times and then returned the toy. Her son never knew it left his room. (We put in fresh batteries as a thank you, though.)

Cabling between floors

If your computers are located on different floors, you have more work to do. You need additional cable because your cable length measurement must include the height of the room on the first floor. If you have one computer in the basement and another on the second floor, you need sufficient cable length to make the trip.

You have several approaches to consider, and here are a couple of suggestions based on my own experiences:

✔ If the rooms are stacked, one above the other, run the cable through the inside of the walls, near a corner. If radiators or pipes are present, use the opening around the pipes. If closets are stacked, use them to your advantage. (Read the section, "Cabling between non-adjacent rooms," earlier in this chapter, for tips on cabling through closets.)

✔ If the rooms are on opposite ends of the house, use the basement for the concentrator (for 10BaseT), or as a crossover for coax. (By this, I mean you can drop the cable from one computer down into the basement, run the wire along the basement ceiling, and then pop the wire up through the floor of the next room you need to cable.) Use the openings around pipes to come up to the computers. (Houses with radiators are usually filled with pipe runs.) If no pipes are there, use the inside of the wall.

After you drill your holes and find the space in the wall or next to a pipe, put a weight on the end of sturdy twine and drop it down to the basement. Then tape the cable in the basement to the string and haul it up.

If you think that you may want additional electrical outlets for the computer room above the basement in the future, haul the electrical wire up when you bring up the network cable. Later, you can have an electrician connect the wire to the breaker box in the basement and to new outlets in the room.

Chapter 3

Installing Networking Software

$\bullet$

In This Chapter

▶ Installing the software drivers for the network interface card

▶ Configuring the network interface card

▶ Installing network protocols and services

▶ Testing the Network Neighborhood

$\bullet$

*A*fter you finish the physical installation of the network interface card (NIC) for each computer — see Chapter 1 — and connect your computers' NICs with cable (see Chapter 2), you must install the Windows drivers for each computer's NIC. *Drivers* are files that the operating system uses to communicate with the NIC hardware.

In addition, Windows needs a way to communicate with the other computers on your home network, and that, too, requires you to install special files.

In this chapter, I tell you how to install all the files you need so that your computers' NICs can start communicating with one another.

Installing NIC Drivers

When you start your computer, Windows 95 and Windows 98 can find the NIC most of the time because of Plug and Play. (See Chapter 1 to find out how to install the NIC.) The Windows Plug and Play feature reviews all the hardware in your computer during startup, and when a new Plug and Play hardware component is detected, the software installation procedure begins automatically.

If your computer doesn't support Plug and Play, the fact that your NIC is enabled for Plug and Play may not count. You probably need to perform a manual installation.

Older NICs are not Plug and Play enabled; so if you don't purchase brand new hardware (some people obtain hardware from a company that's upgrading to newer and faster hardware), you probably need to install the drivers manually. That procedure is covered in this section, too.

Running the NIC setup

Refer to the documentation that comes with the NIC to see what the setup procedures are. Some NICs have jumpers that you must arrange; some NICs have software programs that establish the settings. If you have an older NIC and can't find the documentation, you can call the manufacturer or find the company on the Internet to obtain any setup information or software you need.

Some NIC instructions call this step "preinstallation."

Many NIC setup programs run in an MS-DOS session, and the documentation instructs you to choose Start⇨Run and then type a command in the Open text box of the Run dialog box.

Most of the time, the setup program can determine which settings are available for the NIC. These settings involve an IRQ level and an I/O address, which are technical specifications that guarantee your NIC has a unique position in the technical scheme of things for your computer. (I won't bother you with all the technical explanations, because it's only important to know that they're unique to this piece of hardware.)

You can use the setup program that comes with the NIC to specify a particular IRQ level and I/O address.

Sometimes you need to wait until you've finished the installation (with incorrect specifications) and then correct the specifications, such as when the default settings for the NIC conflict with the settings for another device on your computer.

Determining available settings

Determining the unused IRQ and I/O settings ahead of time is faster and more efficient than waiting until later. You can determine the unused IRQ and I/O by following these steps:

1. **Right-click the My Computer icon on the Desktop and choose Properties from the shortcut menu that appears.**

   The System Properties dialog box opens.

2. **Click the Device Manager tab.**

   A list of all the devices in your computer appears.

3. **Click Print.**

   The Print dialog box for Device Manager opens.

4. **Select System Summary and then click OK.**

   A summary report of the resources in your computer prints. These reports are usually about three pages long.

The IRQ Summary section of the report lists all the IRQs currently in use, and any missing number is available (numbers range from 00-15).

The I/O Port Summary section of the report lists all the I/O addresses currently in use. When your NIC setup program presents possible I/O addresses, select one that isn't being used by another device. Then follow the instructions that came with your NIC to set the IRQ and I/O specifications.

Plug and Play installation

If the Plug and Play feature kicks in, you see a message telling you that Windows has found a new device. Then the Add New Hardware Wizard opens automatically to begin the process of installing the drivers, as shown in Figure 3-1.

Figure 3-1:
It's much easier to install hardware when Windows finds the hardware and runs the installation wizard automatically.

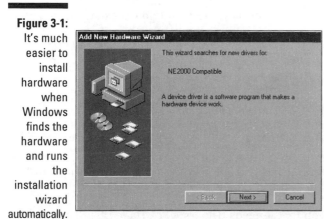

Setting jumpers

Older NICs don't use software to configure the settings. Instead, they use jumpers. A *jumper* is a small piece of plastic that "jumps" across pins, and whether or not pins are "jumpered" determines the settings. The NIC comes with documentation that explains all the possible settings and how to position the jumpers to create the setting you need.

I've run across jumper-set NICs when home users obtain older NICs from their employers (who updated to more modern network hardware). Changing jumpers requires removing the card, so check the Device Manager before you install the NIC to avoid removing the card to make changes.

The wizard recognizes the NIC and automatically looks for the correct driver files. Depending on the NIC you purchase and the instructions that come with it, you need to install either Windows drivers or the drivers supplied by the manufacturer of the NIC.

The wizard also recognizes the configuration of your Plug and Play NIC and installs it with all the correct specifications. However, sometimes Windows makes a mistake and the specifications aren't correct. You can correct the problem and change the specifications quite easily. See the section "Configuring the NIC," later in this chapter.

Using the Windows drivers

If the documentation for the NIC indicates that you need to use Windows drivers, you need to have your Windows CD in the CD-ROM drive. If your Windows operating system was installed by the computer manufacturer, the files you need are probably on your hard drive and no CD exists for you to worry about.

Hold down the Shift key when you insert the CD to prevent the disc from starting its AutoRun program.

The wizard automatically heads for the Windows driver files.

Using the manufacturer's drivers

If the documentation for the NIC indicates that you need to use the drivers supplied by the manufacturer, insert the floppy disk that came with your NIC in drive A. (If the NIC came with a CD instead of a floppy disk, insert the CD.)

When the wizard tells you that it needs drivers, click Have Disk. Then enter the drive letter for the disk that holds the software drivers in the dialog box that asks for the drive letter.

After the files are transferred to your hard drive, Windows displays a message telling you to restart your computer in order to have the new settings take effect. Click Yes to restart Windows.

Installing drivers manually

If your NIC isn't Plug and Play, or if Windows fails to detect it during startup, you need to install the drivers manually. Relax, it's easy. In fact, you're performing the same tasks that the Add New Hardware Wizard performs, except that you actually have to do the work. (Don't worry, it isn't very much work.) Follow these steps to install the drivers for your NIC:

1. **Choose Start⇨Settings⇨Control Panel.**

   The Control Panel opens.

2. **Double-click the Network icon.**

   The Network dialog box opens, with the Configuration tab in the foreground.

3. **Click Add.**

   The Select Network Component Type dialog box opens.

4. **Select Adapter and click Add.**

   The Select Network Adapters dialog box opens (see Figure 3-2). A list of manufacturers appears in the left pane. The adapters made by each manufacturer appear in the right pane after you select a manufacturer.

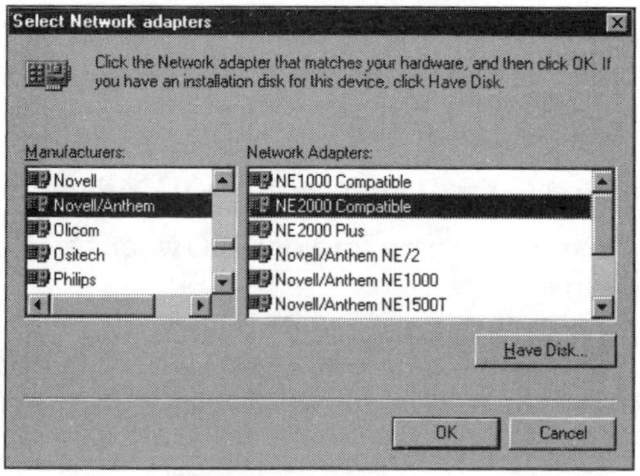

Figure 3-2:
The Select
Network
Adapters
dialog box.

5. **Depending on the instructions that come with your NIC, either choose a manufacturer and model from the dialog box or click Have Disk. Then click OK.**

6. **Follow the instructions onscreen to complete the installation of the NIC.**

If you select a manufacturer and model from the dialog box, you need to have your Windows CD in the CD-ROM drive (unless your computer came with Windows preinstalled).

If you select Have Disk, you need to use the manufacturer's floppy disk in drive A or the CD in the CD-ROM drive.

After the files are copied to your hard drive, the System Settings Change dialog box appears informing you that you must restart the operating system to have the new settings take effect. Click Yes to restart the operating system.

Configuring the NIC

After you restart your computer, you need to check the configuration of the NIC. If any problems exist with the configuration, you need to resolve them immediately.

Checking the installation settings

During the installation of the drivers, Windows determines the settings of your NIC. The determination may or may not be accurate. You need to check the settings attached to the NIC to make sure that they're accurate, which you can do by following these steps:

1. **Right-click the My Computer icon on the Desktop and choose Properties from the shortcut menu that appears.**

   The System Properties dialog box opens.

2. **Click the Device Manager tab.**

3. **Click the plus sign next to the listing for Network Adapters.**

   Windows reveals the specific entry for your NIC when the Network Adapters category expands.

4. **Select your NIC and click Properties.**

   The Properties dialog box for your NIC opens, with the General tab in the foreground.

If everything is fine, the Device Status section of the dialog box displays a message that says the device is working properly. If a problem exists, the message warns you that the device is not working properly.

If a problem exists with the NIC settings, the Network Adapters listing is probably already expanded when you select the Device Manager tab. The listing for your NIC probably has a symbol over its icon, either an exclamation point or an X. The symbol indicates that a problem with the settings for the NIC exists.

In either case, you should check the specific settings. Click the Resources tab to see the settings (see Figure 3-3). If the dialog box indicates there's a problem, see the next section, "Changing the settings."

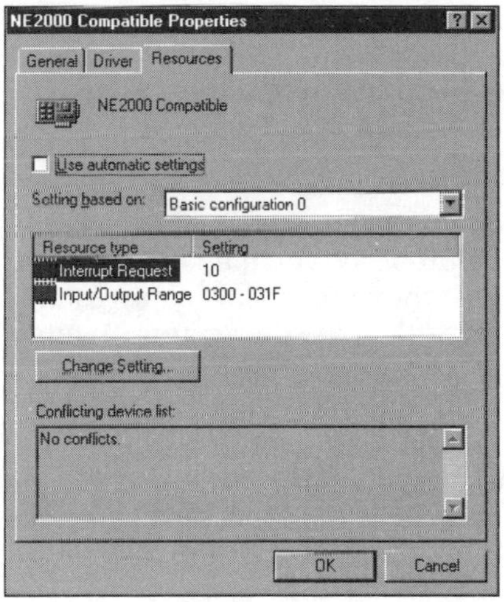

Figure 3-3:
The Resources tab of the Properties dialog box.

Changing the settings

You may need to change the NIC settings if you couldn't successfully install the NIC or if Windows couldn't correctly identify the NIC, the IRQ level, and the I/O address.

If everything didn't work properly and the settings are incorrect, you must correct them. This is sometimes complicated and sometimes easy. Sorry, but I can't be more specific than that. Follow along to see which set of circumstances matches your situation.

When IRQ and I/O settings don't match the NIC settings

You know what the IRQ and I/O settings are either from the documentation that comes with the NIC, or from the preinstallation setup program that you can run (see the section "Running the NIC setup," earlier in this chapter).

To set the IRQ and I/O settings to match the NIC settings, follow these steps:

1. **Select the incorrect setting.**

   If both the IRQ and I/O settings are wrong, select each one, one at a time.

2. **Click the Change Setting button.**

   The Edit Interrupt Request dialog box or the Edit Input/Output Range dialog box opens.

3. **Change the setting to match the physical setting of the NIC.**

   Type the correct number, or use the arrows to select a new setting.

4. **Click OK three times to close all the open dialog boxes.**

When the settings match but have a conflict

If the settings that appear match the settings you configured for the NIC but the installation still isn't working properly, you may have a conflict with another device. You need to re-run the preinstallation program for your NIC to change the setting that has a conflict (see the section "Running the NIC setup," earlier in this chapter).

Don't re-run the preinstallation program for your NIC blindly. You could spend half your life guessing the settings. Refer to the section "Determining available settings," earlier in this chapter, to make sure you know which IRQ or I/O settings are available and are not being used by another device.

Installing Network Protocols and Services

To complete the installation of your network files, you have to install protocols and services. You also have to name your computer and tell the networking software about the workgroup you belong to. In this section, I explain what protocols and services are and how to install them.

Computers that are connected in a network have to talk to each other. That's how they find each other and exchange files. In order to talk to each other, all the computers must speak the same language.

The computer jargon for the language that computers use to communicate is called *networking protocol*. You need to install at least one networking protocol on each computer on your network.

The "mouthpiece" for communications between computers is the NIC. The process of connecting the language to the mouthpiece (the protocol to the NIC) is called *binding*. After the protocol is bound to the NIC, your computers can talk to each other.

Windows provides a number of protocols, including these three commonly used protocols:

- ✔ **NetBIOS Extended User Interface (NetBEUI):** This protocol is a simple, efficient one that works on peer-to-peer networks and Windows NT client/server networks. See Chapter 1 to learn about the different types of networks.

- ✔ **Internetwork Packet Exchange (IPX/SPX):** This protocol was developed by Novell for its NetWare network operating system. (NOS is the jargon for network operating system.) Microsoft also has its own flavor of IPX/SPX. Use this protocol if you have NetWare servers on your network (not commonly found in home networks).

- ✔ **Transmission Control Protocol/Internet Protocol (TCP/IP):** This protocol is the one used on the Internet and is also used by many companies for running large networks. Mobile users find it especially useful for dialing into network servers.

You may have installed TCP/IP when you set up Dial-Up Networking in Windows. For information about setting up Internet connections, refer to *Windows 95 For Dummies,* 2nd Edition, or *Windows 98 For Dummies,* both by Andy Rathbone, or *Windows NT 4 For Dummies* by Andy Rathbone, and Sharon Crawford (all published by IDG Books Worldwide, Inc.).

Adding a protocol

The NetBEUI protocol is probably the best choice for a home network, unless you have some terribly complicated network issues involved in your home network. (Of course, if you did configure a complicated and uncommon network configuration, you probably have enough knowledge to install the appropriate protocol on your own.)

You need the Windows CD in order to access the files for the protocol you install.

Installing the NetBEUI protocol is a simple, straightforward task that you can accomplish by following these steps:

1. **Choose Start➪Settings➪Control Panel.**

   The Control Panel opens.

2. **Double-click the Network icon.**

   The Network dialog box opens, with the Configuration tab in the foreground.

3. **Click Add.**

   The Select Network Component Type dialog box opens (see Figure 3-4).

Figure 3-4:
You can select the type of network component you want to add in the Select Network Component Type dialog box. In this case, Protocol is selected.

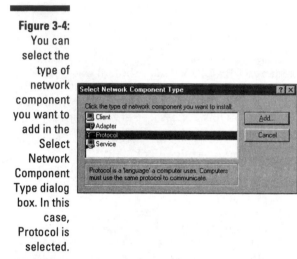

4. **Select Protocol and then click Add.**

   The Select Network Protocol dialog box opens (see Figure 3-5).

Figure 3-5:
Select a manufacturer and a protocol provided by that manufacturer in the Select Network Protocol dialog box.

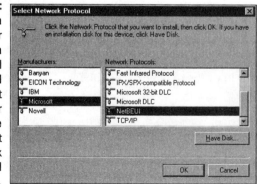

5. **Choose Microsoft from the Manufacturer list, and choose NetBEUI from the Network Protocols list.**

6. **Click OK.**

   You return to the Network dialog box.

7. **Click OK in the Network dialog box.**

   The necessary files are transferred to your hard drive. The Systems Settings Change dialog box opens and prompts you to restart your computer.

8. **Restart your computer.**

Adding network services

You can ask for specific services from the network, using the protocol you installed for inter-computer communication. (Refer to the section "Adding a protocol," earlier in this chapter, to find out about installing protocols.) For example, sharing resources on your computer with other computers is a service that the network provides. Using the resources available on other network operating system servers (such as NetWare) is also a service.

In fact, lots of services can be shared. For home networks, you usually think only in terms of sharing resources, such as drives, folders, and printers and other peripherals. But you can also share these services commonly installed for home networks: File and Printer Sharing for Microsoft Networks, Client for Microsoft Networks, and Microsoft Family Logon (the last two are client services you can use for logging onto the network). You can install more than one service.

The first service that you probably want to add is File and Printer Sharing for Microsoft Networks so that you can share your files and your printer with users on the other computers. Then, if you want to log onto your network with a user name, you can add one of the client services. I discuss these options in this section.

You need to have your Windows files available, so make sure the Windows CD is in the CD-ROM drive before you begin.

Adding the File and Printer Sharing service

Because the File and Printer Sharing service is so common, you don't have to go through the Add Services dialog box to install it — Microsoft provides a button for quick access to the installation of this service. Follow these steps to add the File and Printer Sharing service to your system:

1. **Choose Start⇨Settings⇨Control Panel.**

   The Control Panel opens.

2. **Double-click the Network icon.**

   The Network dialog box opens, with the Configuration tab in the foreground.

3. **Click File and Print Sharing.**

   The File and Print Sharing dialog box opens (see Figure 3-6).

Figure 3-6:
Tell
Windows
you want to
share your
files, your
printer,
or both
resources
in the File
and Print
Sharing
dialog box.

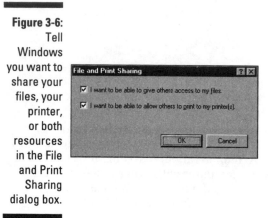

4. **Select the resources you want to share and click OK.**

Adding Network Client services

Client services are added to networks in order to provide a way for individuals to log onto the network. In a client/server network (where all the computers on the network are connected to one server computer), the server authenticates the logon name and password. In a peer-to-peer network (where all the computers on the network can access all the other computers), the logon provides a method of keeping track of users and their preferences. See Chapter 6 for more information about logon names and individual user preferences.

When you double-click the Network icon, as described in the following steps, you may see that the Client for Microsoft Networks is already installed. If that's the case, you don't have to install it again (in fact, Windows won't let you install it again).

To add client services to your network configuration, follow these steps:

1. **Choose Start⇨Settings⇨Control Panel.**

   The Control Panel opens.

2. **Double-click the Network icon in the Control Panel.**

   The Network dialog box opens, with the Configuration tab in the foreground.

3. **Choose Add.**

   The Select Network Component Type dialog box opens.

4. **Choose Client and then click Add.**

   The Select Network Client dialog box opens (see Figure 3-7).

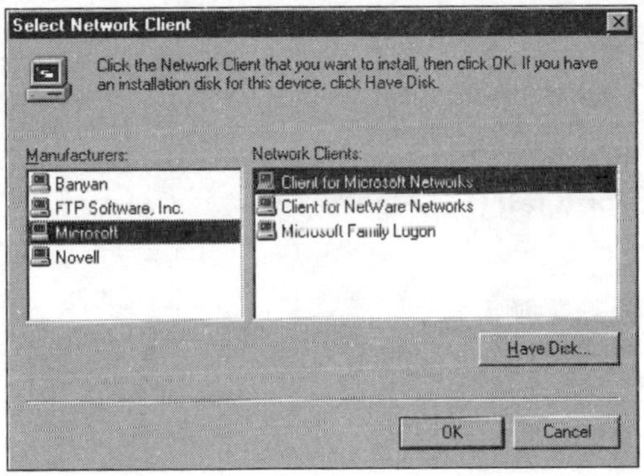

Figure 3-7:
Choose the
client
service you
want to use
on your
network in
the Select
Network
Client
dialog box.

5. **Choose Microsoft from the Manufacturers list in the left pane.**

   The Network Clients available from Microsoft appear in the right pane.

6. **Choose a client service from the right pane.**

   Choose Client for Microsoft Networks to log onto the network with your user name. Choose Microsoft Family Logon to select your name from a list of users. (Read Chapter 6 to find out more about logging on.)

7. **Click OK.**

   The necessary files are transferred to your hard drive, and you return to the Network dialog box.

8. **Click OK in the Network dialog box.**

   The Systems Settings Change dialog box opens, prompting you to restart the computer.

9. **Restart your computer.**

Naming computers and workgroups

The Microsoft networking system is fussy about keeping things straight. The networking services want to know who's who, who's where, and what's what. Because of this compulsive attitude, you must give each computer on your network a unique name. In addition, you must name the group that exists when all the computers that are linked on the network get together.

To name computers and workgroups, follow these steps:

1. **Choose Start⇨Settings⇨Control Panel.**

   The Control Panel opens.

2. **Double-click the Network icon.**

   The Network dialog box opens.

3. **Click the Identification tab (see Figure 3-8).**

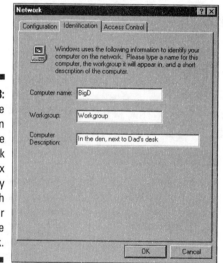

Figure 3-8:
Use the Identification tab of the Network dialog box to identify each computer on the network.

4. **Enter a unique name for this computer.**

   You can use up to 15 characters for the name.

5. **Enter a Workgroup name.**

   The *workgroup name* is the name you use for the group of computers that comprise your home network. You can use the default name of Workgroup or invent a different name. Make sure that all the computers on the network use the same workgroup name.

6. **Optionally, you can enter a Computer Description.**

   The description you enter can be viewed by other computer users if they use the Details view in Network Neighborhood.

7. **Choose OK.**

   Your computer is ready to participate in the network.

   The Systems Settings Change dialog box opens, prompting you to restart your computer.

8. **Restart your computer.**

9. **Repeat these steps for each computer on the network.**

Testing Network Neighborhood

After all computers on your home network have been configured for adapters, protocols, and services, they're ready to hang out together in their own neighborhood, the Network Neighborhood.

Checking the computers in the Neighborhood

Click the Network Neighborhood icon on the Desktop to see the computers on your network. As you can see in Figure 3-9, you see an icon for the entire network as well as an icon for each computer on the network.

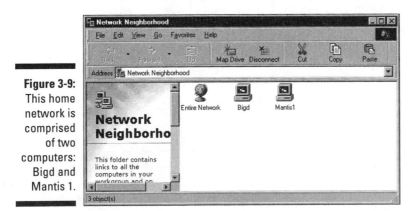

Figure 3-9: This home network is comprised of two computers: Bigd and Mantis 1.

If a computer is missing, or if an error message appears telling you that Windows cannot find the network, you have a problem. Look for these possible culprits:

- ✔ Check the adapter configuration on each computer. Make sure that you don't detect any settings conflicts.

- ✔ Check the cable connections.

- ✔ Make sure that all the computers have the same workgroup name in the Identification tab.

- ✔ Make sure that you installed the same protocol on all the computers.

Opening individual computers

The fact that all the computers on your network have made it to the Network Neighborhood isn't enough. The point of a network is sharing resources, including files, printers, and peripherals. So you need to make sure that these resources are being shared successfully.

Double-click an icon for a computer in the Network Neighborhood window. If the resources are shared, you can see the shared resources that have been established for that computer. Nothing happens when you double-click a computer's icon until resources are shared, because nothing exists to show you.

So, to avail yourself of the benefits of a network, you need to establish shared resources on every computer. For handy information on configuring shares, see the following chapters of this book for everything you need:

- ✔ Chapter 9 explains how to share files and folders.

- ✔ Chapter 12 explains how to share printers.

- ✔ Chapter 13 explains how to share peripherals, such as Zip drives and CD-ROM drives.

Part II
Networking with Telephone Lines

The 5th Wave   By Rich Tennant

"That reminds me-I installed the NICs for our
telephone line network last week."

In this part . . .

This part explains how to set up a network using your household telephone lines — the next big thing in the home PC networking realm. I tell you everything you need to know to connect your computers through your household telephone lines, from adding the hardware and software to computers not equipped with the technology to getting a new network-ready computer up and running. (If you'd like to connect your computers using standard cable rather than your household telephone lines, feel free to skip this part and read Part I instead.)

Chapter 4

Installing Telephone Line Networking Hardware and Software

•••

In This Chapter

▶ Buying and installing the hardware

▶ Installing the drivers

•••

A t about the same time this book was delivered to your favorite bookstore, manufacturers were releasing hardware for a new, exciting technology. That technology lets you create a network by connecting computers through your existing household telephone lines rather than using the traditional method of connecting computers using coaxial or 10BaseT (twisted-pair) cable.

Don't worry, you can still use your telephone. You can dial out, and your phone will ring when people call you. The network technology uses paths available in your telephone lines that your phone doesn't use.

The new hardware comes in two forms:

✔ New network interface cards (NICs) are designed to work with your household telephone lines. You can install these NICs in any computer.

✔ New computers have the telephone wiring adapters built into the motherboard.

In this chapter, I discuss the installation of telephone line network interface cards for your existing computers. For information about setting up the new network-ready computers, see Chapter 5.

Getting the Right Hardware

Several manufacturers offer network interface cards that work with your household telephone lines. At the time of this writing, the hardware was so new that I didn't have an opportunity to shop for NICs in order to see all the available products. However, the indications are that you can buy individual cards or kits that contain cards for multiple computers.

You must purchase a NIC that fits the available slot in your computer. The most likely slot types are ISA and PCI. You must also buy cable to connect the NIC to your telephone jack.

Buying telephone line NICs

The documentation that came with your computer includes a description of the type of expansion slot (also called *bus*) available on your motherboard. (Expansion slots are devices into which you place computer cards such as NICs, video cards, and so on.) If you have an older computer, you probably have ISA slots. If you have a newer computer, you probably have a combination of ISA and PCI slots. However, the documentation doesn't tell you which slots already have cards and which are empty. You must open the computer and examine the slots.

You can tell at a glance what type of bus is available if you know what to look for:

- ✔ An ISA bus is usually black. It has metal pins or teeth in the center, and a small crossbar about two-thirds of the way down the slot.
- ✔ A PCI bus is usually white, and it's shorter than an ISA bus. It has a crossbar about three-quarters of the way along its length.

See Chapter 1 for more detailed information about buses and slots, including illustrations of the various bus types so that you can figure out what type of bus is available in each of your computers.

If you have an EISA bus, you can use an ISA NIC.

If all your computers need the same type of NIC, look for a kit that includes cards and cables. If one computer needs a PCI card and the others only have ISA slots available, you must purchase individual cards and cable.

Buying telephone cable

The cable that connects the NIC to the phone jack is telephone cable. It's inexpensive and available everywhere, from supermarkets to computer stores.

If you purchase a kit for your hardware, the cable is probably included. If you purchase individual cards, you must also buy a length of cable for each card.

Installing the Hardware

The first chore is to install the hardware that you need to create your network. This means that you must install the NICs and then the cable.

Installing the NICs

When you open your computer to install the NICs, observe these important precautions:

✔ Don't use a magnetic screwdriver. Magnets and disk drives do not co-exist. (Magnetic fields can delete data.)

✔ Be sure the computer is unplugged (either pull the plug from the wall or pull the plug from the back of the computer).

✔ Discharge any static electricity in your body by touching something metal before you touch anything inside the computer.

✔ Remove any metal jewelry, especially rings. (Gold conducts electricity, including static electricity.)

Here's how to install the NIC:

1. **Remove the metal plate that's on the back of the computer, behind the slot that you want to use for your NIC. Save the screw so that you can use it to attach the NIC.**

2. **Insert the NIC in the slot and attach its end plate to the back of the computer with the screw you removed.**

3. **Close the computer.**

If you need more details, including illustrations, see Chapter 1.

Installing the cable

Installing the cable for your network is easy. The cable has a connector, called an *RJ-11 connector,* at each end. The two connectors are identical, so it doesn't matter which end goes where.

Plug one connector into the NIC and plug the other connector into the telephone jack in the wall. That's it — you're done!

Installing your telephone

The network connection doesn't interfere with your telephone service, so you can make and receive calls even though your home network is using the telephone lines. Of course, this requires a telephone. But, then, you know that, right?

You can use your wall jack for both a telephone and a network connection at the same time. You just have to adapt the wall jack so that it can do two things at once. Luckily, this is easy to do.

You need to buy a *splitter* (sometimes called a *modular duplex jack*), which is a little doo-hickey that you can purchase for a couple of bucks just about anywhere — at an office supply store, one of those super-duper big megastores, or even the supermarket. The splitter, which is illustrated in Figure 4-1, plugs into the wall jack to give you two places to plug in phone cables instead of just one. You plug the network cable into one connector and your telephone cable into the other connector. It doesn't matter which cable goes where.

Installing the Software

Your telephone line NICs come with software that your operating system needs. The software consists of files called *drivers*. Drivers give your computer the ability to use hardware. They let your operating system set up a communication system among your computer, your hardware, and your software.

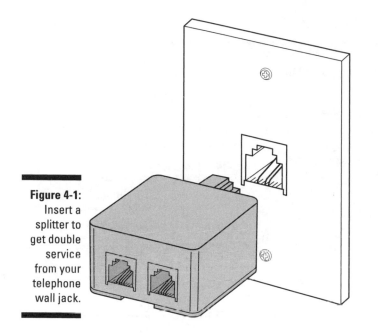

Figure 4-1:
Insert a
splitter to
get double
service
from your
telephone
wall jack.

The software is on a floppy disk or a CD. You have three possible approaches to software installation:

✔ **Drivers:** These are standard drivers that you use with the standard Windows procedures for installation.

✔ **Driver wizards:** Many software companies provide *wizards,* interactive programs that walk you through the process of installing drivers.

✔ **Software wizards:** These wizards install other software in addition to the drivers. Usually, the other software is WinGate Home, which permits everyone on the network to access the Internet simultaneously. In addition, the wizard may provide a way to select the file-sharing and printer sharing features available for networks.

NIC manufacturers include instructions for installing the software. However, I give you some guidelines in the following sections so that you have an idea of what to expect. (Sometimes, documentation isn't written clearly, or the author takes for granted that you understand all sorts of computer jargon. See the Cheat Sheet at the front of this book or the Glossary at the end of this book if you need to brush up on your networking vocabulary.)

In addition to the installation instructions for the software, the documentation should provide the default settings for the hardware. This makes it possible to install the hardware if Plug and Play doesn't work.

What's a network address?

The wizard uses the terminology Network Address Manager, and that term is technically a good description of the server's role. When computers and software are working with the Internet, the concept of an address is important. When a network computer wants to connect to the Internet, it needs a unique IP (Internet Protocol) address, which is a complicated concept that uses a series of numbers with periods between each group of numbers (for example, 198.180.11.1). Those addresses are "managed" by another complicated feature called DHCP (Dynamic Host Configuration Protocol).

Without DHCP, the IP address must be entered manually at each computer every time a computer user wants to use the remote modem and connect to the Internet.

The wizard automatically installs, sets up, and configures IP addresses and DHCP functions, saving you an incredible amount of elaborate technical steps. The software that the wizard installs handles the address management chores for your entire network.

After you install the hardware and start your computer, the Plug and Play feature should find the new hardware and offer to install it. Take the appropriate action, which I describe in the next section.

Installing drivers with Plug and Play

Follow the Plug and Play wizard instructions to install the drivers. When the wizard displays a list of manufacturers, click the Have Disk button. This is necessary because Windows doesn't come with drivers for telephone line NICs, so you can't search for drivers in the Windows database.

Insert the manufacturer's disk with the drivers, and tell the wizard which drive you are using for this installation (either A: or D:, assuming your CD-ROM is drive D — if it isn't, substitute the appropriate drive letter). The wizard presents the Install from Disk dialog box so that you can provide this information.

After the files are copied to your hard drive, you're told to restart your computer. Click Yes to restart. When you're back in Windows, your NICs are completely installed. Go to the next computer and repeat the process of installing the NIC, the cable, and the drivers.

Installing drivers without Plug and Play

Sometimes, Plug and Play doesn't work. Perhaps your computer doesn't support it, or perhaps it just didn't kick in for reasons you'll never know.

You can still install the necessary drivers. Most of the steps depend on your operating system. In this section, I discuss Windows 98 and Windows 95 procedures using the Add New Hardware program.

Installing new hardware in Windows 98

Install the manufacturer's drivers using these steps in Windows 98 if you don't have Plug and Play:

1. **Choose Start⇨Settings⇨Control Panel.**

   The Control Panel opens.

2. **Double-click the Add New Hardware icon.**

   The Add New Hardware wizard appears, with an introductory message. Click Next to begin adding your hardware.

3. **Click Next to let the wizard begin searching for your new hardware.**

   You have no choice; Windows 98 insists on searching for new hardware. The odds are good that Windows 98 won't find the NIC (otherwise, Plug and Play would have worked). But it takes a while for Windows 98 to give up and admit defeat. Relax and get a soda.

   Eventually, Windows 98 concedes defeat and asks you what kind of hardware you're trying to install. You may see a list of possibilities, but the list may not include your new NIC.

4. **If your NIC is listed, select it and click Next; otherwise, select No, The Device Isn't on the List, and then click Next.**

5. **Click Have Disk instead of selecting a manufacturer.**

   Proceed as if you were installing the NIC with Plug and Play, which is covered in the preceding section.

6. **Restart your computer.**

   The next time Windows starts, you see a logon dialog box. Enter your name and, if you wish, enter a password. See Chapter 7 to find out all about passwords.

Installing new hardware in Windows 95

Install the manufacturer's drivers using these steps in Windows 95 if you don't have Plug and Play:

1. **Choose Start➪Settings➪Control Panel.**

   The Control Panel opens.

Figure 4-2:
In Windows 95, you have a choice, and it's usually faster to say No and then perform a manual installation.

2. **Double-click the Add New Hardware icon.**

   The Add New Hardware wizard appears.

3. **Click Next, and the operating system offers you a choice, as shown in Figure 4-2.**

4. **Choose No, and then click Next.**

5. **Click Have Disk instead of selecting an existing manufacturer.**

   Proceed as if you were installing the NIC with Plug and Play, which is covered in the preceding section.

6. **Restart your computer.**

   After your computer starts again, you can log onto this computer with a network logon (Windows presents a logon dialog box), which means the computer has been attached to a network successfully.

Installing drivers with a wizard

If the manufacturer of your NIC supplies a wizard that automates the installation procedure, it's easier to use that wizard than to use the Windows Plug and Play wizard. When you start your computer, Plug and Play will probably find the NIC and attempt to install it. If Plug and Play doesn't start, you can just start the NIC wizard. Follow these steps to use the manufacturer's wizard:

1. **Click Cancel on the Plug and Play dialog box (if it appears).**

2. **Insert the manufacturer's disk or CD that has the wizard.**

   If the wizard is on a CD, it should start up immediately (using a feature called AutoPlay). Follow the instructions, clicking Next to move through all the windows in the wizard.

   If AutoPlay doesn't kick in, double-click the My Computer icon and then double-click the CD icon in the My Computer folder. Look for the file that launches the installation program. The documentation tells you the file name.

   If the wizard is on a floppy disk (which is not very common), insert the floppy disk and follow the instructions in the documentation to launch the wizard. Usually the instructions involve choosing Start⇨Run and then entering *a:file name* in the dialog box. (Substitute the real file name.)

3. **Follow the instructions on the wizard screens, clicking Next to move through all the screens.**

4. **Restart your computer.**

   When your computer starts again, you must add the rest of the network files (see Chapter 3). When that's finished, your computer is part of a network.

Some NIC manufacturers include additional software that's installed with wizard. The software includes WinGate Home, which is included on the CD that accompanies this book.

This is the same installation program I discuss in Chapter 5, so see that chapter for more information. (It seems silly for me to write it twice.)

Chapter 5

Using Network-Ready Computers

*B*ecause of the enormous advantages to home users (and small-business users, too), the ability to connect computers via home telephone lines has caused quite a bit of excitement in the computer hardware world.

To take advantage of the expected popularity, some computer manufacturers now build computers with the telephone line network card built right into the computer's motherboard. This is called an *embedded network card*.

Because everything is still in the development stages as I write this book, I can't go to my local computer store and find all the different computer brands that have this new technology built in.

As a result, in this chapter, I discuss the installation procedures for one particular computer brand and assume that the other computers are designed to work the same way. (The computer I'm working with is the Compaq Presario Internet PC, a new computer designed for home users who want to create a home network using telephone lines.)

Preparing for the Installation Wizard

Most, if not all, of the new ready-for-telephone-line-networking computers are designed to let you install several features. The wizard that comes with the computer covers these procedures:

✓ Installing the drivers for the built-in NICs if you want to use your new computer on a network (which you probably do, or else you wouldn't have purchased this book)

> ✔ Installing software that enables all the users on your network to access the Internet at the same time
>
> ✔ Providing a way to enable file sharing and printer sharing among all the computers on your home network

As an installation program, the wizard works best as a host first and then a client. Let me explain what I mean by that. The wizard software that comes with your new computer assumes that you want to install simultaneous Internet access in addition to networking capabilities. In order to have simultaneous Internet access for all the computers on your network, you must designate a host computer, also called a *server*. The host is the computer with the modem that everybody uses, which is why it's the host — everybody else is a guest. In computer jargon, computers that are using hardware and services on another computer are called *clients*.

The Compaq wizard calls the host (server) computer the Network Address Manager. If you purchased another computer brand, it may use that term or the simpler term "host" or "server." Or, perhaps there's another term invented by your computer manufacturer. Whatever terminology is being used, you just need to understand the server/client (host/guest) relationship needed to share a modem.

You should run the wizard first on the computer that has the modem you want to use. That may or may not be the new computer you just purchased. See the next section, "Preparing for the Network Software," for more information about making this decision.

To make all of this possible, the manufacturer of your new computer has included a CD with the wizard software. Although you can probably double-click an icon on the Desktop to start the wizard from your hard drive, the CD is included so that it can be used on the other computers on your network.

Preparing for the Network Software

Before you install the network software and drivers on your new computer, you have to make some decisions and perform some other easy chores. You must choose a host computer for your modem, install a cable on the new computer, and install the network hardware and software on the other computers. This section guides you through these tasks.

Choosing a host computer for the modem

Your new computer has a modem installed. It's a state-of-the-art modem, rated at the current highest available speed (56 Kbps).

If you want to use this modem for Internet access, the networking software will make sure that it's set up to act as a host modem for all the other computers on the network.

If you have a computer that already has modem capabilities that are more robust than a standard modem, you may want to use that computer as the host for Internet access. The modem types that you can consider using instead of the modem on your new computer are

- An ISDN modem
- An ADSL modem
- A cable modem

(See Chapter 14 for information about the advantages and disadvantages of the various modem types.)

The networking wizard should be run first on the computer that has one of those three options available. Otherwise, you should run the wizard first on your new network-ready computer. Of course, the computer must have a telephone NIC and all the networking features installed before you start.

For this chapter, I'm assuming you want your new computer to be the host. If you want to use another computer, start with that one.

Installing the cable on the new computer

Before you begin setting up your new computer, you should install the cable that comes with the computer. This way, as soon as the software is installed, you can start networking.

If you're going to use the modem in the new computer, you should have a Y-connector (an adapter that is shaped like a capital letter Y) that connects both the modem and the NIC to the length of cable that attaches to your wall telephone jack. The two ends of the top of the Y are connected to the back of the computer (one side in the modem, the other side in the NIC). A single end (the bottom of the Y) is where you attach the cable between the computer and the wall jack.

If you're going to use the modem from another computer, just attach the cable between the NIC that's built into your new computer and the wall telephone jack.

Installing the network hardware and software on the other computers

Unless you purchased two new computers that have telephone line networking built in, you are planning to connect your new computer to an existing (probably older) computer. Incidentally, the computer jargon for an older computer is *legacy computer*.

Follow the instructions in Chapter 4 for installing hardware (NICs and cable) and drivers in the other computers on your network.

Installing the Software on the Host Computer

If you're using your new computer as the host, you should have an icon on the Desktop that starts the networking wizard when it's double-clicked. Depending on the computer manufacturer, the title under the icon varies, but the title should refer to networking. You can also insert the wizard CD, which launches the wizard automatically.

If you're using an existing, older computer as the host, insert the wizard CD in that computer's CD-ROM drive.

The wizard starts by introducing itself, as all wizards do — they're very polite. Click Next to move on to the real stuff.

Some wizards may offer the chance to see an explanation of networking, and you can opt to look at those screens before you begin the installation.

As soon as you start the installation procedure, some files are transferred to your hard drive automatically. These are the files needed to run the setup and configuration programs. Then, additional wizard windows appear so that you can configure your network. Click Next to move through the wizard windows. I discuss the information you need to supply in the following sections.

Naming the computers

You must give each computer on the network a name. Choose a name that describes the computer — for example "kitchen" or "den." The name can have up to 15 characters, but you can't use any spaces. If you want to use two words, place a dash between the words (for example, "Mary's-room"). A dash counts as a character, and so does an apostrophe.

This naming step inserts the name of the computer under the Network icon on the Identification tab. See Chapter 3 for more information about setting up networks, including giving each computer a name.

Installing the host software

The wizard window offers two choices that describe this computer: Either it's the first computer that you're installing on the network (it's a host), or you're adding the computer to an existing network (making it a client).

Tell the wizard that this is the first computer on the network, because the wizard really wants to know which computer you're using as the host. Technically, you're not lying, even if you've already set up another computer with a NIC. After all, this is the first computer that receives this software.

Choosing a setup option

The wizard presents a screen that offers setup options, and it probably has the choices shown in Figure 5-1, even if it doesn't look exactly like this figure.

If you click Custom, you're offered two general choices: Internet access choices and file sharing and printer sharing choices. The next two sections explain these choices.

Internet access choices

The wizard gives you an option to choose whether the computer you're installing the software on connects to the Internet using its own modem (acting as a server/host) or using the modem on another computer (acting as a client).

Because you're starting with the host computer, you don't need to change any options. When you install the software on the client computers, the wizard will find everything it needs on the host and will install the client software automatically. That's why you should start with the host computer and install the hardware on all the computers, giving the computers a way to communicate.

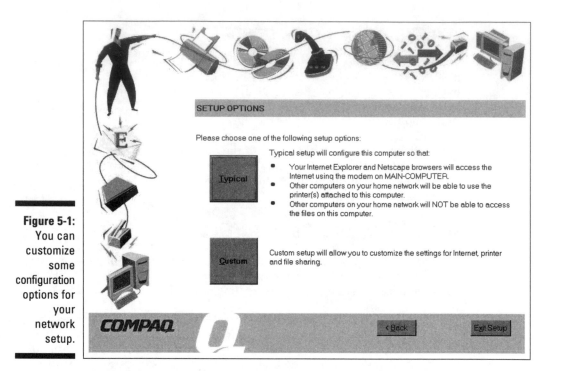

Figure 5-1:
You can
customize
some
configuration
options for
your
network
setup.

File sharing and printer sharing choices

The wizard offers to let you set up *file* and *printer sharing* across the net-work. This means that you can let users on other computers have access to folders and files on your computer and let them use a printer attached to your computer. (See Part V for more about sharing hardware.)

File sharing and printer sharing are useful tools and an important part of networking. However, the way the feature is implemented by the wizard leaves much to be desired. You can perform the same tasks manually, with a great deal more power and control.

See Chapter 3 to find out how to install this feature. See Chapter 9 to find out how to set up drives, folders, and files so that they are shared with other users. Chapter 12 tells you how to share printers with other users.

I prefer a manual configuration for file sharing and printer sharing over the features offered by the wizard. Here's why:

✔ **Entire drives are shared:** The wizard lets you share only drives, not folders. Even if you don't mind making your entire hard drive acces-sible to everybody in the family, you may want to protect one or more folders from prying eyes (your personal correspondence or accounting data, for example). The wizard doesn't support this feature, and to accomplish this, you have to set up sharing manually, as described in Chapter 9. Or you can install this feature through the wizard and then refine it manually later.

✔ **You may not have an installed printer:** If you're running the wizard on your new, network-ready computer, the chances are good that you installed networking before you did anything else. If you haven't yet installed a printer, the only printer that shows up for sharing is the fax (which is not really a printer). Therefore, you can't really set up printer sharing through the wizard. You have to install a printer and then read Chapter 12 to find out how to share it, but that's an easy task.

Finishing the host computer installation

The wizard transfers the necessary files and then tells you to restart the computer. In fact, it offers to perform the task for you. Click Yes to take the computer up on its offer.

When your computer starts again, you see a Network Logon dialog box. You can ignore the Password text box (because no password exists yet) and click OK to continue. Later, you can go back and create a password and create other users. See Chapter 7 for information about creating passwords. Chapter 6 gives you information on adding users to this computer.

Don't click the Cancel button on the Logon dialog box because that tells the computer that you're not performing a network logon. This may interfere with some of the subsequent network chores that you want to perform.

Installing the Software on the Client Computers

You have at least one other computer in your house, or you probably wouldn't have bought this book. Now you can give that other computer the ability to use the modem on the host computer.

The client computer should have a telephone line NIC installed (both physically installed and drivers installed) and the cable connected. Then follow these steps to install the software on the client computer:

1. **Insert the networking wizard CD in the client computer's CD-ROM drive, which should launch the setup program automatically.**

   If the setup program doesn't start automatically, double-click the My Computer icon and then double-click the CD-ROM icon. Look for the file called setup.exe and open it.

The wizard finds the host computer (see Figure 5-2) because you completed the network configuration on this client computer and logged onto the network.

The wizard is easy to use, but you must supply some information. Each computer must have a name, and you have the same options for a custom installation (file sharing and printer sharing) that are discussed in the section "Installing the Software on the Host Computer."

2. **After the installation is complete, restart your computer and log onto your new network.**

Whether you used telephone line network cards on all the computers in your house or you combined those computers with a new, ready-to-network computer, you now have a network.

The chores you performed to create your network weren't much different from the tasks faced by people who installed regular, old-fashioned network cards. You just had an easier time because you didn't have to run network cable through the walls of your house.

Now you can use the information throughout this book to take advantage of the network environment.

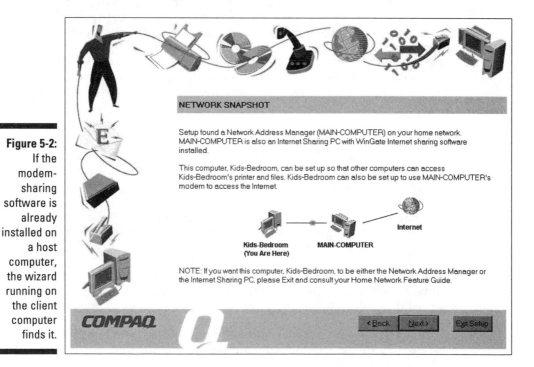

Figure 5-2:
If the modem-sharing software is already installed on a host computer, the wizard running on the client computer finds it.

Part III
Getting Personal

The 5th Wave — By Rich Tennant

"IT WAS CLASHING WITH THE SOUTHWESTERN MOTIF."

In this part . . .

A network makes it easy for everyone in your house to use files on all the computers, but that doesn't mean that you want everyone poking around in your private files. In this part, I tell you how to set passwords to protect privacy. I also tell you how to set up profiles and personalize the Windows Desktop so that each user can feel at home, no matter which computer he's using.

Chapter 6

Profiling Users

S everal people share the same computer in most homes, even if more than one computer resides in the household. One of the nifty features that you can take advantage of when you share the same computer is a profile. Each user has his or her own *personal profile,* which is the computer environment that belongs to that user. Profiles enable you to personalize your Desktop without risking ruin of your decorative effort when the next person uses the computer. (See Chapter 8 for more information about personalizing your Desktop.)

In this chapter, I show you how to set up profile features to provide each user with a personalized computer environment. Typically, the person who's most comfortable with computers takes a lead role in preparing the system for these features, but after the setup is complete, everybody in the household can create a personalized computer environment.

Enabling Profiles

Windows 98 and Windows 95 don't automatically assume that each person who uses a computer wants to make his or her settings permanent. Instead, Windows expects that the same Desktop and menu items can work for everybody. To create customized settings, you have to tell the operating system that you want each user to have a personal profile.

Follow these steps to turn on the profiles feature:

1. **Choose Start⇨Settings⇨Control Panel.**

   The Control Panel opens.

2. **Double-click the Passwords icon.**

   The Passwords Properties dialog box opens.

3. **Click the User Profiles tab.**

4. **Select the Users Can Customize Their Preferences and Desktop Settings option, as shown in Figure 6-1.**

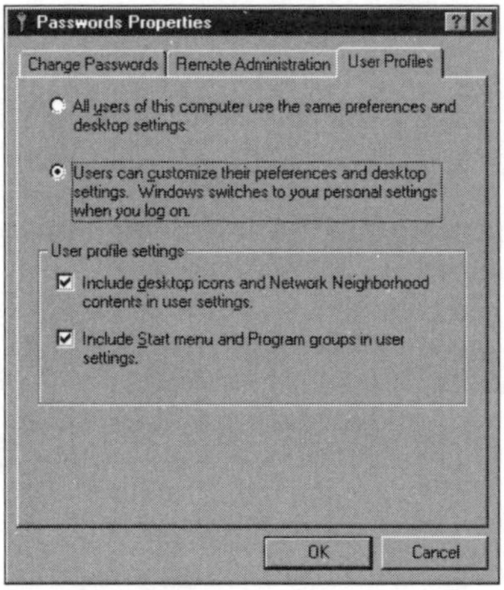

Figure 6-1:
Tell
Windows to
save each
user's
customized
settings.

This selection enables each computer user to save any customized Desktop settings, and those settings are loaded every time that the user logs onto the computer.

If you don't select this option, any changes made by one user are transferred to all other users, which sort of kills the whole idea of having a profile for each user.

5. **In the bottom half of the dialog box, select either or both profile options.**

   The option to include Desktop icons and Network Neighborhood means that each user can make changes to those objects and Windows will remember each user's setup.

   The option to include the Start menu and Program groups means that as each user adds items to the menu (usually by installing software), the menu item appears only when that user is logged on.

6. **Click OK.**

   Now Windows is ready to keep track of all the users who work at this computer.

   The System Settings Change dialog box opens, prompting you to restart the computer.

7. **Restart your computer.**

Don't worry that you won't be able to use software installed by someone else because there's no menu item for that software on your own menu. You can put the menu item on your menu without having to install the software again. (I cover that in Chapter 7.)

Creating Users

After you tell Windows that you want to keep track of each user's settings, it's time to create those users. As you do, Windows sets up folders for each user. Those folders hold all the information about each user's configuration.

User information is also kept in the Registry, which is the database that keeps track of all settings for a Windows computer. The Registry is complicated (and dangerous) to use, but you don't have to risk encountering trouble because all the settings you establish in the Control Panel are transferred to the Registry automatically.

The way that you create users differs depending on whether you're using Windows 98, Windows 95 with Microsoft Internet Explorer 4.0, or Windows 95 without Microsoft Internet Explorer 4.0.

Creating users if you run Windows 98 or Windows 95 with Microsoft Internet Explorer 4.0

If you've installed Microsoft Internet Explorer 4.0 in a Windows 95 system, a Users icon appears in the Control Panel. If you're using Windows 98, Microsoft Internet Explorer 4.0 is installed automatically, so all Windows 98 computers have a Users icon in the Control Panel.

Double-clicking the Users icon enables you to create users who can then access this computer. (Your own logical mind probably figured that out already.)

If you don't want to do all the work yourself, each person in your household can use this tool to create his or her own user file.

Windows provides a wizard to add users to the computer. The first time you double-click the Users icon, the Add User wizard starts automatically. (After the first user is created, double-clicking the Users icon takes you straight to the User Settings dialog box.)

Follow these steps to add a user:

1. **Read the information in the first wizard window and click Next.**

   The first window is just an introduction to the wizard, so you don't have to provide any information.

2. **In the next wizard window, enter the name that you want to use when you log on in the User Name text box.**

   Most people use just a first name, unless there are two people in the household with the same first name. If so, you can use Mom and Sis, or Dad and Junior. Nicknames are fine, too.

3. **Click Next.**

   The Enter New Password dialog box opens.

4. **If you want to use a password, enter the password in the Password text box of the Enter New Password dialog box (see Figure 6-2). Enter the same password in the Confirm Password text box and then click Next.**

   If you don't want to use a password, just click the Next button.

   Either way, the Personalized Items Settings dialog box opens.

   If the entries in the Password text box and the Confirm Password text box don't match, the wizard asks you to enter the password again. You can't see the actual characters you're typing, so use a password that's easy to type. For example, if you frequently make typos when you enter numbers, don't use a number in your password.

5. **In the Personalized Items Settings dialog box (see Figure 6-3), choose the settings that you want to personalize and save in your profile. Also, choose the way that you want these items created. Then click Next.**

   You can personalize the Desktop folder, Documents menu, Start menu, Favorites folder, Downloaded Web pages, and the My Documents folder.

   The items you don't select will remain the same as they are now. Even if you make changes while you're working on the computer, the next time you log on, those items will revert to their current state. See the next section, "Deciding which settings to personalize," for more information on how this works.

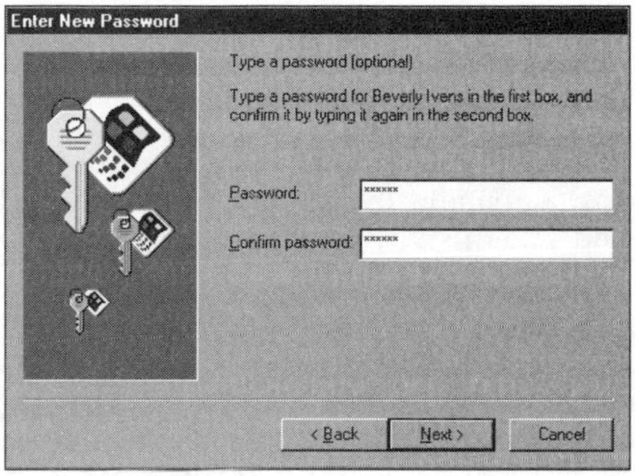

Figure 6-2:
When you
enter a
password,
the
characters
turn into
asterisks so
nobody can
read your
password if
they're
watching
over your
shoulder.

If you tell Windows to create copies of the current items, you're asking that the current Desktop settings serve as the starting point for your configuration efforts. Everything that exists on the current Desktop is automatically copied to your profile. However, if you tell Windows to create new items, you have to build a customized Desktop from scratch.

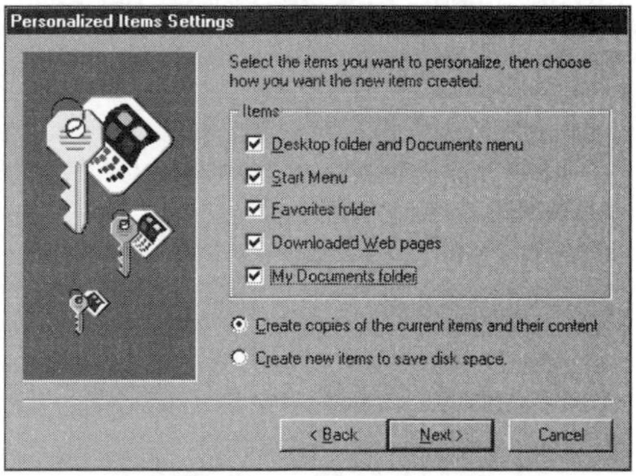

Figure 6-3:
Choose the
settings you
want to
personalize.

6. In the Ready to Finish dialog box, click Finish.

Windows takes a few seconds to set up folders and files for a new user. (You see an animated dialog box as this activity proceeds.) Then you return to the User Settings dialog box, where your user name is listed.

7. **In the User Settings dialog box, click <u>N</u>ew User to set up another user, or choose Close if you're finished for now.**

Every time you log onto the computer with this user name, your customization efforts are saved according to the options you set.

The next time you double-click the Users icon in the Control Panel to add a user, the wizard won't start automatically. Instead, you'll see the User Settings dialog box. To add a new user to the computer, click New User to start the wizard.

Deciding which settings to personalize

The Personalized Items Settings dialog box (the third screen of the wizard that sets up new users) offers several choices for each user's personalization. Here are some guidelines to help you make selections:

- **Desktop folder and Documents menu.** Select this option to save your personal settings for the Desktop and the Documents menu item on your Start menu.

- **Start Menu.** Select this option to save the changes that you make to the Start menu, including Program groups and items.

- **Favorites folder.** Select this option to save your settings for your Favorites folder, which holds links to your favorite Web sites as well as links to programs and documents that are on your hard drive.

- **Downloaded Web pages.** Select this option to save temporary Internet files and cookies in your own personal folders. (Temporary Internet files are called the *cache. Cookies* are pieces of data that Internet sites place on your hard drive in order to identify you when you visit those sites.)

- **My Documents folder.** Select this option to make the Desktop My Documents folder a private folder for yourself.

Creating users if you run Windows 95 without Microsoft Internet Explorer 4.0

Windows 95 does not have a Users icon in the Control Panel (unless you install Microsoft Internet Explorer 4.0). The system creates a new user when someone logs onto the computer with a user name that hasn't been used previously. Follow these steps to create a new user in Windows 95:

1. **Choose Start⇨ Sh<u>u</u>t Down.**

    The Shut Down Windows dialog box opens.

2. **In the Shut Down Windows dialog box, choose Close All Programs and Log On as a Different User.**

   After a few seconds, the Welcome to Windows dialog box opens with the name of the previously logged on user displayed in the User Name text box.

3. **Change the name in the User Name text box to the name that you want to add, as shown in Figure 6-4.**

Figure 6-4:
Creating a
new user is
just a
matter of
entering a
new name
during
logon.

4. **If you want to use a password, enter a password in the Password text box.**

   Windows 95 does a quick chcck on the user name, and if it doesn't exist, the operating system assumes that a new user is being created (which is, of course, exactly what's happening).

5. **In the Set Windows Password dialog box (see Figure 6-5), reenter your password in the Confirm New Password text box and click OK.**

   The password that you originally entered is already inserted in the New Password text box (an asterisk replaces each typed character).

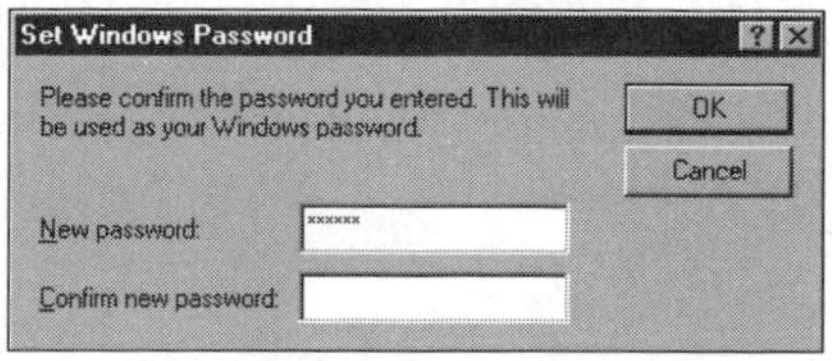

Figure 6-5:
Set up the
password
that you
plan to use
when
logging
onto the
computer
with this
user name.

6. **If you chose to skip a password when you logged on, the New Password text box is empty. Click OK to confirm that you intentionally didn't enter a password when you logged on.**

The technical term for no password is a *null password*.

The Windows Network dialog box opens, asking you to confirm that you want to save any configuration options you change for your own personal Desktop (see Figure 6-6).

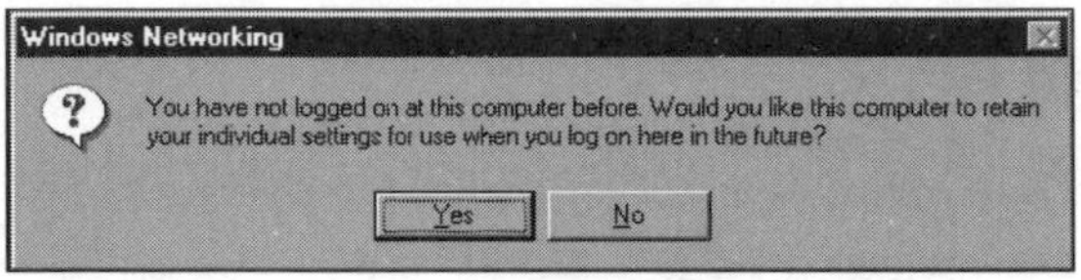

Figure 6-6:
Hello, you
must be
new here.
Are you
planning to
come back?

> **Windows Networking**
>
> ? You have not logged on at this computer before. Would you like this computer to retain your individual settings for use when you log on here in the future?
>
> [Yes]   [No]

7. **Click Yes to indicate that you want a separate profile maintained for this user logon name.**

Windows 95 creates the appropriate Registry entries and folders.

Incidentally, I've seen the dialog boxes in Steps 5 and 6 presented in the opposite order — that is, you're asked about maintaining your personal settings before you're asked to confirm the password. The variation may be the result of Windows 95 versions working in different ways or the effects of upgrade installations. (Several versions of Windows 95 exist, including a version written specifically for brand new computers in which the manufacturer installs the operating system.)

You can create a new user by merely logging on with a new and different user name in Windows 98 as well as Windows 95. However, you don't have the opportunity to set the options for personalized settings that are available in the Users applet. If you use this method of creating a new user in Windows 98, you can later double-click the Users icon in the Control Panel to open the User Settings dialog box to personalize the user configuration.

See Chapter 7 for lots of detailed information about working with passwords, including forgotten passwords.

Changing user options

In Windows 98, the Users icon in the Control Panel isn't just for creating users; you can also manage users there. Managing means that you can change the options for users, copy an existing user's setup to a new user, or delete any user names you don't need anymore.

Copying a user's settings to a new user

Say you have a user who has a really terrific configuration. The good news is that you can use that configuration to set up a new user. Usually, you find the following: a Programs menu that shows everything that's been installed, lots of handy shortcuts on the Desktop, and an absolutely beautiful and highly decorative Desktop. Follow these steps to clone a new user from an existing user:

1. **Choose Start⇨Settings⇨Control Panel.**

   The Control Panel opens.

2. **Double-click the Users icon.**

   The User Settings dialog box opens.

3. **In the Users list box, select the user with the configuration that you want to copy.**

4. **Click Make a Copy to open the Add User wizard.**

5. **Follow the instructions for adding a new user, clicking Next to move through each of the wizard's windows.**

   The wizard asks for a user name, a user password, and a confirmation of the password.

That's all there is to it — the new user has a terrific Desktop waiting!

However, you may encounter some serious problems with this cloning approach. If you choose a user to clone who's been working at this computer for some time, all the documents in that user's personal My Documents folder are cloned. Internet cookies are cloned. Everything that's linked to the user is cloned.

To avoid that problem, remove the check mark from Favorites folder, Downloaded Web pages, and My Documents folder when you get to the Personalized Items Settings wizard window.

The best way to use the Make a Copy feature is to create a user, customize the Desktop and Start menu items, and then use that user only for copying the configuration to new users. You may want to name the user "clone" or "perfect person."

Deleting a user

If your User list contains a name that's no longer used on this computer (perhaps Junior lost his computer privileges), get rid of it. You not only dump the name, but you also clear out all the folders that are attached to the user, which frees up disk space.

You can't delete the user who is currently logged on.

Changing a user's password

You can change passwords in the User Settings dialog box, but you have to know the current password in order to do it. This, of course, eliminates the ability to fix things when a user forgets a password. (See the section "Using the Family Logon feature," later in this chapter, to find out how to handle passwords that somehow slip from memory.)

You can also change passwords in the Passwords Properties dialog box in the Control Panel. However, the Passwords Properties dialog box only works for the currently logged on user; the User Settings dialog box is appropriate for any user.

Follow these steps to change the logon password:

1. **Choose Start⇨Settings⇨Control Panel.**

   The Control Panel opens.

2. **Double-click the Users icon.**

   The User Settings dialog box opens, displaying a list of users in the Users list box.

3. **Select the appropriate user name.**

   The Users list box shows the highlighted user name.

4. **Choose Set Password.**

   The Change Windows Password dialog box opens, as shown in Figure 6-7.

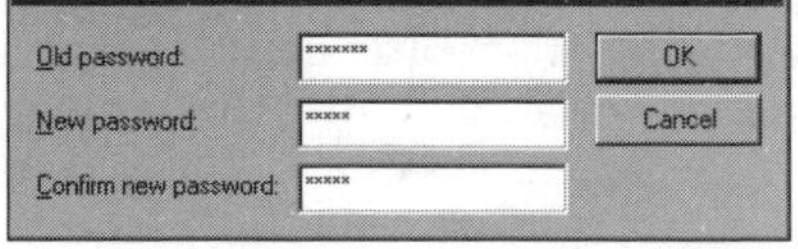

Figure 6-7:
Type carefully because you can't see the characters you're entering.

Change Windows Password		
Old password:	*******	OK
New password:	*****	Cancel
Confirm new password:	*****	

5. **Enter the old password in the Old Password text box.**

6. **Enter the new password in the New Password text box.**

7. **Enter the new password again in the Confirm New Password text box.**

   If you make a mistake, you're invited to try again.

8. **Click OK to return to the User Settings dialog box.**

   A message appears to announce that you now have a new password.

9. **Click Close to close the User Settings dialog box.**

Changing user settings

You can change the items that a user can personalize by selecting the user's name and choosing Change Settings. When the Personalized Items Settings dialog box opens (see Figure 6-8), you can select or deselect items to indicate what this user can personalize. Most of the time, you make these changes for your own logon name, but if you're acting as the home network administrator, you may have reasons to work on other user names.

Figure 6-8:
Some users
don't feel
the need to
personalize
every item.

Logging On

When profiles are enabled, a logon dialog box opens every time you start Windows, and in addition to entering your name in the User Name text box, you must enter a password in the Password text box to complete the logon procedure. The way that you approach passwords depends on the way you configured passwords for your user name. Any of the following scenarios may apply:

 ✔ If you have a password, enter it in the Password text box and click OK (or press Enter).

 ✔ If you don't have a password, just click OK or press Enter.

 ✔ If you don't want to use your own personalized settings, click Cancel or press Esc.

It's not necessary to use passwords when you share a computer with other users. In fact, passwords in this case don't provide much security because they're easy to bypass by pressing the Esc key. Having a unique user name simply saves your configuration changes so that every time you log on, you see the Desktop you designed for yourself. See Chapter 7 to explore security and secrecy on your home network.

Switching to another user

Okay, you powered up your computer and logged on. You balanced your checkbook, sent a letter to Mom, and played a game. Now somebody else wants to use the computer.

Luckily, you don't have to shut down the computer to enable the next user to log on and load his or her personalized Desktop. (I say "luckily" because the shutdown process is time-consuming, and the startup process can seem endless.) Windows provides a feature called a *logoff.* (Computer users have turned that phrase into a noun.) Here are the ways to initiate the logoff procedure:

 ✔ In Windows 98, just click the Start button and click Log Off *<username>*, where *username* is the current logged on user. Then click Yes.

 ✔ In Windows 95, you face a bit more work — there are three clicks instead of two. From the Start menu, choose Shut Down, and then choose Close All Programs and Log On as a Different User. Click Yes.

The logon dialog box opens within seconds so that the next user can log on.

When the logon dialog box returns, the name of the last user who logged on appears in the User Name text box. The new user must remove that name and replace it with his or her logon name and password (if he or she has one).

Bypassing logon

The most common reason for users to bypass the logon is because they don't know the password required for a successful logon — not always a sign of some sinister intent. Being human, users sometimes just forget their own passwords.

You can easily skip the logon procedure in Windows 98 and Windows 95. To bypass the logon procedure, click the Cancel button on the logon dialog box, or press the Esc key. See, I said it was easy.

When you bypass the logon, the Desktop that appears is the Desktop that was in effect when profiles were enabled on the computer. Call it the default Desktop.

If you turned on the profile feature immediately after installing Windows, the default Desktop is quite sparse. The only Desktop icons are those that appear as a result of installation choices. The Programs menu has only a few items (also the result of installation choices) such as Windows Explorer, the MS-DOS Command Prompt, and the Accessories you installed. You may also find a Startup folder, but it's probably empty.

If you used the computer for a while — installing software, creating Desktop shortcuts, and so on — before you enabled the profiles feature, the default Desktop offers those elements.

Anyone who uses the default Desktop can make changes to it. A new default Desktop results from saving those changes. The default Desktop has two uses:

- ✔ It's the Desktop for users who skip the logon procedure.
- ✔ It's the Desktop that's used when you create a new user.

You can deliberately skip the logon just for the purpose of making changes to the default Desktop. Then, from this Desktop, create a new user. You preset the basic settings for that user with this Desktop.

Using the Family Logon feature

So you can't believe that users frequently forget their passwords? Wait till you hear that users also fail to recall their names (okay, not their real names, their logon names). Most of us use nicknames or first names or some cute appellation for a logon name. Most folks don't choose to log on as Bentley T. Backstroke, Jr. The more likely logon choice is Bentley, Bent, or Junior.

Forgetting your logon name is not all that unusual, and I've found that it's a far more common event for people who have strange and esoteric logon names at work. If your company assigns you a logon name of 77645G567 (some companies use names like that) and you decide to use Sammy on your home computer, you can expect a brain fog to settle in when you look at that home-based logon dialog box. You're sure you're not supposed to use that weird logon from work, but you're not really certain what you entered when you set yourself up as a user on your home computer. Was it Sam? Sam Smith? Ssmith? Sam S?

You can bypass the logon (see the previous section, cleverly titled "Bypassing logon") and use the default Desktop to open the Users list in the Control Panel where you find your name on the list. Then you can log on again.

Or, you can avoid that effort and time by taking advantage of a clever logon device called the Family Logon. After the logon's enabled, the Family Logon dialog box — rather than a traditional logon dialog box — opens when the operating system starts up. This Family Logon dialog box lists all the users registered on this computer, as shown in Figure 6-9. You just have to select your name, enter your password (if you have one), click OK, and you're in!

Figure 6-9:
With Family Logon, you don't have to remember your own name.

Enter Password

Microsoft
Windows98

Select user name:

Allen
Bill
Mike
Sarah

Password:

OK   Cancel

Family Logon is available if your computer is running Windows 98 or Windows 95 with Microsoft Internet Explorer 4.0. If you're using Windows 95 without Internet Explorer 4.0, sorry, you're stuck with having to remember your logon name.

Installing the Family Logon feature is easy. Before you begin, however, choose one of following tasks, depending on your Windows setup:

✔ If you're using Windows 98, put your Windows 98 CD in the CD-ROM drive.

✔ If you're using Windows 95 with Microsoft Internet Explorer 4.0 and you received Internet Explorer 4.0 on a CD, place the CD in the CD-ROM drive.

✓ If you're using Windows 95 with Microsoft Internet Explorer 4.0 and you downloaded Internet Explorer 4.0 from the Internet, you don't have to do anything because Windows remembers the location of your Microsoft Internet Explorer 4.0 files on your hard drive.

Hold down the Shift key when you insert a CD to prevent the CD's program from opening automatically. (For more information about disabling the AutoPlay feature that automatically starts the CD, see Chapter 13.)

Follow these steps to install the Family Logon feature:

1. **Choose Start➪Settings➪Control Panel.**

   The Control Panel opens.

2. **Double-click the Network icon in the Control Panel.**

   The Network dialog box opens, with the Configuration tab in the foreground.

3. **Click Add.**

   The Select Network Component Type dialog box, shown in Figure 6-10, opens.

Figure 6-10:
It's easy to add the Microsoft Family Logon to your network components.

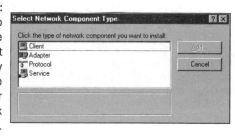

4. **Choose Client and click Add.**

   The Select Network Client dialog box opens.

5. **In the Select Network Client dialog box (see Figure 6-11), choose Microsoft from the Manufacturers pane on the left.**

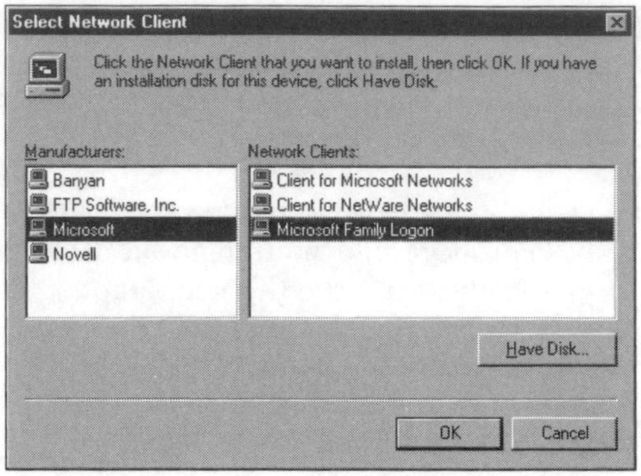

Figure 6-11:
Installing
network
services
requires
choosing a
manufacturer
and a
service.

Select Network Client

Click the Network Client that you want to install, then click OK. If you have an installation disk for this device, click Have Disk.

Manufacturers:
- Banyan
- FTP Software, Inc.
- Microsoft
- Novell

Network Clients:
- Client for Microsoft Networks
- Client for NetWare Networks
- Microsoft Family Logon

Have Disk...

OK   Cancel

6. **Choose Microsoft Family Logon from the Network Clients pane on the right.**

7. **Click OK.**

   You're back at the Network dialog box, and the necessary files are copied from Microsoft Internet Explorer 4.0 or Windows 98.

8. **In the Primary Network Logon text box, choose Microsoft Family Logon.**

9. **Click OK.**

   The Systems Settings Change dialog box opens to tell you that these settings take effect after you restart your operating system.

10. **Click Yes to restart the system.**

   When Windows starts again, the Family Logon dialog box opens so that you can select your user name and enter your password if you have one.

Logging Off

After you finish working on the computer — and nobody's standing over your shoulders waiting impatiently to be the next in line — play it safe and log off. Otherwise, the next person who sits down in front of the computer may just start working, which can change your configuration. When the computer is up and running, people tend to forget they need to log off the previous user and log themselves on. Going right to work is just too tempting.

 If you don't use passwords, you may want to erase your name from the Select User Name text box in the logon dialog box that appears after you log off. (Just use the delete key to erase the letters.) Removing your name prevents the next user from accidentally clicking OK or hitting the Enter key, thus getting to your Desktop. Such a move happens more often than you may imagine, and the result is two surprised and disappointed users. Your Desktop is different the next time you log on, and the user who changed your Desktop is annoyed when he logs on properly and the changes he made aren't on his Desktop.

When you log off, any open software windows are closed for you. Before the logoff procedure starts, you're given an opportunity to save any data that you've changed since the last save.

If you have an operating system window open, such as the Control Panel or My Computer, you can expect to find it open when you log on again. The same is true even if lots of other users log on in the meantime — the window just waits for you to return. Another user can't see the open window on the Desktop (unless she left the same window open when she logged off).

Viewing Your Personal Profile

Your personal profile is a collection of the configuration options you set for yourself. Every time you make changes to the Desktop or install software, the results are stored in your profile. When you log onto Windows with your own user name, your own user profile is loaded when Windows starts.

Displaying profile information

You can see the elements in your profile by looking in the folders that contain your profile information. When you know how to find and identify profile elements, you can take advantage of the tricks and tips available for changing your profile easily. To see the elements in your profile, follow these steps:

1. **Choose Start⟹Programs⟹Windows Explorer.**

   The Explorer window opens.

2. **Click the plus sign to the left of the folder in which your Windows software is stored (usually named Windows).**

   The subfolders under your Windows folder are displayed in the left Explorer pane.

3. **Click the plus sign to the left of the subfolder named Profiles.**

   Folders for each user on the computer are displayed in the left Explorer pane.

4. Click the plus sign to the left of the subfolder for your logon name.

You can see the subfolders for your own personal profile in the left Explorer pane, as shown in Figure 6-12.

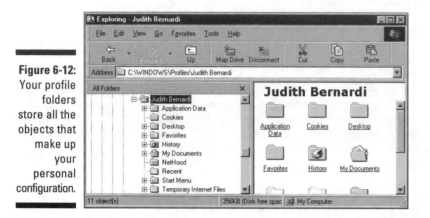

Figure 6-12: Your profile folders store all the objects that make up your personal configuration.

Looking in your Desktop folder

Click the Desktop folder to check out the subfolders and shortcuts it contains. The objects that you see in the folder represent the objects you find on your Desktop when you log onto Windows. As shown in Figure 6-13, you can have folders and shortcuts on your Desktop.

Here are some tidbits of information to note when you view your profile's Desktop folder:

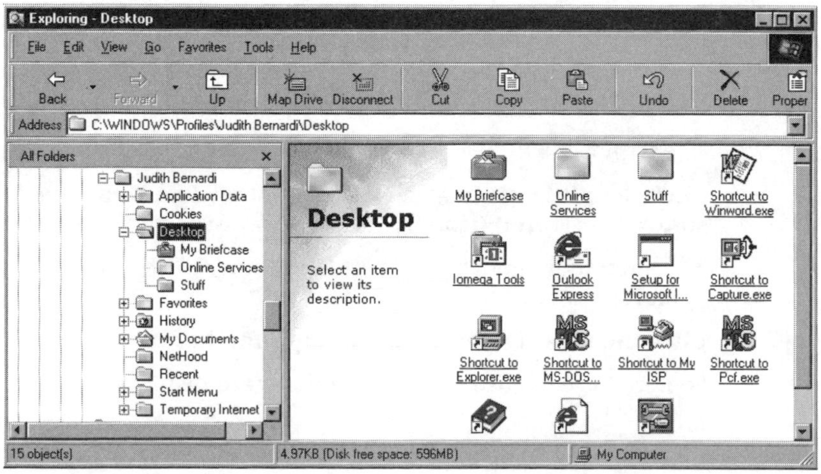

Figure 6-13: The objects in your Desktop folder probably differ from these, because this folder represents the user's configuration decisions.

> ✔ The default Desktop icons aren't represented in your profile Desktop folder. Those icons include My Computer, Network Neighborhood, the Recycle Bin, and the My Documents folder.
>
> The My Documents folder is a default Desktop folder in Windows 98, but not in Windows 95.
>
> ✔ You may not have either a Briefcase folder or an Online Services folder on your Windows 98 Desktop, because they appear as a result of selecting them during installation of Windows 98. They don't appear on your Desktop by default.
>
> Windows 95 doesn't offer an Online Services folder during installation.
>
> ✔ The objects in the profile Desktop folder are linked to your real Desktop. If you delete or add an object in either place, the change is made in both places.

Viewing your Start Menu folder

You can view and manipulate the items that appear on your personal Start menu within your personal profile folders. Use these steps to view your personal Start Menu folder:

1. **Choose Start⇨Programs⇨Windows Explorer.**

   The Explorer window opens.

2. **Click the plus sign to the left of your Windows folder.**

   The left Explorer pane displays the subfolders under the Windows folder.

3. **Click the plus sign to the left of the Profiles folder.**

   The left Explorer pane displays the user folders.

4. **Click the plus sign to the left of your profile folder.**

   The left Explorer pane displays all the subfolders in your personal profile.

5. **Click the plus sign to the left of your Start Menu folder and also click the folder itself.**

   The left Explorer pane displays the subfolders under your Start Menu folder, and the right pane displays the contents of your Start Menu folder.

6. **Click the plus sign to the left of your Programs folder and also click the folder itself.**

   The left pane displays the subfolders on your Programs menu, and the right pane shows the listings that appear on your Programs menu, as shown in Figure 6-14.

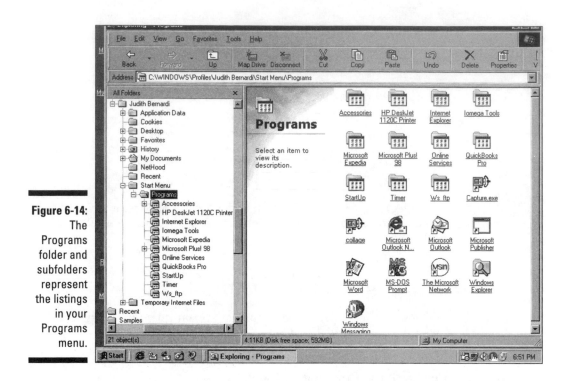

Figure 6-14:
The
Programs
folder and
subfolders
represent
the listings
in your
Programs
menu.

Subfolders under the Programs folder represent program groups that appear on your Programs menu. You can use the objects in these folders to change the way your Programs menu presents items. Common manipulations include the following:

- ✔ **Create folders to hold groups of program items.** You can create a new subfolder in the Programs folder and then move related program items into that folder. This action is useful if your Programs menu is very long.

- ✔ **Move items from a subfolder to the Programs folder.** This is a handy trick if you use a particular accessory frequently and don't want to move down another level when you open it from the Programs menu.

To discover more about creating folders in Windows 95 and Windows 98, look into *Windows 95 For Dummies,* 2nd Edition, and *Windows 98 For Dummies* (both are written by Andy Rathbone and published by IDG Books Worldwide, Inc.).

You can also copy Programs menu items from other users' personal folders. You find out how to accomplish that task in Chapter 8.

Chapter 7

Setting Passwords and Maintaining Secrecy

● ●

In This Chapter

▶ Working with passwords

▶ Remembering your password

▶ Keeping your private stuff secret

● ●

*T*his chapter is about passwords and secrecy, but I'm going to be a nice person and start by telling you the truth: Windows 98 and Windows 95 provide no real security.

Sure, you can make up passwords for logging on, and you can install software so that it appears only on your Programs menu and no one else's. And yes, you can change file attributes to make a file hidden or unable to be changed. You find out how to do these things throughout this book.

But none of it means a thing! Anybody who understands how to maneuver around a hard drive and manipulate files in Explorer can get past all the security measures that you put into place.

So, in this chapter I explain how to set up security measures, and then I explain how to get around them. I do this for two reasons:

▶ If you understand the ways to get around the security measures, you'll be able to design a better security plan.

▶ If one family member absolutely needs to get around the security imposed by another family member and has a valid reason, you can handle the problem. (Don't let anyone else read this — it means that you're the administrator and that you're in charge of the computer.)

Keep in mind, however, that software programs usually have a way to impose security that works better than anything you can design. I cover that subject in this chapter also.

Working with Passwords

Password protection in Windows 98 and Windows 95 is called a security wall. It isn't a brick wall — it's more of a straw wall. Straw walls can keep out those people who don't know how to get past straw. People who know their way around computers aren't intimidated by passwords, but at least you can protect yourself against people who don't have computer expertise.

Changing passwords

Some people feel more secure if they change their logon password often. Frequently, these are the same people who say, "Oh, do it yourself — here's my password," when someone needs a data file from the computer. Eventually, the password is known by so many other people that it may as well be taped to the front of the monitor — "John's password is gojohn. Help yourself."

Actually, changing your password periodically is a good habit, even if you don't give out your password to everyone in the immediate five-county area. Your computer security does increase when you take this step — in case you've given out your password to someone who doesn't know how to get around the logon dialog box. Some people change passwords because they acquired the habit at work — many companies insist on password changes at regular intervals.

To change your password, you have to know the old password, so this feature is not a cure for a forgotten password. The solution for that problem is covered later in this chapter, in the section "Help! I Forgot My Password."

In Windows 98, you can change your password in either of two places, both of which are in the Control Panel: The Passwords Properties dialog box, or the User Settings dialog box.

In Windows 95, only the Passwords dialog box is available (unless you've installed Internet Explorer 4.0, which adds the Users icon).

Changing passwords in the Passwords Properties dialog box

The Passwords Properties dialog box is available to change the password of the user who is currently logged on. Double-click the Passwords icon in the Control Panel to see the dialog box shown in Figure 7-1.

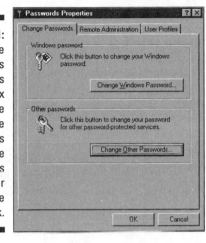

Figure 7-1:
Use the
Passwords
Properties
dialog box
to change
the
passwords
you use
for this
computer
and for the
network.

You have two choices available for passwords in this dialog box:

- ✔ **Windows password:** This is the password you use for logging onto the computer.

- ✔ **Other passwords:** These are the passwords you use for other password-protected network activities, such as logging onto a network server.

  If you haven't configured the computer for other logon activities, such as logging onto a Windows NT network server or a Novell NetWare server, this choice is not available. Home networks usually are not set up for these additional network activities.

To change your logon password, click the button marked Change Windows Password. When the Change Windows Password dialog box opens, as shown in Figure 7-2, fill in all three text boxes and then click OK.

Figure 7-2:
You have
to know
the old
password if
you want to
create a
new one.

Change Windows Password		
Old password:	********	OK
New password:	*****	Cancel
Confirm new password:	*****	

If you're working on a computer that has network logons, you have an opportunity to change the other passwords at the same time that you change the Windows password, as long as you're planning to use the same password for both password types. If you want to set a different password for the other network services, you have to use the Other Passwords choice in the dialog box. The dialog box for Other Passwords is the same as the dialog box for the Windows password.

You can use this dialog box to change from one password to another, to change from no password (null password) to a real password, or to change from a real password to a null password. When you enter your password, you won't see the characters you type because they're displayed as asterisks. This prevents anyone who is looking over your shoulder, from seeing your password.

1. **Enter the old password.**

   If the old password is a null password, just leave that text box blank.

2. **Enter the new password.**

   If the new password is a null password, leave the text box blank.

3. **Confirm the new password by entering it again.**

   If the new password is a null password, leave the text box blank.

4. **Click OK to close the dialog box.**

If you entered everything correctly, you see a message telling you that the password was successfully changed. If you made a mistake, the message tells you that you entered information incorrectly:

✔ If you made a mistake when you entered the old password, the error message tells you that the Windows password you typed is incorrect. Click OK and enter the old password again.

   If you continue to fail when entering the old password, you obviously have forgotten the password that you used to log onto the computer. Because this is highly improbable, you may have assumed that you are the current logged on user, but instead you've begun working at the computer without noticing that someone else had logged on and then left the computer. Click the Start button to see the name in the Log Off choice. If it's not your name, select the Log Off choice and then log yourself on.

✔ If you made a mistake when you repeated the password in the Confirm New Password text box, the error message tells you that the new and confirmed passwords don't match. Click OK and reenter the password in the confirmation box.

If you fail more than once when you're trying to confirm a new password, you may have chosen a string of characters that invites typos. Start again with a password that's easier to enter.

Changing passwords in the User Settings dialog box

You can change the password for any user in the User Settings dialog box. If you change someone else's password, I hope you do so because that person asked you to. Changing another user's password as a practical joke is not sporting. When you double-click the Users icon in the Control Panel, you see the User Settings dialog box, as shown in Figure 7-3.

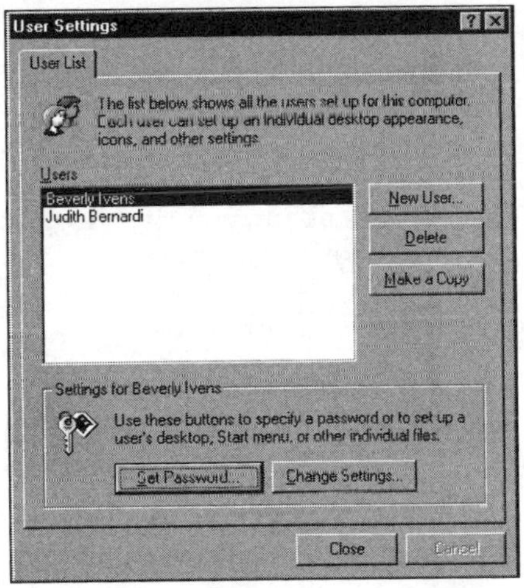

Figure 7-3:
You can change the password for any user on this computer in the User Settings dialog box.

Select the user name that you want to work with and click Set Password. The dialog box that opens is the same dialog box that's displayed when you use the Passwords Properties dialog box (refer to Figure 7-2). Enter the old password and the new password, and then confirm the new password.

Help! I Forgot My Password

People forget their passwords. It's a common, frequent problem. You usually forget your password the next time you try to log on after a password change, but using a password for weeks or months and then suddenly forgetting it is not rare.

Recognizing the symptoms of a user who forgets a password is easy. When the logon dialog box opens, the user stares at it for a moment and then shrieks or moans, "Oh no." The user usually is frozen in front of the computer for several seconds and then experiences a panic attack. (The symptoms vary according to the way that person handles panic.)

The problem of a forgotten password is easy to solve, so the user has no reason to panic. In this section, I go over the steps for the solution, which illustrates why we say that Windows 95 and Windows 98 are operating systems devoid of security.

Remember that you cannot issue a new password by changing the current password, because you have to know the old password in order to effect the change.

The way to solve the problem of a forgotten password is to delete the Windows file that holds the password. That file is checked against your password entry whenever you log on.

Sometimes users don't really forget their passwords. The problem may be with the user's password file. If a password file becomes corrupted, or someone inadvertently deletes it, the password won't work.

To delete the password file, you must log onto the computer. Fortunately (or unfortunately, depending on how you feel about security), logging on without a password is as easy as pie. Follow these steps:

1. **In the Logon dialog box, click Cancel or press Esc.**

   Presto! You're on the computer.

2. **Double-click the Windows Explorer icon or the My Computer icon and go to the folder that holds your Windows files (usually named Windows).**

3. **Press F3 to open the Find dialog box.**

   You want to find files with the extension .pwl, which is the extension that Windows assigns to password files. The Find dialog box should indicate that it is searching your Windows folder (see Figure 7-4).

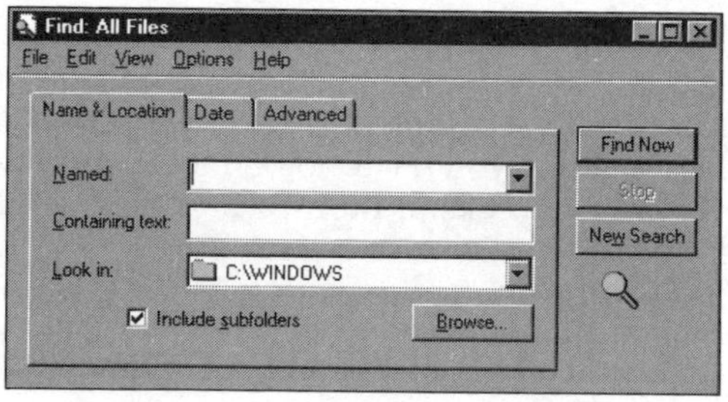

Figure 7-4:
The Look in text box should say "Windows" when you search your Windows folder for files.

![Find: All Files dialog box. Tabs show Name & Location, Date, Advanced. Fields for Named, Containing text, and Look in (C:\WINDOWS). Include subfolders checkbox checked with Browse button. Buttons: Find Now, Stop, New Search.]

4. **In the Named text box, enter pwl (or *.pwl) and click Find Now.**

   The Find dialog box shows a list of all the files that your computer found with the .pwl extension.

5. **Select your password file from the list that appears in the Find dialog box.**

   You can recognize your password file because it has the first eight letters of your logon name, followed by the extension .pwl. If your logon name has a space in it, the space is ignored in the password file name.

   You could also head right for your password file in the Windows folder, instead of using Find.

6. **Press Del to delete the file.**

   Windows asks you to confirm the fact that you want to delete the file.

7. **Click Yes to confirm that you want to delete the file.**

Your computer no longer has any record of your password. You are password-less. Is that anything like being speechless?

Searching for character strings instead of extensions

In Windows 98 and Windows 95, you don't have to use the old DOS method of entering ***.pwl** to look for files with the .pwl extension. You can search for any text, including extensions, by merely entering the letters. However, when you search for a string of characters, Windows finds every instance of that string. If the string is included in file names, you see those file names listed in the search results, too.

For example, in this figure, the string "pwl" is part of a file name.

Usually, the old DOS method of searching for an extension with *.<extension> is the best idea.

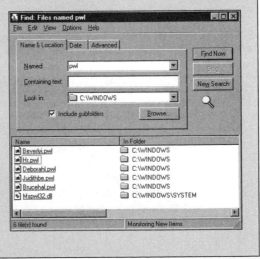

Creating a new password

After you've deleted your password file, your computer has no record of a password for you. This is the same as having a null password. You don't have to do anything else except log off and log on again with your own name. But you probably want to have a password, just in case. This section gives you two options for creating a new password: You can create a new password immediately after deleting the old one, or you can wait to create a new password until the next time you log on.

Creating a new password at the next logon

The way you fill out the Logon dialog box at your next logon determines your new password:

- If you want to keep the null password, enter your logon name, skip the password text box, and click OK. Your password file is re-created with a null password.

- If you want to create a new password, enter a new password in the password text box of the Logon dialog box. When you click OK, you're asked to confirm the password by typing it again. A new password file is created for you, and the password you entered is saved as your new password.

- If you're using Family Logon, your name appears on the list of users for this computer, but the password text box is grayed out and inaccessible. Click OK to log on with a null password, because you have no choice.

You can go to the Passwords icon in the Control Panel to change your password at any time. Whenever you create a new password, try to remember it.

Creating a new password before the next logon

If you want to enter a new password before you log on again, you can't use the Passwords icon in the Control Panel because it's connected to the current logged-on user — remember, you didn't log on as yourself because you forgot your password.

However, if you are using Windows 98, or Windows 95 with Internet Explorer 4.0, you can double-click the Users icon in the Control Panel and create a new password for your logon name before you log on again. Here's how to create a new password and a new password file at the same time:

1. **Double-click the Users icon in the Control Panel and select your logon name.**

2. **Click Set Password.**

3. **Skip the Old password text box, and enter a new password in the New Password text box.**

   Windows doesn't find an old password because you wiped out the password file for this user.

4. **Enter the new password again in the Confirm Password text box.**

5. **Click OK and then click Close to close the User Settings dialog box.**

   Windows creates a new password file.

6. **Choose Log Off from the Start menu and then log on again as yourself.**

If you once again forget the password, start these steps all over again, but this time, don't enter any passwords anywhere. That means you'll have a null password.

Another security device that you can employ in Windows is a password-protected screen saver. Information about using this feature is available in Chapter 8.

Hiding Files and Folders

You can hide files and folders so that other users of the computer don't see them in Windows Explorer or My Computer. This is a way to hide a program that you don't want anyone else to use or a file that you don't want anyone to see.

For each security measure, a workaround exists — a way to break through the security. Breaking this security measure is easy if you know how; I explain how in this section.

Understanding view options

By default, Windows 95 and Windows 98 don't show hidden files or folders in Windows Explorer or My Computer. If you hide a file or folder object, nobody will see it. Whether an object is hidden depends on its attributes, and you can change the attributes quite easily. See the following section, "Changing attributes for files and folders," for information on how to do that.

The operating system also automatically prevents the display of certain files needed by the operating system and software programs as a way of protecting them against accidental deletion.

Changing attributes for files and folders

To prevent other users from seeing a file or folder, you have to hide it by changing one of its attributes to "hidden." Here are some good reasons to hide files and folders:

✔ People hide folders to prevent other users from accessing the software that's installed in that folder. If the data for the software is also in the folder, you've killed two birds with one stone. This method keeps the kids out of the accounting software.

Actually, because the kids are commonly more computer-literate than the parents, this technique is also frequently a way to keep parents out of the kids' software.

✔ People hide files to prevent anyone from seeing data. If you hide a data file from view in Windows Explorer and My Computer, the file is also hidden from view when you use the Open dialog box to see the data files in Windows software.

Changing the attribute of a file or folder to make it hidden is very easy:

1. **Right-click the object in Windows Explorer or My Computer and choose Properties from the shortcut menu that appears.**

2. **In the Properties dialog box, click the check box next to Hi_d_den (see Figure 7-5).**

3. **Click OK.**

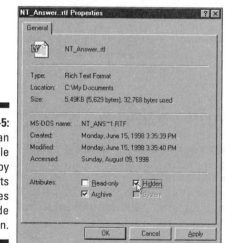

Figure 7-5:
You can hide a file or folder by changing its attributes to include Hidden.

Using DOS commands to set attributes

If you're comfortable with DOS, you can open an MS-DOS window and use the **attrib** command. Enter **attrib <setting> <foldername>**, or **attrib <setting> <filename>**, where a setting of +h sets the Hidden attribute, and a setting of -h turns off the Hidden attribute. Here are some examples:

- ✔ **attrib +h c:\mystuff** hides the folder named mystuff.

- ✔ **attrib +h c:\mystuff*.*** hides all files in the mystuff folder (but doesn't hide the folder).

- ✔ **attrib +h c:\mystuff*.doc** hides all files with the extension .doc in the mystuff folder.

- ✔ **attrib +h c:\mystuff\smith*.*** hides all files with file names that begin with smith (useful if your name is smith and you save personal files with a naming convention such as smithchecksjuly).

Accessing hidden files and folders

Even you won't be able to see the files and folders you've hidden, but you can access them manually. This means that you have to remember the name of the folder or file you secreted.

Accessing hidden objects in Windows 98

Windows 98, as well as Windows 95 with Internet Explorer 4.0 installed, presents an Address bar in Windows Explorer that you can use to access files and folders.

To get to a hidden folder, choose Windows Explorer from the Programs menu and enter the path to the folder in the Address bar. For example, if you hid the folder named Checkwriting, enter **c:\checkwriting**. Then you can open the file you need.

To get to a hidden file, select its folder in Windows Explorer. The path to the folder appears in the Address bar automatically — for example, C:\mystuff. All you have to enter is a backward slash, followed by the name of the hidden file, so that you end up with something like this: C:\mystuff\myfile.txt.

When you're working in a software program (such as a word-processing program), open a hidden file by typing its name into the File Name text box of the Open dialog box. Hidden files aren't displayed in the list of files that appears in the Open dialog box.

Accessing hidden objects in Windows 95

In Windows 95, to get to a hidden folder, choose <u>T</u>ools➪<u>G</u>o To from the Windows Explorer menu bar. When the Go To Folder dialog box opens, as shown in Figure 7-6, enter the path to the folder that you want to work with.

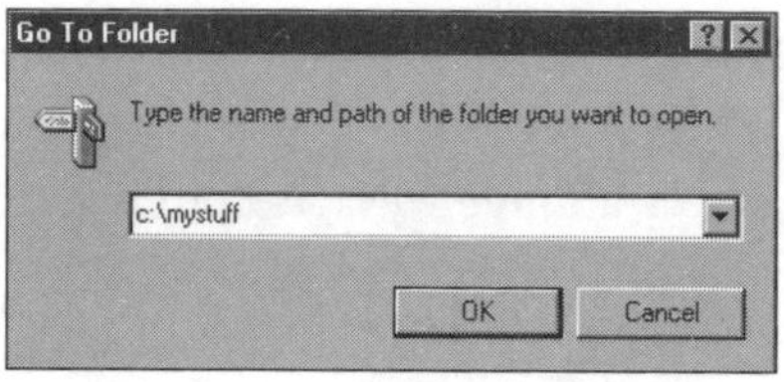

Figure 7-6:
Move to a
hidden
folder by
entering its
path in the
Go To
Folder
dialog box.

You can't get to a hidden file in Windows Explorer or My Computer with Windows 95. If you want to use a hidden file, you must "unhide" it (use the DOS command **attrib -h c:\mystuff*filename.ext***) or change the way that Windows Explorer displays files so that hidden files are visible (covered in the section "Viewing hidden files — the workaround").

When you're working in a software program (such as a word-processing program), open a hidden file by typing its name into the File Name text box of the Open dialog box. Hidden files aren't displayed in the list of files that appears in the Open dialog box. The software opens the file.

Viewing hidden files — the workaround

Hiding files can be a waste of time because forcing Windows to show you hidden files is easy. Here's how:

In Windows 98, choose <u>V</u>iew➪Folder Options. Click the View tab and scroll to the Hidden Files section in the Advanced Settings box (see Figure 7-7). Select Show All Files and click OK.

In Windows 95, choose <u>V</u>iew➪<u>O</u>ptions from Windows Explorer or My Computer, click the View tab, select Show All Files, and then click OK.

Many people don't know that they can change the default settings in Windows Explorer or My Computer, and if people like that share your computer, you can use this feature to keep your stuff private.

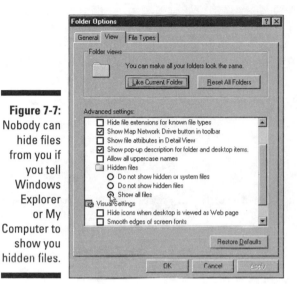

Figure 7-7:
Nobody can
hide files
from you if
you tell
Windows
Explorer
or My
Computer to
show you
hidden files.

Using Software to Secure Files

Most software written for Windows contains a feature that enables you to keep other users out of your files. This feature works a bit better than the operating system's security device of hiding files, but it's not foolproof.

Creating file passwords

No universal set of keystrokes exists that works for all software programs, but you should look in the Save dialog box of your Windows software application to find the options for password-protecting the document that you're saving. Some programs have a check box that you have to click; other programs have a button (named Options or Advanced) that opens a new dialog box where you can select password protection for the file. At some point, you are asked to enter the password, and then you are asked to enter it again to confirm it.

If you password-protect a file and then forget the password, you are absolutely out of luck. You have no way to open the file.

When any user selects the file to open it, a dialog box opens asking for a password. Figure 7-8 shows the Password dialog box for Microsoft Word 97 (which may be different from the dialog box that your software displays).

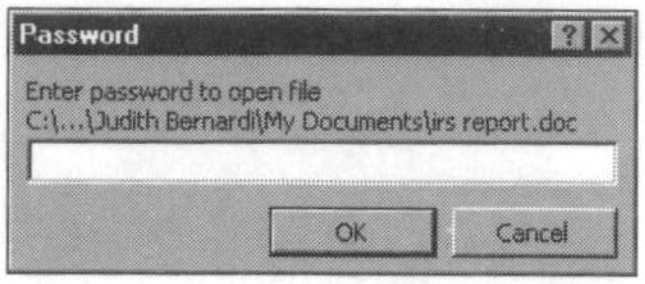

Figure 7-8:
The correct password is the key for unlocking a document that's protected.

Password

Enter password to open file
C:\...\Judith Bernardi\My Documents\irs report.doc

OK   Cancel

The software won't open the file without the correct password entry (see Figure 7-9).

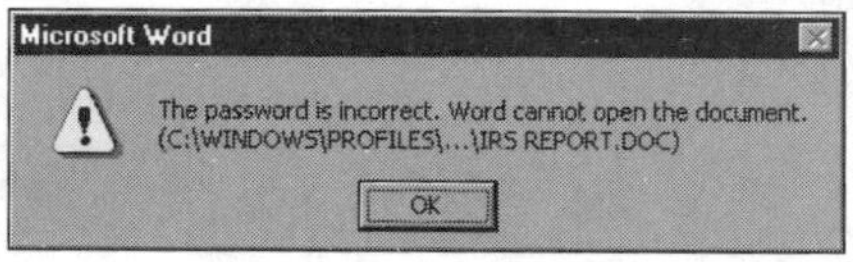

Figure 7-9:
Sorry, no way!

Microsoft Word

⚠ The password is incorrect. Word cannot open the document.
(C:\WINDOWS\PROFILES\...\IRS REPORT.DOC)

OK

Creating modification passwords

Some software programs offer two password levels — one to open a file and another to modify it. This is useful if you don't mind permitting other users to see the file, but you're fussy about who can change it. Password-protected modification should be used when you want to permit modifications as long as you give permission, via password.

Read-only files can't be modified under any circumstances

You don't need a password if you just want to protect a document against modification. You can use the read-only option that's available in the Save dialog box. It's not connected to passwords because a read-only file can't be changed by anyone (including you). If changes are made, the document must be saved with a different file name.

Some software, such as Microsoft Word 97, presents a dialog box when you open a read-only file. The dialog box asks if you'd like to open the file without the read-only attribute, which sort of undermines the intent.

If a document is password-protected against both opening and changing, anyone who tries to open it (including you) must fill out two passwords. After entering the correct password to open the document, the password for modifying the document is requested.

If the modification password is unknown or incorrect, the document can be opened in *read-only mode,* which means that changes cannot be saved. When the user attempts to save the document, a dialog box opens with the message that the document is protected as a read-only file. Then the Save As dialog box opens so that the file can be saved with a different name. This protects your original document from modification.

Defeating software file password protection

The only way to defeat software password protection is to delete the password from the protected file. You probably wouldn't do that to a file you protected, but anyone you give the password to could perform that action. Here's how to beat the system:

1. **Enter the correct password to open the file.**

2. **Choose File⇨Save As from the menu bar.**

3. **Use the options on the Save As dialog box to delete the password.**

4. **Click Save.**

 I'm told that some software programs lock out changes to password protection so that the scenario for beating the protection doesn't work. I haven't seen any programs that provide protection against such changes, but they could exist.

Knowing that password protection has a workaround should make you think twice about giving anyone the password to a file that you want to protect. If it doesn't, here's another scenario that you should think about: Suppose the user who has your password changes the password instead of removing it? Now you won't be able to get into your own file.

Using password-protected software

Some software programs have a password feature that prevents users from loading the software without the right password. Many accounting software programs use this device.

Another protection scheme is to load the software opening screens or menus and then prohibit access to specific parts of the software by asking for a user name and a password. Each user can be configured for access to certain software features. For example, many accounting software programs can be configured to permit users into one area (perhaps entering bills or writing checks) but not others — for example, the payroll module is frequently restricted to all but a few users.

Personal checkwriting and bookkeeping software usually provides password protection. For example, Quicken and QuickBooks, both popular with home users, have password-protection features.

Software security that is linked to the ability to open the software files is usually impenetrable.

The ultimate security for your data files is to save documents on a floppy disk. Then hide the disk (but don't use your underwear drawer — it's the first place people look for secret stuff). The downside of this security "feature" is that floppy-disk saving is incredibly slow. Also, you have a bunch of floppy disks after a while, and keeping track of the files becomes difficult. However, if security is a priority, saving documents to a floppy is the way to make sure that nobody else will ever see your data.

Chapter 8

Personalizing Your Desktop

● ●

● ●

*T*he Windows Desktop is very much like a physical desktop: It holds the stuff you need to get your work accomplished (and a few things that merely serve as pleasant distractions). You can put tools, pictures, and decorative items on your Desktop.

When your computer is set up for multiple users (that is, *profiles* are enabled), each user gets his own Desktop when he logs on. You can take advantage of this for aesthetic or security reasons.

When I was growing up, I shared a room with my sister, and we had totally different tastes. If I could have enabled profiles for our room, as soon as I walked into the room, the wall colors, the bedspreads, the knick-knacks on the bureau, and everything else all changed to the design I'd created. Then, when my sister entered the room, the room would instantly redesign itself to reflect all of her weird design efforts.

Profiles are a great feature for families and businesses that have more users than computers. Because people have to share computers, profiles provide a way for the computers to memorize each user's preferences. When you log onto a computer using your logon name, your personal profile is loaded. All the changes you make to the Desktop are saved in your profile.

Working with the Default Desktop

The first time you launch Windows after you install the operating system, the Desktop you see is the default Windows Desktop. It features icons and menu items that represent the choices you made during the operating system installation.

You can add software (which means another choice is added to the Programs menu), create Desktop shortcuts, decorate the Desktop with patterns or wallpaper, and even change the look of dialog boxes and software windows. Each time you make a change, the result is a new default Desktop. It's the default Desktop for this computer, because it's the only Desktop. Every change you make is saved. Windows calls it the default Desktop, but you can think of it as the Desktop design that is currently in effect.

When you decide to use profiles on the computer to give each user who logs on the opportunity to save his or her personal settings, the default Desktop is used as the base configuration. At that point, the changes you make to the Desktop affect your personal Desktop and are not transferred to the default Desktop. The only way the default Desktop can be altered is if it loads and a user then changes the Desktop settings — something that only happens if a user bypasses the logon process. (Read Chapter 7 to find out how to bypass the logon process.)

Personalizing Desktops

The scope of personalized elements that you can apply to your Desktop is enormous. You can decorate the Desktop by using colors and pictures, and you can put tools on the Desktop. Sounds like the same thing you can do with your physical desk, doesn't it?

Changing the appearance of the Desktop

Most of the Desktop design features are available in the Display Properties dialog box, which you get to by following these steps:

1. **Right-click on a blank spot on your Desktop.**

2. **Choose Properties from the shortcut menu that appears.**

   The Display Properties dialog box opens.

The features and options available in the Display Properties dialog box differ depending upon the operating system you installed, and whether you installed additional features for the operating system. For example, if you installed Plus! for Windows 98 or Windows 95, you have more options available for changing your display.

Some video controllers and monitors have software installation routines that add options to your Display Properties dialog box. The combinations of all the possible features are endless, so this section is an overview of the general kinds of decorative changes that you can make to your Desktop.

For detailed information about using the Display Properties dialog box, read *Windows 95 For Dummies,* 2nd Edition, or *Windows 98 For Dummies,* both written by Andy Rathbone and published by IDG Books Worldwide, Inc.

Figure 8-1 shows the Display Properties dialog box for a standard installation of Windows 98, and Figure 8-2 shows the Display Properties dialog box for a standard installation of Windows 95. The dialog box you see on your computer may have additional tabs, and some tabs may have additional features.

Figure 8-1:
Windows 98 offers configuration options for special effects and displaying your Desktop as a Web page.

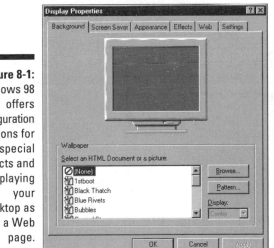

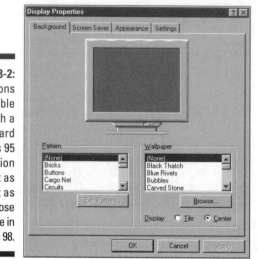

Figure 8-2:
The options available with a standard Windows 95 installation are not as robust as those available in Windows 98.

Creating Desktop backgrounds

Desktop backgrounds can be as simple or as decorative as your taste warrants. You can decorate your Desktop with a pattern or wallpaper.

You can choose from many *patterns* (design elements that fill your entire screen), and you can even design your own if Windows doesn't provide one that strikes your fancy. Use one of these methods to choose a pattern from the Display Properties dialog box:

✔ In Windows 98, click the Pattern button on the Background tab. Then scroll through the Pattern list box to find a design that you like.

✔ In Windows 95, find the Pattern list box on the Background tab and then scroll through the choices until something catches your eye.

As you click on the name of each pattern, you can see the design in the dialog box's preview box. Select the pattern that you want to put on your Desktop, and then click OK. (In Windows 98, click OK again in the Display Properties dialog box.)

Wallpaper is a picture that's placed in the middle of your screen. The wallpaper choices that come with Windows are graphics (for example, clouds or bubbles) rather than pictures of people or scenery. If you want to use one of the built-in wallpaper designs, select it from the Wallpaper list box on the Background tab of the Display Properties dialog box.

You can substitute a real picture for your wallpaper if you have a picture file that you want to use. Click the Browse button and go to the folder where you stored the image that you want to put on your Desktop. Here are some guidelines for picture files:

✔ Windows 98 can use any picture file that has the extension .bmp, .gif, or .jpg.

✔ Windows 95 can only use picture files that have the extension .bmp.

✔ In both Windows 98 and Windows 95, if you're on the World Wide Web, you can right-click on any graphic on a Web page and choose Set as Wallpaper from the shortcut menu that appears.

The Display Properties dialog box offers choices for the placement of wallpaper. The default setting is to center the wallpaper on your screen, as shown in Figure 8-3. (In this case, a photo was scanned in, saved on the hard drive, and set as wallpaper. You can also download pictures from the Internet, as explained in the preceding list.)

You also have the option of *tiling* the picture. This means repeating the picture enough times to fill the screen (see Figure 8-4).

Figure 8-3: Put a favorite family photo on your Desktop, just as you would on your physical desk.

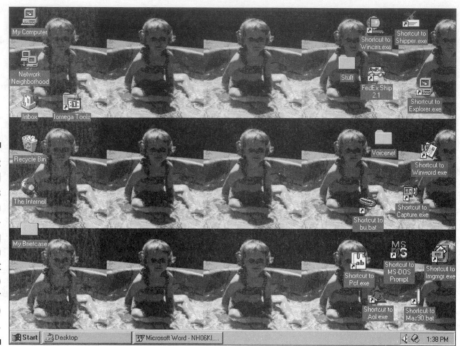

Figure 8-4:
Tiled
pictures
can be a
little over-
whelming
and can
make it
hard to
see your
Desktop
shortcuts.

Windows 98 and Windows 95 Plus! offer an additional placement option for wallpaper — stretch. If you select the stretch option, your wallpaper picture is stretched to fill the screen. This sometimes creates a very distorted picture, which you may or may not find attractive.

Using screen savers

Years ago, anything that was displayed on the computer screen for a long time actually burned itself into the screen. No matter what you were doing on the computer, a faint, ghostly display of the burned-in image remained on your screen. That image was usually the menu that appeared when the computer started up. Screen savers were invented to avoid this problem.

Screen savers are programs that appear on your monitor's screen, entertaining you with either not-so-entertaining pitch blackness or cool pictures or animations when a specified amount of time has elapsed without any keyboard or mouse activity. The default time for Windows 98 is 14 minutes, and the default time for Windows 95 is 1 minute.

Today, color monitors are manufactured with a different technology and burn-in is no longer a problem. However, screen savers are more popular than ever, for two reasons:

✔ **They're fun.** Screen savers can be amusing, pretty, clever, and even funny.

✔ **They provide security.** You can password-protect a screen saver so that you are the only person who can make it disappear. This prevents someone from using your computer if you step away from your desk for a while.

Windows comes with a number of built-in screen savers, and plenty more are available on the Internet or in stores. People trade screen savers the way they used to trade baseball cards.

Using a screen saver involves two steps: First you have to choose a screen saver, and then you must configure its behavior. The following two sections walk you through both of these tasks.

Choosing a screen saver

Choose a screen saver by following these steps:

1. **Right-click a blank spot on your Desktop and choose Properties from the shortcut menu that appears.**

   The Display Properties dialog box opens.

2. **Click the Screen Saver tab in the Display Properties dialog box.**

3. **Click the arrow to the right of the Screen Saver list box and choose a screen saver from the list that appears.**

   The preview box on the Screen Saver tab shows you what the screen saver looks like (see Figure 8-5).

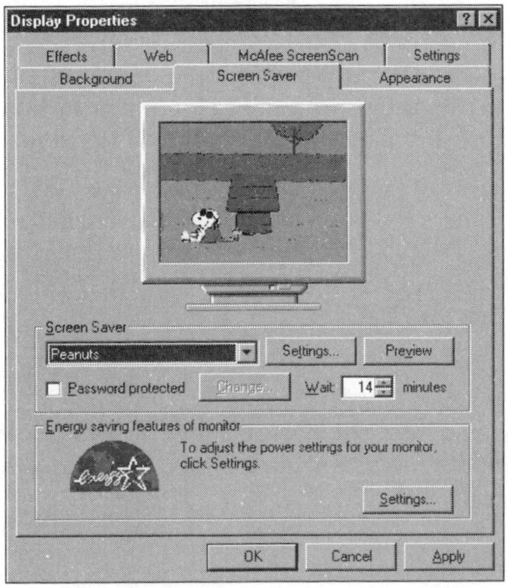

Figure 8-5: You can get a preview of the screen saver, along with its animated effects.

If the preview in the dialog box window doesn't let you see enough of the screen saver to make a decision about displaying it, click the Preview button. The screen saver will take over your screen and run until you press a keyboard key or move the mouse.

If you don't want any special configuration options to control the screen saver's behavior, just click OK at the bottom of the dialog box. The screen saver will occupy the screen when the specified amount of time has elapsed without any keyboard or mouse action.

If you download screen savers from the Internet or get some from a friend, you need to put them in the appropriate folder so that they show up in the list of available screen savers in the Display Properties dialog box. Windows 98 and Windows 95 keep screen savers in the \Windows\System folder.

Using screen savers with profiles enabled

Windows 98 and Windows 95 have a small problem with screen savers if a computer is configured for profiles. Everybody gets the same screen saver, although each user can have his or her own settings for the screen saver configuration. (See the next section, "Configuring the screen saver," for more information.)

The Windows 98 support team at Microsoft doesn't call this a bug — they call it a design element. The Windows 95 support team told me that they're working on it, which is jargon for recognizing that it's a bug.

The problem arises because Windows 98 and Windows 95 store the name of the screen saver you select in one place and store the configuration settings you select in another place. Here's the problem:

 ✔ The name of the active screen saver is stored in a file named System.ini, which is located in your Windows folder. Each computer has only one System.ini file. Each time any user changes the screen saver, all users see that screen saver.

 ✔ The configuration options for screen savers that are selected by individual users are stored in the Registry. This means that each user of a computer can have specific settings for the way the screen saver behaves under his or her profile.

Configuring the screen saver

You can change the appearance and the performance of a screen saver with the options available on the Screen Saver tab of the Display Properties dialog box.

Screen saver settings

Click the Settings button in the Display Properties dialog box to change the setup of the screen saver that you selected. Each screen saver has its own set of configuration options. For example, a screen saver named 3D Pipes has quite a few options for changing the setup (see Figure 8-6). Other screen savers may permit changes to the speed of animation only.

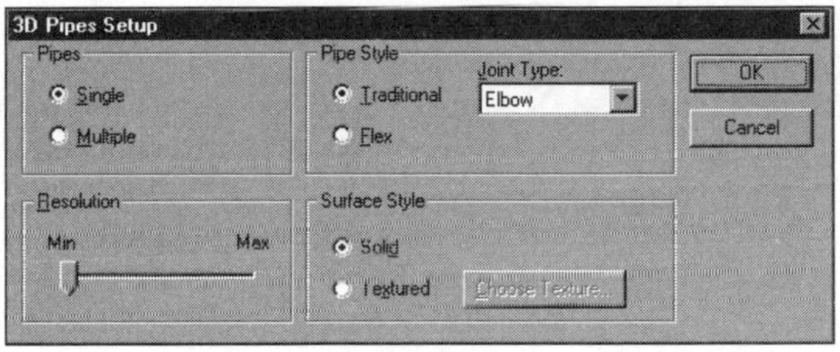

Figure 8-6:
This screen saver setup lets you change the shapes and graphics that appear when the screen saver runs.

Elapsed time setting

You can specify the amount of idle time that must elapse before the screen saver appears. Use the arrows in the Wait box to increase or decrease the number of minutes (or type the number directly in the Wait box). You can choose any number between 1 and 60.

Password-protecting a screen saver

One great advantage to screen savers is the amount of security that they can provide for your computer. You can attach a password to a screen saver so that the screen saver doesn't go away immediately when the mouse is moved or a key is pressed. Instead, a password dialog box is displayed, and if you don't know the password, the screen saver stubbornly remains on the screen. To add a password to a screen saver, follow these steps:

1. **Right-click a blank spot on the Desktop and choose Properties from the shortcut menu that appears.**

   The Display Properties dialog box opens.

2. **Click the Screen Saver tab and select a screen saver from the list in the Screen Saver list box.**

3. **Click the Password Protected check box to place a check mark in the box.**

   The Change button becomes accessible (it's grayed out if no check mark appears in the Password Protected check box).

4. **Click the Change button.**

   The Change Password dialog box opens, as shown in Figure 8-7.

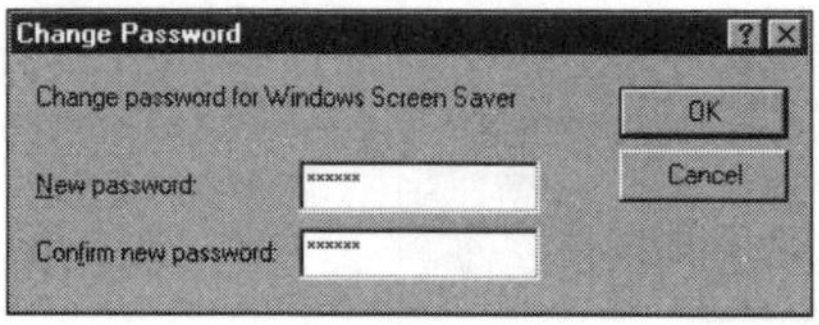

Figure 8-7:
You can
attach a
password
to a screen
saver.

5. **Enter a password in the New Password text box.**

   Asterisks replace the characters you type so that nobody can see what you're typing.

6. **Press the Tab key to move to the Confirm New Password text box and enter the same password again.**

   If you do not enter the password exactly as you entered it in the New Password text box, you are asked to enter the password again.

7. **Click OK.**

   A message appears to tell you that the password has been successfully changed.

8. **Click OK to close the Change Password dialog box.**

9. **Click OK again to close the Display Properties dialog box.**

In older versions of Windows 95 (everything except OSR2) problems may occur with the screen saver if your password exceeds 14 characters. Double-click the Systems icon in the Control Panel to see what version of Windows 95 you have.

When the specified amount of time has elapsed, your screen saver takes over your screen. However, when you press a key or move the mouse, the screen saver doesn't go away. Instead, the Windows Screen Saver dialog box appears, asking you to enter the screen saver password in the text box. After you enter the password, click OK. One of the following things will happen:

- **The password is accepted.** The screen saver disappears, and you're returned to your screen. Whatever was on the screen when the screen saver kicked in is there, waiting for you to continue your work.

- **The password is incorrect.** If this is the case, a dialog box appears with the message, "The password that you typed is not correct. Try typing it again." Enter the password again and click OK.

If you forget the password for your screen saver, or if you're trying to break into someone's computer and don't know the password, you're out of luck! You cannot bypass a password-protected screen saver. The following restrictions apply when a password-protected screen saver is running:

- The Windows key on a Windows keyboard, which usually provides access to the Start menu when you press it, doesn't work.

  You cannot get to the Start menu to go back to the Display Properties dialog box and change the password. Nor can you use the Shut Down menu item to perform a normal shut down procedure.

- Pressing Ctrl+Alt+Esc to see a list of running programs (and close any programs, such as the screen saver) does not work.

In fact, the only way to get past this screen saver is to turn off the computer. This is a bad idea because Windows doesn't shut down properly if you don't perform a correct shut down procedure. When you start the computer again, Windows will take some extra actions to check your hard drive, but you may do some damage to any open programs or documents.

Troubleshooting screen savers

Sometimes, screen savers don't kick in, even though an appropriate amount of inactivity has elapsed. Several things may cause this problem.

Keyboard key or mouse button is active

The most common reason for screen saver failure is that technically either the keyboard or mouse is not really inactive. I've received hundreds of calls from users who opened the conversation with the statement that their screen savers weren't working. I always start the troubleshooting with the same words: "Please look carefully at your keyboard and your mouse to see what is leaning on a key or a button." After an embarrassed laugh, or a muttered "Oops," I always ask, "What was it?" Answers have included a book, a cigarette lighter, a pack of cigarettes, a sandwich, and "you wouldn't believe it."

DOS software isn't configured for screen savers

DOS programs don't permit a screen saver to kick in unless the screen saver setting has been specifically configured as active. To make sure that your DOS software lets the screen saver run, follow these steps:

1. **Choose Start⇨Programs⇨Windows Explorer.**

   The Explorer window opens.

2. **In the left Explorer pane, click the folder that contains the DOS program.**

   The contents of the folder are displayed in the right Explorer pane.

3. **In the right Explorer pane, right-click the program file for the DOS software.**

   This is the file that launches the software, and it probably has an extension of .exe, .com, or .bat.

4. **Choose Properties from the shortcut menu that appears.**

   The program Properties dialog box opens.

5. **Click the Misc tab.**

6. **Check the box next to Allow Screen Saver, as shown in Figure 8-8).**

7. **Click OK.**

Now your screen saver will appear while you're using this DOS software — after the specified period of inactivity has elapsed, of course.

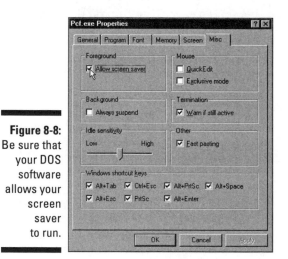

Figure 8-8:
Be sure that your DOS software allows your screen saver to run.

System items are active in Windows 95

It's usually safe to assume that the screen saver will kick in no matter what you're doing on your computer. But a couple of situations prevent your screen saver from running if you're using Windows 95. Watch out for these things:

- **A menu is open.** If you've opened a menu, such as the Start menu, and then stopped working at the computer, the screen saver will not kick in. Close the menu or make the appropriate menu selection to resolve the problem.

- **A system modal dialog box is active.** A dialog box that requires a response from you (for example, a dialog box that asks "Are you sure you want to delete this file?") is called a system modal dialog box. Your screen saver won't kick in while any system dialog box that requires input from you is open.

Windows 98 doesn't have these problems.

Using a screen saver on demand

If your screen saver is password-protected, one security loophole can cause problems. Your screen saver doesn't kick in until the specified amount of time with no activity has elapsed. If you leave your desk, your computer is vulnerable until that time period has elapsed.

You can plug this security hole by creating a screen saver shortcut that kicks in on demand. Follow these steps to accomplish this:

1. **Choose Start⇨Programs⇨Windows Explorer.**

   The Explorer window opens.

2. **Click the plus sign next to your Windows folder in the left Explorer pane.**

   The subfolders are displayed in the left Explorer pane.

3. **Click the System subfolder in the left Explorer pane.**

   The contents of the System subfolder are displayed in the right Explorer pane.

   Windows 98 doesn't display the contents until you click the underlined link that says Show Files.

4. **Right-click and hold down the mouse button while you drag the file for your screen saver to the Desktop.**

   To find the screen saver, look for a filename ending with the extension .scr that matches the screen saver selection you made.

5. **Release the right mouse button and choose Create Shortcut(s) Here from the menu that appears.**

A shortcut to your screen saver is on the Desktop. Double-click it to start your screen saver whenever you have to leave your desk.

Adding Software to Your Programs Menu

Adding software to the Programs menu on a computer with profiles enabled creates an interesting problem — the changes one user makes to the Programs menu aren't reflected on the Programs menus for the other users.

For example, if your spouse logs on and installs a bookkeeping program, he or she can start the program from the Programs menu. If you want to use the program, however, you can't open your own Programs menu and click on the listing because it isn't there. You have to put it there yourself!

You can add a listing for any program installed on the computer to your Programs menu. The listings in the Programs menu are nothing more than shortcuts that have been placed in the Programs folder in your personal profile — you only have to copy the shortcut into your own Programs folder.

You can obtain the program shortcut from the program itself, but taking the shortcut from the existing program listing in your spouse's folder is so much easier. In fact, because many programs install groups of listings, this is the only way to ensure that you have all the choices. Follow these steps to copy a program listing from one user's Programs menu to your own Programs menu:

1. **Choose Start⇨Programs⇨Windows Explorer.**

   The Explorer window opens.

2. **In the left Explorer pane, click the plus sign to the left of the Windows folder.**

   The subfolders under the Windows folder are displayed in the left Explorer pane.

3. **Click the plus sign to the left of the Profiles folder.**

All the profile folders for the computer are displayed in the left Explorer pane.

4. Click the plus sign to the left of the profile that has the Programs menu listing that you want to add.

All the subfolders for this profile are displayed in the left Explorer pane.

5. Click the plus sign to the left of the Start menu folder to reveal the Programs folder, and then click on the Programs folder.

All the folders (groups) and individual items on the Programs menu are displayed in the right Explorer pane (see Figure 8-9).

6. Right-click the program item that you want to add to your own Programs menu and choose Copy from the shortcut menu that appears.

7. Click the plus sign to the left of your own profile folder.

All the subfolders for your profile are displayed in the left Explorer pane.

8. Click the plus sign to the left of your Start menu folder to reveal your Programs folder.

Figure 8-9: Groups and items on the Programs menu are represented by folders and shortcuts in the Programs folder.

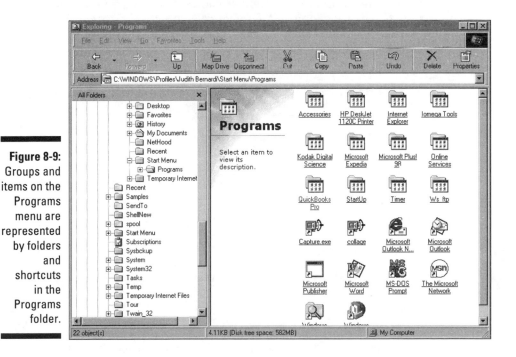

9. **Right-click on your Programs folder and choose Paste from the shortcut menu that appears.**

The program listing is copied to your own Programs menu.

Creating Desktop Shortcuts

You can put lots of tools on your Desktop so that you can get your work done faster. The most useful Desktop tool is a shortcut, which enables you to access an item without opening a menu.

Creating shortcuts to programs

If you use a few software programs frequently, you can create shortcuts to those programs on the Desktop or on the Start menu.

You create a program shortcut by dragging the program file item to the target location, either the Desktop or the Start menu. When you drag a program file to either target, Windows knows that you aren't moving the program to a new location and automatically creates a shortcut. Program files have extensions of .exe, .com, or .bat. Files with other extensions have to be dragged with the right mouse button (see "Creating shortcuts to documents" later in this section for more information).

To put a shortcut to a software program on your Desktop, follow these steps:

1. **Choose Start➪Programs➪Windows Explorer.**

The Explorer window opens.

2. **Locate the program file that you want to have as a shortcut and drag it to the Desktop.**

Press and hold the left mouse button to drag the file.

 When you release the mouse button, the shortcut appears on the Desktop.

The first Desktop shortcut you should create is a shortcut to Explorer.

To put a program listing directly on the Start menu (so you don't have to navigate through the other menu groups), drag the program file's icon to the Start button. The program item appears at the top of your Start menu, as shown in Figure 8-10. This is especially useful for software that's listed a couple of layers down on the Start menu. For example, opening a game requires you to move through the Start menu, the Programs menu, the Accessories menu, and the Games menu. That's too much work!

Figure 8-10:
Create a
listing on
the Start
menu for
quicker
access to a
program.

Creating shortcuts to documents

If you have a document that you use as a template or as boilerplate language, put a shortcut to that document on your Desktop or your Start menu. For example, I have boilerplate documents for letterheads, faxes, invoices, and memos. Each boilerplate document is ready to go, waiting for me to add the name of the recipient and the text that I want to include on a particular occasion. Graphics, letterhead text, font selections, and other details are already saved. To create a shortcut for a document, follow these steps:

1. **Open Windows Explorer.**

   Using an Explorer shortcut is easier than opening the Start menu and the Programs menu and then clicking on the Windows Explorer listing, so check out the preceding section to find out how to create that shortcut.

2. **Locate the document for which you want to create a shortcut.**

   Usually the file is in your My Documents folder. In Windows 98, you can find the My Documents folder in \Windows\Profiles*your logon name* if profiles are enabled. Windows 95 does not create individual My Documents folders in the \Windows\Profiles folders.

3. **To put a shortcut on the Desktop, right-click the document object, drag it to the Desktop, and choose Create Shortcut(s) Here from the menu that appears when you release the mouse button.**

4. **To put a shortcut on the Start menu, drag the document object to the Start button.**

   You don't have to right-click and drag an item to create a Start menu shortcut because Windows knows that you're creating a shortcut, not moving a document to the Start menu.

Creating shortcuts to folders

You can create a Desktop shortcut to any folder in your Windows system, giving you quick access to the contents of the folder. The folder that you probably use most often is My Documents. Windows 98 provides a shortcut to your My Documents folder, but Windows 95 doesn't. To create a shortcut to your Windows 95 My Documents folder, follow these steps:

1. **Open Windows Explorer.**

   By now, you've probably created a Desktop shortcut to Explorer, but if not, choose Start⇨Programs⇨Windows Explorer. The Explorer window opens.

2. **Find the folder for which you want a Desktop shortcut.**

   In this example, I use the My Documents folder, but these steps work for any folder.

3. **Right-click the folder and drag it to the Desktop.**

4. **Choose Create Shortcut(s) here from the menu that appears when you release the mouse button.**

   The folder shortcut appears on the Desktop.

To work on a file, double-click the Desktop shortcut folder and open the file. The software that created the file opens with the selected file in the software window.

The Desktop shortcut to the folder is a clone of the real folder. When you add or remove items from one, the changes are reflected in the other. The My Documents folder usually grows (has items added) through software as you create and save documents. You can clean up the folder by removing unneeded files (especially backup files that are created by the software) from the Desktop folder, eliminating the need to open the software.

Creating shortcuts to printers

Occasionally, someone asks me for a printed copy of a document. To comply, I have to open the software program in which the document was created, click the Open button on the program's toolbar, find the document, select it, click the Print icon on the program's toolbar, and close the program. Whew! That's too much work.

So I created a shortcut to the printer on my Desktop. Now, I only have to find the file in the My Documents folder on my Desktop and drag it to the printer shortcut on my Desktop. The software that created the document opens automatically, the document is loaded in the software window and sent to the printer, and the software closes. I don't have to do anything; it's all done on autopilot. Cool!

To create a printer shortcut on your Desktop, follow these steps:

1. **Choose Start➪Settings➪Printers.**

   The Printers folder opens.

   You can also open the Printers folder from the My Computer folder on your Desktop.

2. **Right-click the printer icon and drag it to the Desktop.**

3. **Choose Create Shortcut(s) Here from the menu that appears when you release the right mouse button.**

Now you can drag documents to the printer shortcut to make printing an automatic procedure.

This shortcut works even if the printer that you use isn't connected to your computer and is instead attached to another computer on your home network. See Chapter 12 for information about sharing printers across the network.

Creating a shortcut to the Desktop

After you create a bunch of useful shortcuts on your Desktop, you need to get to the shortcuts easily and quickly (otherwise, what's the point in creating them?). Usually, you have software windows open on your screen and can't see the Desktop.

In Windows 98, your taskbar has a toolbar with a button that you can click to see the Desktop. However, Windows 95 provides no similar tool, but you can create your own. Use these steps to create a taskbar button that you can use to get to your Desktop quickly:

1. **Double-click the My Computer icon.**

   The My Computer folder opens.

2. **Choose View➪Toolbar to see the My Computer toolbar in the folder window.**

3. **Click the arrow to the right of the folder list text box, which currently displays My Computer as the viewed folder.**

   A list of folders displays.

4. **Click the up arrow on the scrollbar to see the Desktop listing (see Figure 8-11).**

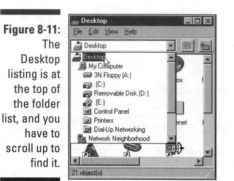

Figure 8-11:
The
Desktop
listing is at
the top of
the folder
list, and you
have to
scroll up to
find it.

5. **Click on the Desktop listing to select it.**

   The contents of the My Computer folder change to display the objects on your Desktop.

6. **Click the minimize button at the top-right corner of the folder window.**

   The Desktop folder is minimized, and a Desktop button appears on your taskbar.

Now you can click the Desktop button on the taskbar to open a window that displays your Desktop and all the items on it, along with any other open windows on your screen. You can re-size the Desktop window to suit your needs or taste. As long as you remember to minimize the Desktop window instead of closing it, it will remain on your taskbar. In fact, when you shut down Windows 95 and restart the computer, the Desktop button will still be on the taskbar.

Part IV
Communicating Across the Network

The 5th Wave   By Rich Tennant

"Doug insisted on it. He says it's the only place he can get work done."

In this part . . .

Sharing was probably one of the first lessons you learned as a kid, and it's just as important when you're setting up your home network as it was when you were three years old playing in the sand box. One of the best reasons to set up a network is that you aren't limited to the resources on the computer you're currently using — you can grab files from other network computers without leaving your seat. This part tells you how to share resources among all the computers on your network, how to find and access those resources, and how to map shortcuts to resources you frequently access on other computers.

Chapter 9

Viewing All the Computers in the House

. . . .

In This Chapter

▶ Configuring your computers to share resources

▶ Creating shared resources

▶ Configuring security for remote access

▶ Accessing remote computers

▶ Accessing shared resources on computers

▶ Accessing password-protected resources

. . . .

*A*fter you install the network hardware, install the cable to connect the computers, and configure the operating system to recognize and use those items (see Chapters 1,2, and 3 if you're networking with standard cable; see Chapters 4 and 5 if you're networking with telephone lines), your computers are members of the network.

That means each computer can see the other computers on your network. That's jargon, because we know that computers don't really have eyes and can't see anything. But you can sit in front of one computer and can see another computer using your computer's perspective, which is the view you see through Network Neighborhood. (Looking up from your screen and seeing another physical computer across the room doesn't really count.)

The Network Neighborhood icon on your Desktop is your window to the computers that are connected to your network. Double-click the Network Neighborhood icon to see your neighborhood (mine appears in Figure 9-1).

The fact that you see a computer in Network Neighborhood means the computer is running and has the necessary hardware and software to use network services. That's all it means. It doesn't necessarily mean that you can look inside the computer to see the files contained within it or that you can copy files from one computer to another. You have to set up all those features, and I cover that in this chapter.

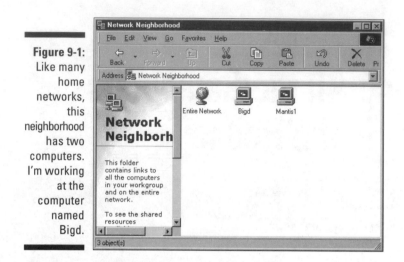

Figure 9-1:
Like many
home
networks,
this
neighborhood
has two
computers.
I'm working
at the
computer
named
Bigd.

Setting Up Sharing

If you want to share the resources in your computer (such as drives, folders, or any peripherals that are attached to your computer), you have to configure the computer for sharing.

The word *sharing* is used a lot in network computing, and it means creating resources on one computer that can be accessed by users on other computers. As a noun, a *share* is a resource that's been configured for access by remote users. For example, if you configure your C: drive for sharing, that drive is known as a share.

The term *remote user* means a user who's accessing one computer but sitting in front of a different computer. If you ever use your home computer to dial into the office and use the software on the office computer, you're a remote user. When you're accessing a remote computer, the computer you're sitting in front of is called the *local computer*.

To set up sharing, you have to enable the sharing feature. Then, you can decide whether you want to limit what people can do to your files (for example, users may copy files but not delete them), or you can decide which users can visit your shared resources and which users are locked out.

Enabling shared resources

The first task is to enable sharing by telling Windows that you want remote users to be able to access resources on your computer. To configure your computer for sharing, follow these steps:

1. **Choose Start⇨Settings⇨Control Panel.**

   The Control Panel opens.

2. **Double-click the Network icon.**

   The Network dialog box opens, with the Configuration tab in the foreground.

   Another way to open the Network dialog box is to right-click the Network Neighborhood icon and choose Properties from the shortcut menu that appears.

3. **Click the File and Print Sharing button.**

   The File and Print sharing dialog box opens, as shown in Figure 9-2.

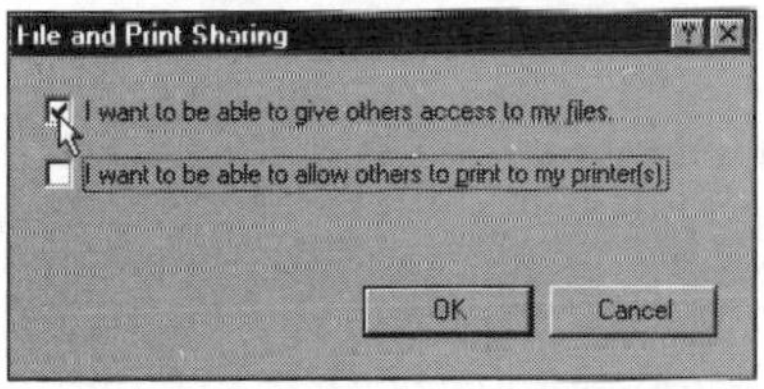

Figure 9-2:
Turn on the
sharing
feature with
a click of
the mouse.

File and Print Sharing
☑ I want to be able to give others access to my files.
☐ I want to be able to allow others to print to my printer(s).
OK   Cancel

4. **Select I Want to Be Able to Give Others Access to My Files.**

   If you have a printer attached to your computer and you want to share it with remote users, you can select the second option, too. You can find information about sharing printers in Chapter 12.

5. **Click OK.**

You return to the Network dialog box. Technically, you've enabled sharing and the task is complete. You can choose OK to close the dialog box (you have to restart the computer for these new settings to take effect). However, you should go to the next phase, setting up controls, before you finish with this dialog box.

Setting up access controls

Controlling access means devising a scheme to control which users can access your computer and what they can do when they get there. You might decide that you don't want to let every user on your network use every shared resource you create. Perhaps some shares should be limited to certain users. You can prevent wholesale access by imposing access controls. You can use two types of access controls:

- ✔ **Share-level controls,** which enable you to control access on a share-by-share basis. This is the default access control.

- ✔ **User-level controls,** which enable you to control access on a user-by-user basis. This control type is only available if users log onto a network server that validates user names and passwords. Having home networks configured for server validation is unusual, so you probably won't be able to use this feature.

Controls for shared resources only apply to people who are accessing your computer from a remote computer. Anyone who uses your computer directly can access a folder without being hampered by the controls you set.

You configure the specific controls when you create the shared resource (covered later in this chapter). Right now, you just have to tell Windows whether you're planning to use share-level controls or user-level controls. Follow these steps to specify your control method:

1. **Click the Access Control tab on the Network dialog box.**

   If you closed the Network dialog box after enabling sharing, right-click the Network Neighborhood icon and choose Properties from the shortcut menu that appears to open the Network dialog box again.

   The Access Control dialog box displays, as shown in Figure 9-3.

2. **Select Share-level Access Control, unless you have configured your network so that users log onto a server.**

   The share-level option is preselected for you. If you're using a server for logons in your network, see the "User-level controls" sidebar before deciding whether you want to take advantage of that option.

3. **Click OK.**

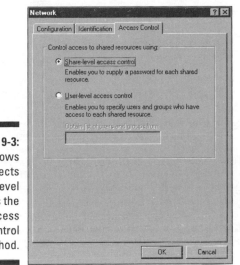

Figure 9-3:
Windows
preselects
Share-level
as the
access
control
method.

Understanding share-level controls

As you set up and configure each shared resource on your computer, you're going to be asked about the controls that you want to impose on that share. In this section, I discuss the two types of share-level controls so that you can understand what you're doing when you get there. You can find specific information about setting up shares in the section "Sharing Drives and Folders" later in this chapter.

Access type controls

With access type controls, you can restrict how a remote user can manipulate the folders and files in your computer. Every time you create a share, you have three choices of access types for that share:

  ✔ **Read-Only.** Remote users can open and copy documents from your hard drive, but can't make changes to them or delete them. If you choose this option, you can either require a password to admit only certain users to the share, or you can give read-only access to every remote user.

  ✔ **Full.** Remote users can manipulate and use folders and files on your hard drive just as if they were working directly at your computer. If you choose this option, you can either require a password or let all remote users have full access to your hard drive.

  ✔ **Depends on Password.** The passwords that you create contain one of the access rights. As a result, the actions that users can perform depend on the passwords they use. If you choose this option, you must create a password for each type of access.

User-level controls

The User-level Access Control option is available only if users log onto a server that authenticates their user names and passwords. To perform those authentication services, the server maintains a list of users.

If you select the User-Level Control option, you can list the users who can access each shared resource you establish. You must select names from the list maintained by the server.

With user-level controls in place, nobody needs a password to access your shared resources (they've successfully entered their passwords during logon). If they're on the list, they're in. You enter the names of the favored users when you create the shared resource.

Password controls

You can protect your shared resources by attaching a password to each share you create. Then you just give that password to certain users. For example, you might decide to create a shared resource for the folder that contains the files for your household budget. You'd probably decide to give the password for that folder to your spouse and not to your kids.

Remember that if you want to work on your own files from another computer, you're a remote user just like any other remote user. You have to know the password to get into your files.

The share-level control passwords are entered when you actually set up the shared resource (which I cover in the next section, "Sharing Drives and Folders").

If you want to keep a certain folder totally secret from any remote user, give it a password. Then don't give anyone the password. In fact, you can use a string of characters that don't mean anything (which prevents anyone from guessing and gaining entry). If you don't remember the password, you can change it at any time. Unlike logon passwords, you don't have to know the old password for a share in order to change it to a different password.

Sharing Drives and Folders

After you've enabled sharing on your computer, you can create the resources that you want to share with remote users. The most common shares are hard drives and folders, because those are the containers for files. However, you can also share peripherals, such as CD-ROM, Jaz, Zip, and floppy drives. See Chapter 13 for information about sharing these peripherals.

Sharing a hard drive

For home networks, sharing all the folders and files on the hard drives of every computer is common. This is a convenient way to make sure that you can find and use files no matter which computer you use.

For example, suppose you began working on a document last week while you were sitting at the computer in the den. Today, you have time to do some more work on that document, but another family member is using the computer in the den. The computer in the kitchen is free, so you can work there. You don't have to ask the person using the computer in the den to stop and copy your file to a floppy disk, and then carry that floppy disk to the kitchen (the computer jargon for that method of sharing files is called *sneakernet*). Instead, you can access your file in the den directly from the computer in the kitchen. This is one of the coolest advantages of networking.

The ability to see a hard drive on another computer isn't automatically granted. You have to configure the hard drive for sharing, which includes naming the share, deciding what people can do with the folders and files they access on the drive, and also deciding whether you want to use passwords. Whew! Sounds like a lot of work. Don't worry, it isn't; it's easy and you can accomplish everything in a couple of minutes by following these steps:

1. **Double-click the My Computer icon.**

2. **Right-click the hard drive you want to share (usually Drive C).**

3. **Choose Sharing from the shortcut menu that appears.**

   The Properties dialog box for the drive opens, and the Sharing tab is in the foreground. The Not Shared option is selected, and all the other options in the dialog box are grayed out and inaccessible.

4. **Select Shared As.**

   The options in the dialog box are now available, as shown in Figure 9-4.

5. **Enter a name for this share in the Share Name text box.**

   Choose a name that describes the share. For example, for the computer in the den, DenDriveC would be a good name.

6. **Optionally, enter a descriptive phrase about this share in the Comment text box.**

   You can use the Comment text box to add more description about this share (for example, "Hard drive on the den computer"). The text in the Comment text box appears to remote users if they use the Details view of Network Neighborhood. (By default, Network Neighborhood displays an Icon view instead of the Details view.)

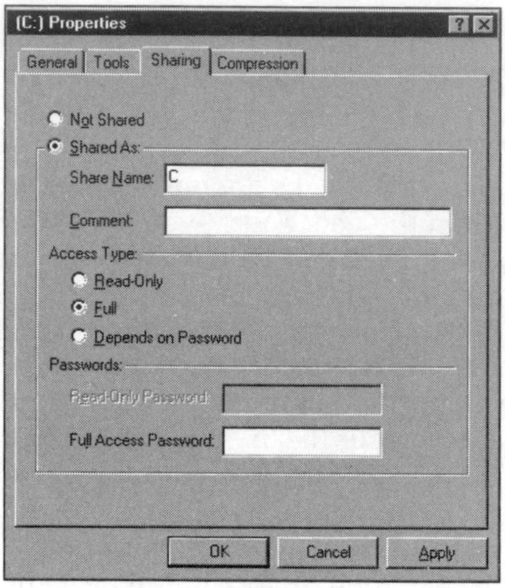

Figure 9-4:
Windows
automatically
picks the
letter of the
hard drive
as the
share
name, but
you can
change it to
something
that
provides a
better
description
for remote
users.

[C:] Properties   ? X

| General | Tools | Sharing | Compression |

○ Not Shared
● Shared As:

    Share Name: C

    Comment:

Access Type:
    ○ Read-Only
    ● Full
    ○ Depends on Password
Passwords:

    Read-Only Password:

    Full Access Password:

[OK]   [Cancel]   [Apply]

7. **Select an Access Type.**

   Specify the access type for this share using the guidelines in the section "Access type controls" earlier in this chapter.

8. **If you want to require a password, enter the password in the appropriate Password text box.**

   If you selected Depends on Password as the access type, you have no choice in the matter — you must enter a password for each access type.

9. **Choose OK.**

   If you entered a password (or multiple passwords), a Password Confirmation dialog box appears so you can enter the password again to confirm it. Then choose OK.

You return to the My Computer window, where a hand appears under your hard drive icon. The hand indicates that the drive is a shared resource. All the shares that you create will display that hand icon.

If you don't enter the password correctly in the Password Confirmation dialog box, a message appears that says, "The password you typed is incorrect." Click OK to return to the dialog box and re-enter the password. If your entry is incorrect again, choose Cancel and start over with a password you can enter without making typos.

Creating shared folders just to make them visible

You may have another reason for creating a shared resource for a folder, even if you don't want to change the security configuration for that folder. Every shared resource is individually visible in Network Neighborhood and Windows Explorer. Creating a separate folder share makes it easier for remote users to get to that folder. You're saving the remote user the trouble of searching through the shared hard drive to find the folder.

For example, you may have subfolders under the My Documents folder to hold special files that are popular with all family members. A subfolder for the family's favorite recipes is handy for whomever is preparing dinner tonight. A subfolder for names and addresses of friends and relatives is in constant demand.

A remote user who wants to use one of these subfolders has to start with the shared hard drive and then drill down through folders and subfolders to find the right folder. If you create a specific share for the folder, it appears in Network Neighborhood and Windows Explorer as soon as you click the icon for the computer.

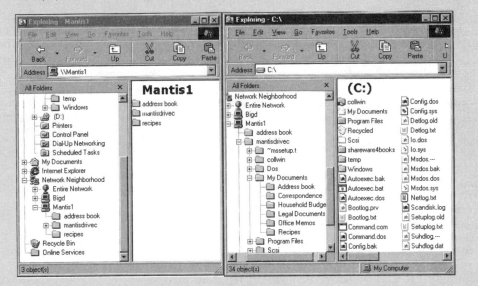

In the figure, drive C of the computer named Mantis1 is shared, which means that all the folders on the drive are also shared. Two subfolders in the My Documents folder are very popular: address book and recipes.

The Explorer window on the left shows the display when Mantis1 is expanded from a remote computer. The popular subfolders have been configured as specific shares. Notice how easy it is to get to those subfolders.

The Explorer window on the right shows the display when those subfolders have not been set up as specific shares. Notice how a remote user has to drill down through the hard drive and the My Documents folder to get to the popular subfolders.

Sharing folders and subfolders

When you establish a share, everything within that share is automatically shared, too. If you share a hard drive, all the folders on that drive are shared. This is known as a *parent-child relationship*. Folders are children of parent drives, and subfolders are children of parent folders.

In a parent-child relationship, the child inherits all the characteristics of the parent. That means that if you create a certain type of access or a password for a parent, a remote user who successfully accesses a parent has the same access to the children.

The most important thing to remember about this parent-child inheritance scheme is that all files are children (the folder is the parent). When you configure folders as shares, you're also configuring the files contained in those folders.

You can interrupt the inheritance factor by changing the configuration of any folder child. For example, you can give full access to your hard drive to every remote user, and then protect one particular folder by changing its security with a password or a different type of access (or both). Or you can configure a folder for sharing with one configuration, and then change the configuration for a subfolder. You can change the configuration of a child to be either more restrictive or less restrictive than its parent.

 Actually, you can emulate one of the access controls for specific files. The access control Read-Only is available for individual files. Right-click the file you want to control and choose Properties from the shortcut menu that appears. Then select Read-Only from the Properties dialog box.

 You may decide that you don't want to share your hard drive, but you do want to share certain folders on your hard drive. If so, you must create a separate share for each folder (there is no lateral inheritance — in other words, no brothers, sisters, or cousins).

You can create as many folder shares as you want, using these steps:

1. **Choose Start⇨Programs⇨Windows Explorer.**

   The Explorer window opens with all the folders on your hard drive displayed in the left pane.

2. **Right-click the folder that you want to share and choose Sharing from the shortcut menu that appears.**

   The Properties dialog box for the folder opens (see Figure 9-5). The Not Shared option is preselected even if the folder is on a shared drive, because this folder is not itself specifically configured as a share.

This message indicates that the folder is on a shared drive.

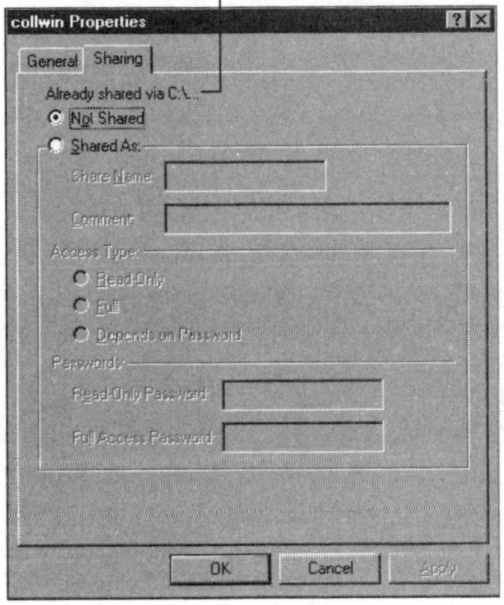

Figure 9-5:
Even
though this
folder is
already
shared
because it's
on a shared
drive, you
can create
a separate
share for it.

3. **Select Shared As.**

   The other options in the dialog box become accessible.

4. **Enter a name in the Share Name text box.**

   Windows automatically inserts the name of the folder, which is usually a good choice. However, you can change the name if you wish.

5. **Optionally, enter a description of this share in the Comment text box.**

   The description that you enter in the Comment text box appears to remote users if they use the Details view of Network Neighborhood. (By default, Network Neighborhood displays icons instead of details.)

6. **Choose an Access Type and enter a password if you want to use passwords.**

   See the section "Access type controls," earlier in this chapter, for information about access types and passwords.

7. **Choose OK.**

   You return to the Explorer window, where the folder icon has a hand under it, indicating that it's a shared resource.

When a remote user looks at your computer in Network Neighborhood or Windows Explorer, the user sees no indication that a share is password protected. The first clue comes when the user tries to open the share and sees a dialog box asking for the password. Therefore, you may want to use the Comment text box to tell users that the share needs a password.

You can repeat these steps to configure any other folder or subfolder on your computer as a shared resource.

Changing passwords for shares

Sometimes a password for a share becomes so well known that even casual visitors to the household can sit in front of one computer and access shares on another computer. That's when you know the password has outlived its usefulness. It's time to create a new password and give it to a limited number of users. Changing the password for a share is very easy; just follow these steps:

1. **Choose Start⇨Programs⇨Windows Explorer.**

   The Explorer window opens.

2. **Right-click the shared resource for which you want to change the password and choose Sharing from the shortcut menu that appears.**

   The Sharing tab of the object's Properties dialog box appears.

3. **Delete the existing password.**

4. **Enter a new password.**

5. **Choose OK.**

   The Password Confirmation dialog box appears.

6. **Enter the password again to confirm it.**

7. **Choose OK.**

The new password goes into effect immediately.

Accessing Shares

Say, for example, that one of the computers on your home network is in your bedroom. That's the computer you always use. You've shared your hard drive, and in addition you've created shares for some specific folders. For those folders, you've controlled the access type, sometimes requiring passwords. None of this means anything when you work at your computer; you create, change, and delete files without seeing any error messages. You don't need a password to get into a folder.

Now you have to work on a specific document that you've been working on at home for a special project at work. It's due tomorrow. You find your daughter working at the computer in your bedroom.

You tell her you need the computer. She tells you that if she doesn't finish this book report, she'll fail English, mess up her grade point average, fail to finish high school in the top percentile of her class, and lose any chance of a scholarship, and you'll have to shell out big bucks for her college education. You go to the computer in the den.

Assuming somebody else with an equally good story isn't already working at the den computer, you can accomplish your work from there. That's one of the reasons you set up a network at home.

If you find a family member playing a game at a computer that you want to use for some important task, and you ask that person to give up the computer, you might hear something like this: "But this is doing wonderful things for my eye-hand coordination." Some parents actually fall for that line. Don't buy it! Snort, laugh, or stare with a fixed gaze (whatever usually works) until the computer is yours.

Now you're a remote user, and you're facing the same procedures that all remote users encounter when they want to use your computer. It doesn't matter that you're the person who set up all this security; to the computer in the bedroom, you're just another remote user. You'd better remember all those passwords.

Opening shares

Locating the shares that you need on a remote computer is easy, and you have a couple of choices for the tools you can use: Windows Explorer or Network Neighborhood. You'll find some differences between these tools, mostly in the way objects on the remote computer are displayed. Try each tool to see which you prefer.

Using Windows Explorer

If you like the hierarchical view of a computer's contents, you may prefer working with Windows Explorer when you access a remote computer. Here are the steps to take to accomplish this:

1. **Choose Start⇨Programs⇨Windows Explorer.**

   The Explorer window opens.

2. **Scroll down in the left pane to find the Network Neighborhood icon and click the plus sign to the left of the icon.**

   The computers in your network are displayed in the left Explorer pane.

3. **Click the plus sign to the left of the remote computer that you want to access.**

   The shares configured for that computer are displayed in the left pane.

4. **If the only share is the hard drive, or the folder you need isn't displayed as a share, click the plus sign to the left of the hard drive.**

   The folders on the hard drive of the remote computer are displayed in the left pane (see Figure 9-6).

Explorer's hierarchical display of drives, folders, and files

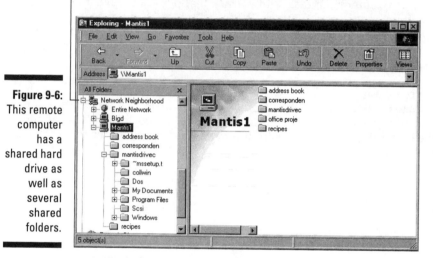

Figure 9-6: This remote computer has a shared hard drive as well as several shared folders.

5. **Click the folder that contains the file you want to work with.**

   The contents of the folder are displayed in the right Explorer pane.

You can copy, move, open, or otherwise manipulate the file. You can find more information about all the procedures you can perform with files on remote computers in Chapter 10.

Using Network Neighborhood

Double-click the Network Neighborhood icon to display all the computers on the network, and then double-click the icon for the remote computer that you want to use. Network Neighborhood displays all the shares for that computer (see Figure 9-7).

In many home networks, the only shared resource for each computer is the hard drive. You must open the hard drive to display all the folders, and then open the correct folder to find the file that you want to use. Sometimes you have to open one or more subfolders to get to your file.

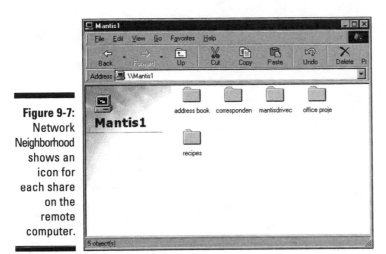

Figure 9-7:
Network
Neighborhood
shows an
icon for
each share
on the
remote
computer.

Network Neighborhood doesn't present the hierarchical view that Windows Explorer displays. Depending on your preferences and your familiarity with the contents of the remote computer, you may prefer the Network Neighborhood window, even though you have to keep opening folders one after another.

However, you can have the best of both worlds with just two clicks of the mouse:

1. **Right-click on any folder (or drive) in Network Neighborhood.**

2. **Choose Explore from the shortcut menu that appears.**

   Windows Explorer opens, and the folder or drive you selected is highlighted and expanded if it has folders (see Figure 9-8).

Opening password-protected shares

When you want to access a share on a remote computer, you can't tell whether the share is protected by a password until you try to open the share. Follow these steps to open a share that's protected by a password:

1. **Double-click the Network Neighborhood icon.**

   The Network Neighborhood window opens and displays all the computers on your network.

   Alternatively, you can open Windows Explorer and click the plus sign to the left of the Network Neighborhood icon to display all the network computers in the left Explorer pane.

Figure 9-8:
Use
Network
Neighborhood
to select a
shared
resource,
and then
use
Windows
Explorer to
drill down
through all
the folders
and files.

2. **Double-click the icon for the computer that you want to use.**

   A window opens, displaying all the shares on the computer that you selected.

3. **Double-click the icon for the share that you want to use.**

   The Enter Network Password dialog box appears, as shown in Figure 9-9.

Figure 9-9:
What's the
magic
word?
Without it,
you're not
going to
look inside
this folder.

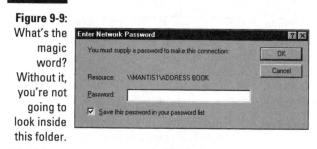

4. **Enter the password for this share.**

   You can't see the characters you type because Windows substitutes asterisks for each character.

5. **Click the Save This Password in Your Password List check box.**

   Windows adds this password to a password list file that's maintained on your local computer, and the next time you want to open this share, you won't have to enter the password.

6. **Click OK.**

   The drive or folder opens, and you can head for the file you want to use.

If you don't enter the password correctly, the error message shown in Figure 9-10 appears. Click OK to return to the Enter Network Password dialog box.

Figure 9-10:
Bzzzzz,
wrong!

Microsoft Networking	✕
✕ The password is incorrect. Try again.	
OK	

You can try again, and again, and again. After a while, if you keep getting the error message, odds are you're not making a typo; you're using the wrong password. Either your memory is inaccurate or the password was changed and nobody told you. Click Cancel on the Enter Network Password dialog box to end the attempt.

Understanding the password list file

If you select the option to save a password for a share in your password list file, Windows writes the password (along with the share it's linked to) to a special file on your computer called a password list file. The file is named *yourlogonname.pwl* (the pwl extension stands for password list).

When you log onto your computer, your password list file is automatically loaded into the computer's memory. This makes the information in the file available immediately whenever it's needed. The jargon for the process of loading passwords into memory is called *password caching*.

Windows supplies a software tool that you can use to edit the password file. It's called the Password List Editor, and the executable filename is Pwledit.exe. The program has to be installed using Add/Remove Programs in the Control Panel. The files for the program are on the Windows CD-ROM. In Windows 98,

the Password List Editor is in the \tools\reskit\netadmin\pwledit folder. In Windows 95, the files for the program are in the \admin\apptools\pwledit folder.

When you use the Password List Editor, the password list file for the current logged-on user is opened in the software window. All the other password list files on the computer are locked while you're logged on, so you can't edit another user's password list file.

You can't read the passwords in the password list file while you're using the editor (they're encrypted), but you can see the list of shares that have passwords attached. If you know the password for a share is wrong, or you suspect the password is corrupt, you can delete the entry for that share's listing.

Using the Password List Editor is not a good idea if you're inexperienced and uncomfortable with computer operating systems.

Solving password list problems

The first time you access a password-protected share, you must enter the correct password. If you select the option to remember the password, the password you enter is saved in your password file, linked to that shared resource. You can open that share any time without entering the password again. But occasionally, you may discover a problem with the saved password.

Share password has changed

If the password for the share is changed, your password stops working. When you attempt to open the share, you see an error message telling you that the password in your password list isn't correct (see Figure 9-11).

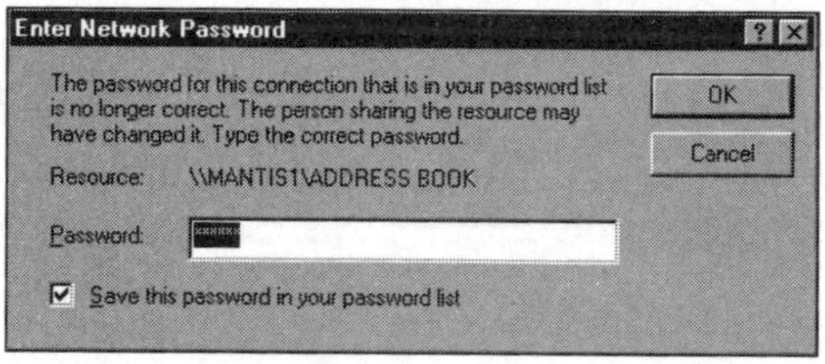

Figure 9-11:
Uh oh, somebody changed the pass-word — hopefully you have the new password.

The old password is in the Password text box and it's highlighted. As soon as you begin entering characters, the old password is deleted, and the new characters appear in the Password text box.

Because the Save This Password in Your Password List option is selected, you can access this share without a password after you enter the new password (well, at least until it's changed again). Click OK to open the share.

Password list file is corrupt

Sometimes you see an error message that your password no longer works, even if the password for the share you're trying to open wasn't changed. Your password list file probably has a problem. For some reason, password list files become corrupted. Sometimes, you can't figure out why; it's just one of those things. Sometimes, it's because somebody decided to edit the password file (and, sometimes, that somebody is you) and performed the task badly.

If you see an error message telling you that your password is no longer correct for the share you're trying to open, and you're absolutely sure that the password wasn't changed, you probably have a corrupt password list file. You have two tasks in front of you, and the order in which you perform them doesn't matter:

- ✔ You still have to open the share so you can get your work done.
- ✔ You have to delete the corrupt password list file.

To open the share, enter the password manually and choose OK.

To delete the corrupt password list file, follow these steps:

1. **Choose Start⇨Programs⇨Windows Explorer.**

   The Explorer window opens.

2. **In the left Explorer pane, double-click the folder that holds your Windows files (the folder is usually named Windows).**

   The right pane in a Windows 98 system displays a warning about opening this folder. Click Show Files to display the files in the Windows folder.

   In Windows 95, the right pane displays the files in the Windows folder.

3. **In the right Explorer pane, find your password file and select it.**

   The file has the filename *your logon name*.pwl.

4. **Press Delete to delete your password list file.**

   Windows asks you to confirm the fact that you want to delete this file. Click Yes.

After you've deleted your password list file, you have to enter passwords manually for shared resources again. However, if you continue to select the Save This Password in Your Password List File option, you'll rebuild your password list file.

Chapter 10

Using Files on Remote Computers

*O*ther users are creating files on other computers all the time. Occasionally, you may want to see one of those files. In fact, you may want to work on one of those files. Perhaps you want your very own copy of a file that currently resides on another computer.

If you find yourself working on different computers at different times, you probably have files on all of them. That can be nerve-wracking. Imagine that you're sitting in front of the computer that you use most of the time, looking for that letter to Aunt Mathilda. You know you started it yesterday, and today you want to finish and mail it. But where is it? You look through all your document subfolders; you even use the Windows Find command to search for it. It's nowhere to be found. Think back — could it be that you began the letter on the computer in the den? And now you want to work on the computer in the kitchen?

You don't have to get up and walk to a remote computer to use a file that's on it, whether you or another household member created the file. Let the network cable do the work by transferring the file from the other computer to the one you're using now.

The first thing that you have to do is find the file you want to use. This always takes a couple of steps because files can't be shared resources. That means that they won't appear in the list of resources available to you on other computers. They are, however, contained within the resources available to you, because those resources are drives or folders (or both). I discuss shared resources — what they are and how to create them — in Chapter 9.

Using Network Neighborhood to Find Files

One quick way to see all the shared resources on any computer is to double-click the Network Neighborhood icon.

When you double-click the Network Neighborhood icon, you see all the computers on your network. Figure 10-1 shows a typical home network, consisting of two computers.

Figure 10-1:
Network
Neighborhood
shows all
the
computers
on the
network,
including
the one that
you're
using.

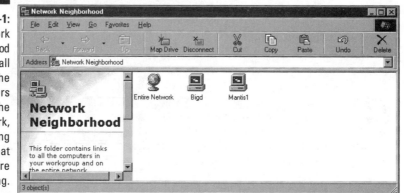

Accessing computers in Network Neighborhood

You can see the shared resources on a remote computer by double-clicking that computer's icon in Network Neighborhood.

By default, the window that opens displays icons for every shared resource on that computer, as seen in Figure 10-2.

If you've configured the shared resources wisely, the name of each resource is a good indication of what it is. See Chapter 9 for more information about setting up shared resources.

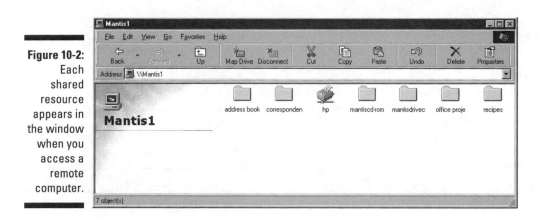

Figure 10-2: Each shared resource appears in the window when you access a remote computer.

If descriptions for shared resources are available, you can see them by choosing View⇨Details from the menu bar. As you can see in Figure 10-3, these descriptive phrases can help you to figure out more easily what's what on a remote computer. When you set up a shared resource, you can use the Comments field to enter the description. (Some shared resource names are obvious enough that descriptive phrases probably aren't necessary.)

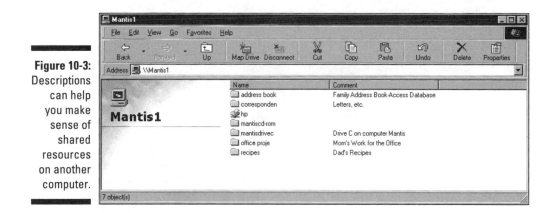

Figure 10-3: Descriptions can help you make sense of shared resources on another computer.

Accessing password-protected shared resources

If the person who created the shared resource wants to limit access to the resource, he or she can create a password (see Chapter 9 for information about creating passwords for shared resources). If that person doesn't tell you the password, you're outta luck. Only the favored few who receive the password can open the shared resource.

Network Neighborhood is redundant

The Network Neighborhood window includes an icon for the entire network. If you double-click that icon, you see an icon for the *workgroup* (the group that the computers on your network belong to). If you double-click the workgroup icon, you see the individual computers in your workgroup, which are the same computers you saw in the original Network Neighborhood window. You're back where you started. The Entire Network icon is really for larger networks that may have multiple workgroups, but that's not the way home networks are configured. So I wouldn't worry about the Entire Network icon.

If you received the password (or you're accessing your own files on a different computer, which means you should know the password because you created it), you have to enter it in the Enter Network Password dialog box that appears when you double-click the resource to open it (see Figure 10-4). Click OK after you type the password.

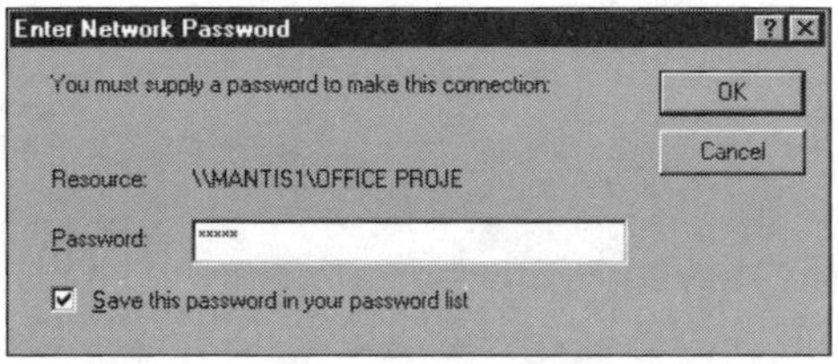

Figure 10-4:
Say the magic word!

Enter Network Password

You must supply a password to make this connection:

OK

Cancel

Resource: \\MANTIS1\OFFICE PROJE

Password: *****

☑ Save this password in your password list

When you enter the password, you don't see the characters that you type because they appear as asterisks. This is a security measure to prevent anyone who may be hanging around from seeing the password.

You have the option to select Save This Password in Your Password List at the bottom of the dialog box; if you select this option, the local computer stores the password. Then, the next time you want to open this shared resource, the local computer fetches the password from your password file and enters it automatically. You won't even see the Enter Network Password dialog box, unless the person who created the shared resource changes the password.

If the password that you enter isn't correct, or you saved the password and the user who created the shared resource changed the password, Windows displays an error message (see Figure 10-5).

Figure 10-5:
Uh oh,
either you
made a typo
or you don't
know the
password.

Microsoft Networking

The password is incorrect. Try again.

OK

If you think that you may have mistyped, click OK and try again. If that doesn't work, click Cancel on the Enter Network Password dialog box. Then find the person who created the shared resource and either get the password or find out why you can't have it.

If you need one particular file from a password-protected folder, ask the owner of the folder to move that file to a different folder if he or she doesn't want to compromise the security of the folder.

Understanding permission levels

Double-click a shared folder to see the files contained in the folder. The *permission level* that's set for the folder applies to all the files in that folder (see Chapter 7 for more information about setting up passwords and granting permissions). The person who created the shared resource decides what type of permission level to grant:

- ✔ **Read-Only.** You can open or copy files in this folder, but you can't delete any files, change the contents of any files, or add anything (files or subfolders) to the folder.

- ✔ **Full.** You can add, change, or delete anything in the folder.

- ✔ **Depends on Password.** Your permission level is either Read-Only or Full, depending on the password that you use.

Unfortunately, you receive no message indicating your permission level for the folder that you use. The only way to find out whether you have Read-Only permission is to do something that requires Full permission (such as saving a file to the folder, or changing the name of a file) and see whether you get an error message. It's like driving in a state you're not familiar with, where you don't know if the state permits right turns on red until you see the first sign that says "No Turn on Red."

Searching for files in Network Neighborhood

Sometimes, the only shared resource on a remote computer is the hard drive. You can double-click the hard drive's icon in Network Neighborhood to see the drive's contents, and then open individual folders to locate the file you need. If you don't know where a file is located, you may have to open a lot of folders.

When you share a hard drive, you automatically share all the folders on the hard drive. You can, however, choose specific folders on the drive and turn off sharing for them, or password-protect them.

Even if you set up several folders as shared resources, finding a specific file can be tedious. If you go through all the menu items on the menu bar, you learn that Network Neighborhood doesn't have a Find command.

Wait, don't panic — a Find command does exist, sort of. You can use the universal Windows Find feature. Here's how:

1. **Choose Find⇨Files or Folders from the Start menu (or press F3).**

   The Find: All Files dialog box appears.

2. **Click Browse.**

   The Browse for Folder dialog box appears (see Figure 10-6).

3. **Click the plus sign next to Network Neighborhood to expand the listing.**

   All the computers in Network Neighborhood are listed in the left pane of the dialog box.

Figure 10-6:
Browse through Network Neighborhood to find the file that you need.

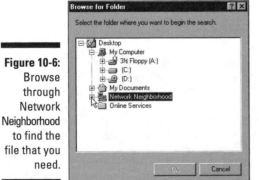

4. **Click the plus sign next to the remote computer to expand it so that you can see its shared resources.**

   The shared resources may be folders, the hard drive, or both.

5. **Select the highest level of the hierarchy for the remote computer and click OK.**

   Usually the highest level of the hierarchy is the hard drive. If you see shared folders but no shared hard drive, you have to search all the folders for your file.

6. **In the Find: All Files dialog box, enter as much of the file name as you know in the Named text box.**

   You can use any string of characters. For example, entering **rob** finds files named robber, Robert, carob, problem, and so on.

7. **Be sure to check the Include Subfolders option.**

   If the shared folders contain subfolders, you want to make sure the search includes those subfolders.

8. **Click Find Now to begin searching.**

The Find dialog box displays a list of all the files that match your search criteria. You can open the file that you need from the list, or you can move to the folder in which the file resides (the name of the folder appears in the list) and open the file from there.

Using Windows Explorer to Find Remote Files

You can also use Windows Explorer to find files on remote computers. In fact, I think finding stuff with Windows Explorer is easier, because you can select a folder in the left pane and see its contents in the right pane. You know at a glance which folders have subfolders, because you see a plus sign to the left of any parent folder.

In addition, if you want to move or copy files from one computer to another, the hierarchical layout of Windows Explorer makes performing those tasks easier.

Opening Network Neighborhood in Windows Explorer

Scroll down through the left pane in the Explorer window to find the Network Neighborhood icon, and then click the plus sign next to it. All the computers on the network appear in the left pane. When you click the plus sign next to a computer name, you see all the shared resources on that computer.

If the remote computer's hard drive is the only shared resource, click the plus sign so that you can see all the folders on the hard drive. Then select the appropriate folder to see its contents in the right Explorer pane. Then find the file you want to use.

Adding remote shares to your Favorites list

In Windows 98 (and Windows 95 with Internet Explorer 4.0), you can use the Favorites feature to get to a shared folder on a remote computer quickly. This nifty trick makes getting to the files you need easier. Did you realize that Favorites aren't just Internet sites? Isn't that cool?

Browse to the folder that you want to use and select it. If the folder isn't specifically configured as a shared resource, open its parent, which is either a shared folder or the hard drive. Expand the parent so that you can select the folder. Then follow these steps to add the folder to your list of favorite sites:

1. **In Windows Explorer, select the folder that you want to mark as a Favorite.**

   The contents of the folder appear in the right pane. You can't mark an individual file as a Favorite, but you can mark the folder in which it resides to make finding the file much easier.

2. **Choose F̲avorites⇨A̲dd to Favorites from the Explorer menu bar.**

   The Add Favorite dialog box appears with the name of the folder appearing in the Name text box (see Figure 10-7).

3. **Change the name to clearly indicate that this folder resides on a remote computer.**

4. **Click OK.**

   Being exact when naming a favorite site is more efficient, so add the name of the remote computer. In this example, because the folder is on the computer named Mantis1, the name **address book on Mantis1**

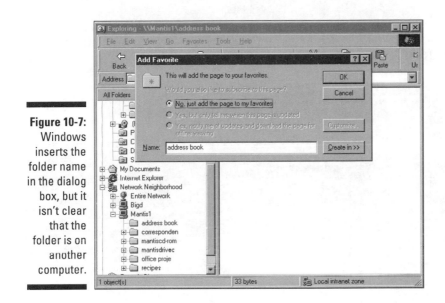

Figure 10-7:
Windows
inserts the
folder name
in the dialog
box, but it
isn't clear
that the
folder is on
another
computer.

makes sense. Another reason to add the name of the computer to the
name of the Favorite is that you may have a folder by the same name on
your own computer. (For example, My Documents is a popular folder to
share. You may want to say **My Documents on Mantis1** in this example.)

The next time you want to use this folder, open Windows Explorer and click
Favorites on the menu bar. The folder appears in the Favorites menu (see
Figure 10-8).

Figure 10-8:
Point and
click to
move to any
site on your
list of
Favorites.

Click the listing. Like magic, Windows Explorer expands the Network Neighborhood window in the left Explorer pane and selects the remote folder (see Figure 10-9).

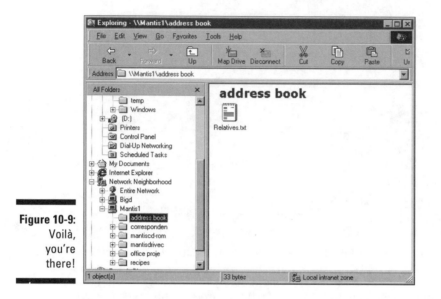

Figure 10-9:
Voilà,
you're
there!

If you have several folders on remote computers that you access frequently, you can organize them so that they're all together in your Favorites list. Follow these steps to create a Favorites folder for a remote computer:

1. In Windows Explorer, choose F_a_vorites⇨_O_rganize Favorites.

The Organize Favorites dialog box appears (see Figure 10-10).

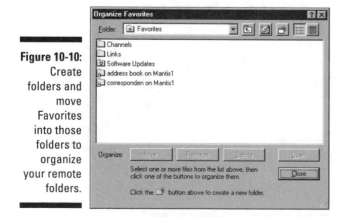

Figure 10-10:
Create
folders and
move
Favorites
into those
folders to
organize
your remote
folders.

2. Click the Create New Folder button on the toolbar.

A new folder, conveniently called New Folder, appears in the Organize Favorites dialog box. The folder's name is highlighted, so that when you begin typing a name for this folder, the characters replace the existing characters.

3. Enter a name for the new folder and press Enter.

Naming the folder after the remote computer that owns the sites you're planning to put in the folder is a good idea. This is especially efficient if you have multiple remote computers on your network.

4. Select the Favorites that you want to place in the new folder.

To select multiple objects, hold down the Ctrl key as you click each item.

5. Click Move.

The Browse for Folder dialog box appears, displaying a list of all the folders in your Favorites listings.

6. Click on the icon for your new folder and click OK.

You're back in the Organize Favorites dialog box. You may see the original listings, but in a second or two they disappear when they move into the folder that you created.

The next time you want to use one of these remote folders, choose Favorites⇨*<folder name>*⇨*<share name>*. As shown in Figure 10-11, the shared resources in the folder that you created appear in a submenu. When you select one, Explorer expands the Network Neighborhood listing and automatically selects that folder so that you can view its contents in the right pane.

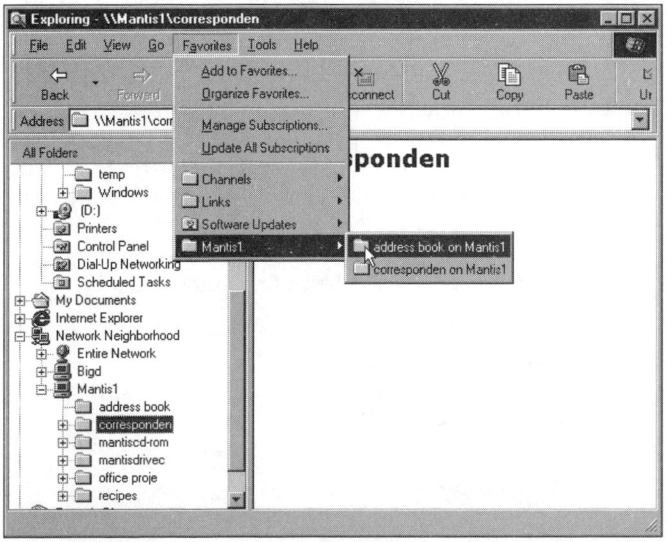

Figure 10-11: The shared folders that you work with are now on a submenu, making it easy to select them in Windows Explorer.

You can create multiple folders to hold Favorites. Create one for each remote computer, or create separate folders to organize remote folders by category.

Working with Remote Files

When you open remote folders to access the files within them, you can do things with those files as if they were on your own computer. The only hindrance that you may face is when a remote folder is configured for limited actions (see "Understanding permission levels" earlier in this chapter). For this discussion, however, I assume that you have full permission to manipulate the files on the remote folder.

Copying files between computers

You can copy a file from a remote computer to your own computer by either dragging or using the shortcut menu.

You can use the exact same techniques to copy files in the other direction, from your computer to the remote computer. Just reverse the processes described here.

Copying by dragging files

If you drag a file from a remote computer to your own computer, you copy it, rather than move it. This is different from dragging a file from one folder to another on your own computer, which moves the file instead of copying it. That's because Windows assumes that you don't want to deprive the user of the other computer of the file. It's a good assumption.

To make dragging files from a remote computer to your own computer easier, open separate windows for each computer. If you use Windows 98, you must configure Explorer to open separate windows for each folder you open. (Windows 95 is preconfigured for separate windows.) Here's how to do that:

1. **Choose Start➪Programs➪Windows Explorer.**

    The Explorer window appears.

2. **Choose View➪Folder Options.**

    The Folder Options dialog box appears, with the General tab in the foreground.

3. **Click the Settings button.**

    The Custom Settings dialog box appears (see Figure 10-12).

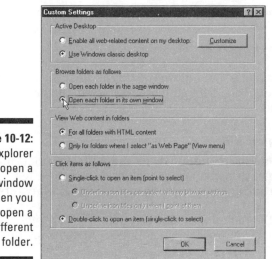

Figure 10-12:
Tell Explorer
to open a
new window
when you
open a
different
folder.

4. **Select Open Each Folder in Its Own Window.**

5. **Click OK, and then click Close in the Folder Options dialog box.**

Now you're all set to use multiple windows for easy dragging. Follow these steps to copy a file using Windows Explorer:

1. **Choose Start⇨Programs⇨Windows Explorer.**

   The Explorer window appears on your Desktop.

2. **Expand the Network Neighborhood listing and then expand the remote computer to select the remote folder that holds the file that you need.**

   The files in the remote folder appear in the right Explorer pane.

3. **In the left Explorer pane, scroll up to the listings for your own computer and right-click the folder that you want to copy the file into.**

   The shortcut menu for the folder appears when you right-click.

4. **Choose Open from the shortcut menu.**

   A separate window opens on your screen, displaying the contents of your local folder.

5. **Right-click on a blank spot on your taskbar and choose an arrangement scheme from the menu that appears.**

   Choose Tile Windows Horizontally or Tile Windows Vertically to see both windows.

6. **Drag the file from the remote folder to the local folder (see Figure 10-13).**

   The file is copied to your local folder.

If you want to copy multiple files, hold down the Ctrl key and select all the files that you need. Then drag one file to the other window, and all the other files come along for the ride.

Copying by right-dragging files

Perhaps you're not very adventurous and you're afraid that you may move the file instead of copying it. Or perhaps you can't remember whether dragging moves or copies when you're working with multiple computers.

To play it safe, drag with the right mouse button (called *right-dragging*). When you release the mouse button, a menu appears. Choose Copy Here.

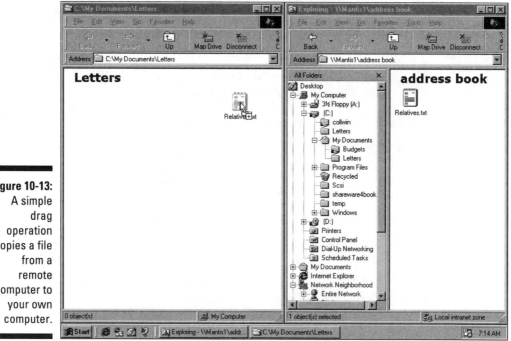

Figure 10-13: A simple drag operation copies a file from a remote computer to your own computer.

Copying with the shortcut menu

You can use the shortcut menu that appears when you right-click an item in Windows Explorer to copy a file. This method eliminates the need for a second window. Follow these steps to copy files from a remote computer to your own computer:

1. **Choose Start⇨Programs⇨Windows Explorer.**

   The Explorer window appears.

2. **Expand the Network Neighborhood listing, and then expand the remote computer to select the folder that holds the file you need.**

   The files in the selected folder appear in the right Explorer pane.

3. **Right-click on the file that you want to copy.**

   The shortcut menu appears. If you want to copy multiple files, hold down the Ctrl key as you click on each file. Then right-click on any file listing to see the shortcut menu.

4. **Choose Copy.**

   The file (or multiple files) is placed on the Windows clipboard.

5. **In the left Explorer pane, right-click on the folder on your local computer into which you want to copy the file.**

6. **Choose Paste from the shortcut menu that appears.**

   The file is copied to your local folder.

Moving files between computers

Sometimes you may want to move a file, thus removing it from the remote computer and placing it on your local computer (or the other way around). This is less common than copying files, but if you used to work on the computer in the den and have decided that you prefer the computer in the kitchen, this is a good way to move your files over to your new computer.

Another reason to move a file instead of copying it is to work on a file that another user started. If you move it and then return it when you finish with it, you don't have to worry about the original user making changes at the same time that you make your changes.

Moving by right-dragging files

You can drag files from the remote computer to your own computer with the right mouse button (called *right-dragging*). If you drag with the left mouse button, you copy the files instead of moving them.

Use the steps discussed in the section "Copying by dragging files" earlier in this chapter to open two windows from Windows Explorer — one for the remote computer and one for your local computer. Then drag the file or files you need from one window to the other, using the right mouse button.

When you release the right mouse button, a menu appears. Choose Move Here. The files move from the original location to the new location.

Using the shortcut menu to move files

If you don't want to open separate windows in order to drag files, you can use the file shortcut menu to cut and paste.

Follow the steps in the section "Copying with the shortcut menu" earlier in this chapter to open Windows Explorer and select the files you want to move. Instead of choosing Copy from the shortcut menu, choose Cut. Then choose Paste to move the files to the folder of your choice on your own computer. (Make sure that you click on the folder to select it before using the Paste command.)

The files move from the original location to the new location.

Deleting files from remote computers

You can delete a file from a remote computer as easily as you delete files from your own computer. Just select the file and press the Delete key. The same thing is true of folders.

The problem, however, is that the Recycle Bin doesn't work across the network. A deleted file is really deleted, so you can't recover it from the Recycle Bin right after you say "oops."

Accessing Remote Files with Software

You don't have to take the trouble to copy or move files to your own computer when you want to work with them in a software program. You can open and save files on remote computers right from the software. In fact, software written for Windows is designed to do this.

Opening files on a remote computer

If you work in a Windows software program and you want to work on a file that's located on a remote computer, you can accomplish that right from the software. Follow these steps to use a remote file in your software:

1. **Click the Open button on the software toolbar, or choose File➪Open from the menu bar.**

   The Open dialog box appears. The folder used by the dialog box is the default folder for the software, which is usually the My Documents folder on your own computer.

2. **Click the arrow to the right of the Look In box and select Network Neighborhood from the list of locations (see Figure 10-14).**

   The Open dialog box displays the computers in the Network Neighborhood.

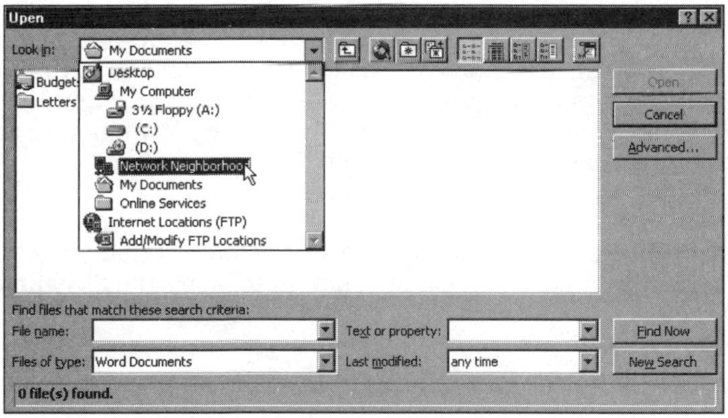

Figure 10-14: Network Neighborhood is available from the Open dialog box.

3. **Double-click the icon of the remote computer that you want to access.**

   Icons for the shared drives and folders on the remote computer appear in the Open dialog box.

4. **Double-click the folder that holds the file you want to use.**

   The files located in that folder are displayed in the Open dialog box.

5. **Select the file and click Open.**

   The file loads in your software window, so get to work!

If the file that you need is located in a subfolder of a shared resource, it won't appear when you double-click the computer's icon (only the folders that are configured for sharing show up in the display). You must open the parent folder (which is a shared folder or the hard drive) and then open the subfolder to get to the file.

Saving remote files

If you open a file from a remote computer, saving it doesn't change its original location. Every time you click the Save button on the toolbar, press Ctrl+S, or choose File⇨Save, you save the file in its original location on the remote computer.

The same thing is true for files that you open in software residing on your local drive — they're saved to the same location every time you click the Save button.

Suppose that you open a file that's on a remote computer and work on it in a software program, and then you decide that you want to have a copy of it on your own computer. Well, doing that is easier than you might think, because you don't have to close the software and use the copy function described earlier in this chapter. You can work on the document and copy it in one fell swoop, using the features in the software program.

The same shortcut action is available for documents that you create on your local computer, if you decide that you want to share the file with a user on another computer.

Saving a remote file to the local computer

You've opened a software program and loaded a document from another computer on the network, using the steps discussed in the previous section. You work on the document, making creative changes and adding brilliant new text. Then your brain comes up with a thought that matches one of these ideas:

✔ The user who created the document likes it just the way it is. If you prefer the changed document, you should keep it on your own computer.

✔ The original document is meant to be used as a template, and you'd prefer to have your own copy of it.

✔ You haven't finished working on the document, and reloading it is faster if the file is in your local My Documents folder.

✔ You know that you want to continue working on the document and just in case the other computer isn't running the next time you need it, you don't want to climb the stairs to the den.

✔ You just want your own copy because you just want your own copy.

For any of those common reasons (or for some reason I didn't think of), you can save the file to your own local computer. To accomplish this, follow these steps:

1. **Choose File⇨Save As from the menu bar of your software window.**

   When the Save As dialog box opens, the saving location is the same remote folder that you opened to fetch the file.

2. **Click the arrow to the right of the Save In text box.**

   If you use Windows 98, select the My Documents folder. If you use Windows 95, select your local hard drive, and then select your My Documents folder.

   If you don't save documents in the My Documents folder, select your local hard drive and then head for the folder that you use for saving documents.

3. **Click Save.**

You now have a copy of the file on your local computer, and the original file remains on the remote computer.

Saving a local file to a remote computer

When you work in a software program and you create an absolutely terrific work of art, a fantastic poem, or a mathematically brilliant budget that helps your family save 20 percent of your income without any deprivation, you should show it off — er, share it.

If you just created the document, you should save it to your local documents folder first, because having your own copy of a document is a good idea. Then follow these steps to save the document on another computer so that other users can share it:

1. **Choose File⇨Save As from the software menu bar.**

   The Save As dialog box appears.

2. **Click the arrow to the right of the Save In text box and select Network Neighborhood from the list of locations (see Figure 10-15).**

   Icons for the computers on your network appear in the Save As dialog box.

Figure 10-15:
You can change your location to Network Neighborhood right in the Save As dialog box.

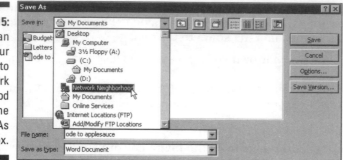

3. **Double-click the icon for the remote computer on which you want to store a copy of your document.**

   The shared folders on the selected computer appear in the dialog box.

4. **Double-click the folder into which you want to save the document.**

   If the folder you want to use is a subfolder of a shared folder, open the shared folder first, and then open the subfolder.

   If the only shared resource is the hard drive, open the hard drive and then open the appropriate folder.

5. **Choose Save to copy the document to the remote location.**

   If you wish, you can also change the name of the document before you save it to the remote computer.

Understanding Documents in Use

Two people can't work on the same document at the same time. When a document is being used by one user, no other users can access the same copy that's being used.

Loading a remote document that's being used

If you try to open a document that's already open on the remote computer, Windows displays a message and offers to make a copy of the document and load that copy in your software window (see Figure 10-16).

Click OK to have a copy of the document placed in your own software window. The copy that you get is from the hard drive of the remote computer, not the software window of the remote user. That means that you get a copy of the file the way it looked the last time the remote user saved it, which may have been three minutes ago, yesterday, or last week. That user is obviously still working on the file, but any changes or additions since the last save aren't copied to your computer.

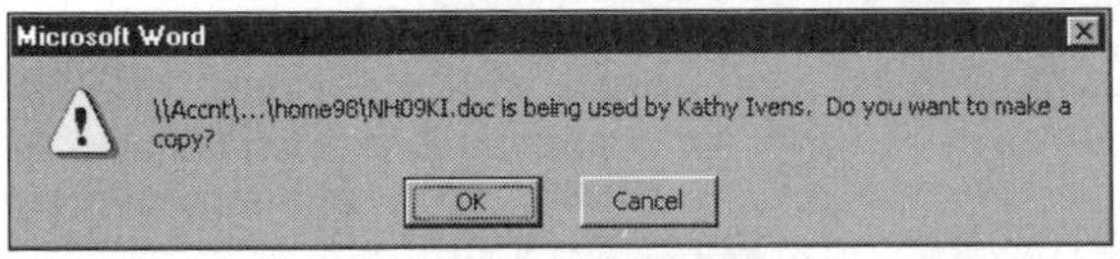

Figure 10-16:
Somebody's
using this
document,
but you can
have a copy
of it.

So, now you have a copy of the file. You can make all the changes and additions that you care to, just as if another user wasn't using the file. Have a ball!

Saving a document that's in use

Eventually, you're going to want to save the file, and that might present a problem. You may run into one of several possible scenarios, and each has an upside and a downside.

The first scenario is that you want to save the file, with your changes, and the first user is still working with the file. An error message appears, informing you that the file is in use. Click OK, and a Save As dialog box appears so that you can save the file under a different name or in a different location. Here are your options:

- ✔ **Use a different file name and save the file in the original location on the remote computer.** For example, add your initials to the end of the existing file name.

- ✔ **Save the file to your local computer.** Click the arrow to the right of the Save In text box and select your local hard drive or the My Documents folder.

  The problem with this option is that you now have two files with the same name, but different content, on the network (albeit on two separate computers). If you think that you and the original user may want to compare and combine the two documents, save the file under a different name when you save it to your local computer.

The second scenario is that you want to save the file, and the first user has finished working with the file. In fact, the first user has saved the file, and the latest saved version contains all sorts of changes and additions.

When you try to save your version of the file, a message appears telling you that the file has been changed and saved by another user. Here are the options that you get in that message (shown in Figure 10-17):

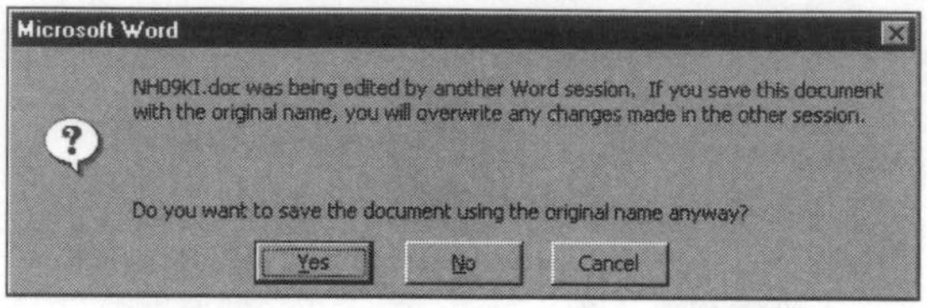

Figure 10-17:
Be careful
about the
method that
you use to
save a
shared file.

Microsoft Word

NH09KI.doc was being edited by another Word session. If you save this document with the original name, you will overwrite any changes made in the other session.

Do you want to save the document using the original name anyway?

[Yes] [No] [Cancel]

- ✔ **Click Yes to save the file.** This option replaces the file that the first user saved. Then leave home because your life is in danger. This is a dirty trick, because you end up overwriting all the work saved by the first user.

- ✔ **Click No to open a Save As dialog box.** Here, you can save the file with a different file name, in a different location (remote computer or local computer), or both.

- ✔ **Click Cancel to return to the document without saving.** Have a discussion with the first user to arrive at a solution, and then return to your computer to save the file. If the first user isn't available, or you can't decide how to handle the situation, the safest route is to choose File⇨Save As and save the file to your own computer with a different file name.

Playing Games across the Network

This is the ultimate "sharing files across the network" experience — a chance to play a game with another household member who's on a different computer in a different room or even on a different floor of the house.

You can download plenty of network games from the Internet, but you can start your Internet gaming experience right from your Windows system. The Microsoft Hearts Network is built into Windows, and after you've connected your computers, you can play the network version of Hearts.

If nobody else is home, or you're not on a networked computer, you can still play Hearts. Your playmates are computer-controlled players.

When you want to play Hearts with other folks on other computers, Windows does the work needed to connect the players. You should know these three things before you start:

✔ The first person to open Hearts must choose to be the dealer, and then everyone else chooses to join the game.

✔ The dealer starts the game when he or she decides that all the available players have joined the game. If you don't have four participants on the network, Windows supplies any missing players.

✔ You must know the name of the computer that the dealer uses. If you don't remember the computer name, you can find it on the Identification tab of the Network dialog box in the Control Panel.

Here's how to get a network game of Hearts started:

1. **Choose Start➪Programs➪Accessories➪Games➪Hearts.**

   The Microsoft Hearts Network window appears, with a dialog box listing options in front of the main window (see Figure 10-18).

   Your name (taken from your logon name) is already in the What Is Your Name? text box. If you want to, change the name to anything that strikes your fancy.

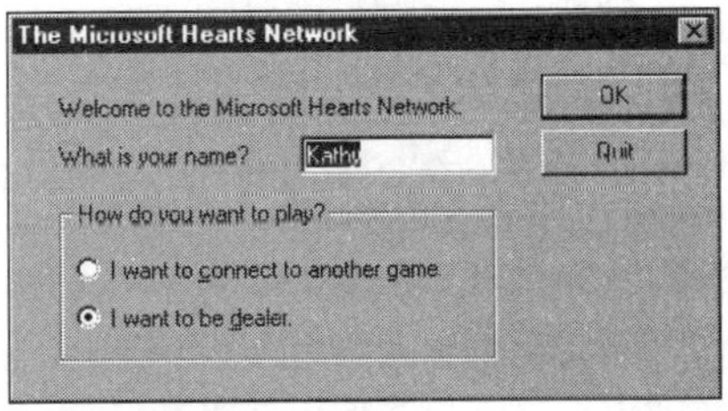

Figure 10-18:
Are you starting a new game or are you joining a game in progress?

2. **If you're the first person on the network to open Hearts, select I Want to Be the Dealer. Then click OK.**

   The Options dialog box goes away and the main Hearts window is on your screen. The Hearts Network is waiting for other players to join the game. Your name appears at the bottom of the window — that's your seat at the table. Skip to Step 5.

3. **If a dealer has already started a game, select I Want to Connect to Another Game, and click OK.**

   The Locate Dealer dialog box appears.

4. **Enter the name of the computer that the dealer is using, and then click OK.**

   The Hearts Network window appears on your screen, and your name is at one of the seats. You're waiting for the dealer to begin the game.

Your name also appears on the dealer's window, so the dealer can keep track of who's joined the game so far.

5. **When all the available players have joined the game, the dealer presses F2 to begin the game.**

   The cards are dealt, and Windows puts players at any seats not occupied by a real person on the network (see Figure 10-19).

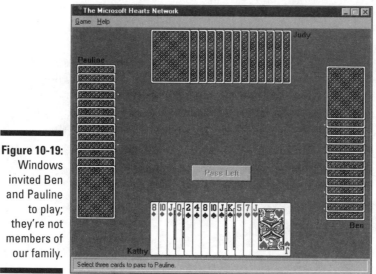

Figure 10-19:
Windows
invited Ben
and Pauline
to play;
they're not
members of
our family.

I'm not going to explain how to play Hearts, for which you should be grateful because my expertise isn't terrific. My kids hand me humiliating losses when we play. I'd have one of them explain the game to you (obviously they're better qualified), but they're not around at the moment. So you'll have to learn the game yourself, if you haven't already played Hearts with a regular deck of cards.

You can change the following options when you play a network game of Hearts:

✔ **Choose Game⇨Options (or press F7) to open the Hearts Options dialog box shown in Figure 10-20.** You can specify the speed at which cards move across the table, and you can also change the names of the players that Windows puts at your table.

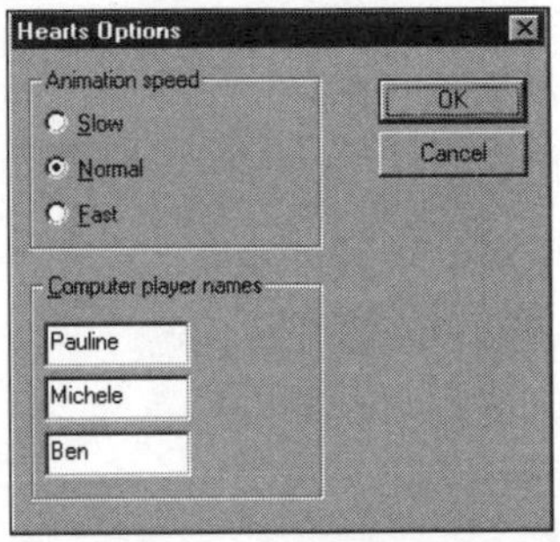

Figure 10-20:
You can
configure
the
animation
speed and
the names
of players.

> ✔ **Choose Game⇨Sound (or press F8) to turn on sound effects.** A check
> mark appears next to the Sound menu item — choose it again to turn
> off sound effects (it's a toggle). The sound effects include the sound of
> breaking glass when a Heart is played, and a "bong" when the Queen of
> Spades is dropped.
>
> ✔ **Choose Game⇨Score (or press F9) to see the current score.**

Games are great ways to waste time (wasting time is good for your psyche),
and network games are a terrific way for the whole family to enjoy computer
contests.

Chapter 11

Mapping Shortcuts to the Network

After you configure all the computers on your network as shared resources, you can take advantage of shortcuts and features for network environments. This chapter covers a couple of nifty features related to computer names, share names, and drive letter designations. You can use this information to make accessing remote computers on your network easier.

Using the Universal Naming Convention

When you work at one computer and access a shared resource on another computer, you're accessing something with a name — you can see the name of a shared folder on a remote computer in Network Neighborhood or Windows Explorer. What's not so obvious is that you're also accessing the remote computer itself by name.

When you access remote resources, you're using a convention called the *universal naming convention* (UNC). The format for displaying the UNC works like this: \\computername\resourcename.

Naming your computers and shared resources

Computers on Windows networks have names; naming a computer is part of the configuration process when you set up the network features on your Windows computer (see Chapters 3 and 5). You can name your computers whatever you want. Some people use descriptive names (Den, Kitchen,

Laptop, and so on); some people use names that reflect the owner or primary user of the computer (Dad, Sis, and so on). And others just give computers names that don't necessarily have anything to do with anything. I have a colleague who named the computers on his home network Zeke and Fred because "when I brought them home and set them up, they looked like a Zeke and a Fred." Hey, whatever works.

In addition to the computer name, you have to consider other names when you work on your network — the share names. Each shared resource has a name, because providing a name is part of setting up the share. See Chapter 9 to find out about creating shares on your computers.

Share names are usually a bit more descriptive than computer names because people tend to use the name of the drive or folder that's being shared. For example, if you have a folder on your computer named Addresses, then you probably named the share Addresses when you configured the folder for sharing.

Understanding when to use a UNC and when to use a path statement

When you understand that a computer has a name and a shared resource has a name, using a formatted style to refer to a particular shared resource on a particular computer makes sense. Once upon a time, a computer nerd said, "Hey, let's call that the UNC." And everybody who needed to access shared resources in this way said, "Okeydokey."

So if you're working on your network and you open a folder named Budgets on a remote computer named Bob, you're working at a UNC named \\Bob\Budgets.

Now this format may look familiar because it's very similar to the way you enter paths when working in MS-DOS. For example, your Windows files are located at a UNC named C:\Windows, which means they're on drive C: in a folder named Windows. Some important operating system files are in a subfolder named System. The path to that subfolder is C:\Windows\System.

In a path, the letter *C* followed by a colon (:) indicates the drive. In the same way, in a UNC statement, a double backslash (\\) followed by a name indicates a remote computer.

Your own computer has a name, too, because it's on a network (remember that you have to name a computer in order to set up networking in Windows). If your computer's name is Bigdaddy, your system files are in \\Bigdaddy\Windows\System. Anyone working at another computer on the network uses that UNC to get to that folder. You can't use the UNC to get there; you must use an MS-DOS path statement because using a UNC statement signals your computer to look to the network to find the folder. When you use the MS-DOS path format, you tell your computer that the target folder is on the local computer.

Viewing UNC and path statements

You can see the path or UNC for any object on any computer when you're working in Windows Explorer if you configure Windows Explorer to display this information. By default, Windows Explorer doesn't display this information. Use these steps to display path and UNC details in Windows Explorer:

1. **Choose Start⇨Programs⇨Windows Explorer.**

   The Explorer window opens.

2. **In Windows 98, choose View⇨Folder Options from the Windows Explorer menu bar. In Windows 95, choose View⇨Options.**

   The Folder Options dialog box opens.

3. **In Windows 98, click the View tab of the Folder Options dialog box. (Windows 95 opens to the View tab automatically.)**

   The View options appear, as shown in Figure 11-1.

4. **Select Display the Full Path in Title Bar. (In Windows 95, the option is called Display the Full MS-DOS Path in the Title Bar.)**

5. **Choose OK.**

Now when you select drives or folders on your own computer or on remote computers, you see the full path or UNC statement in Windows Explorer.

In Windows 98, the path or UNC statement is in the address bar. In Windows 95, the path or UNC statement is at the top of the right Explorer pane.

But there's more to understanding the UNC than knowing what it means when you see the UNC statement in Windows Explorer. You can use the information to move around the network faster and easier as well as to turn a UNC statement into a path statement (using a feature called mapping, which is covered in the next section). You can also use UNC statements with other Windows features such as the Run command on your Start menu. I cover all these cool tricks later in this chapter.

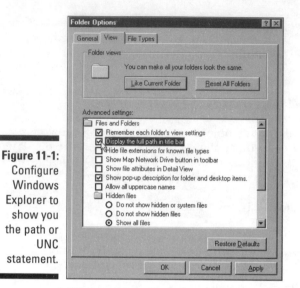

Figure 11-1:
Configure
Windows
Explorer to
show you
the path or
UNC
statement.

Mapping Drives and Folders

If you have a networked computer, you can use a feature called *mapping* to more easily access a shared resource on another computer. Mapping means assigning a drive letter, such as *E: or F:*, to a shared resource on another computer. You can map another computer's drive, folder, or subfolder.

The drive letter you use becomes part of the local computer's set of drive letters, starting with the first letter available after all your local drives have been assigned. The drives you create are called *network drives.*

Understanding drive letters

The computer you use already has at least two drive letters. The floppy drive is A:, and the hard drive is C:. If you have a second floppy drive, that's B:. If you have a CD-ROM drive, it also has a drive letter (probably D:). If you have a Zip, Jaz, or other peripheral drive attached to your computer, a drive letter is assigned to that, too.

To see the drive letters that your computer is already using, open Windows Explorer and click the plus sign to the left of My Computer. All the devices on your computer that have drive letters are displayed in alphabetic order.

For example, say that a computer named Eve, located in the kitchen of a house that has a home network, has three drive letters that belong to local resources:

- ✔ Drive A: is a floppy drive.
- ✔ Drive C: is a hard drive.
- ✔ Drive D: is a CD-ROM drive.

Drive C: is configured as a shared resource named EveDriveC. The hard drive has a lot of folders, of course, and some of them have been configured as shared resources that can be accessed by users on other computers. Eve's shares include the following folders:

- ✔ \AddressBook, which has the share name Addresses
- ✔ \FamilyBudget, which has the share name Budget

The other computer on the network is in the upstairs hallway (in a handy little nook that was just perfect for a computer console). That computer is named Adam, and it has the following resources with drive letters:

- ✔ Drive A: is a floppy drive.
- ✔ Drive C: is a hard drive.

The hard drive on Adam is a shared resource named AdamDriveC. It has lots of folders, too, and these folders have been configured as shares:

- ✔ \LegalPapers, which has the share name Legal
- ✔ \Letters, which has the share name Letters

Figure 11-2 shows both computers with their drive letters and paths.

Of course, when Adam looks at Eve, or Eve looks at Adam, those path statements become UNC statements. Because neither Eve nor Adam configured any drives except drive C: for sharing, floppy drives and CD-ROM drives can't be seen across the network.

Mapping remote resources

If you use a particular share from a remote computer a lot, all the steps you use to open the share eventually seem tedious. You have to double-click the Network Neighborhood or Windows Explorer icon, then you have to find and open the remote computer, then you have to expand the remote computer to see its shares, and then you have to open the share you need. Boring!

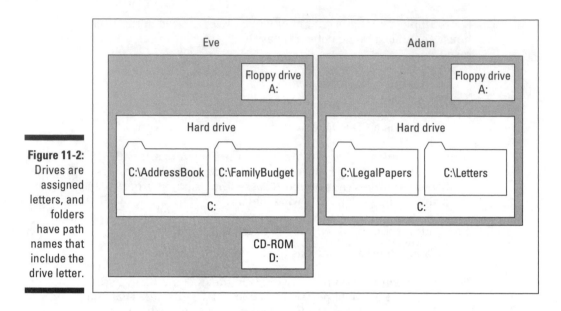

Figure 11-2:
Drives are assigned letters, and folders have path names that include the drive letter.

Now, another fact, which is a related fact (trust me, I will get to the relationship), is that you have all these drive letters you aren't using. Even if you have two floppy drives, a hard drive, a CD-ROM drive, and a Zip drive, most of the letters of the alphabet are unused.

Put the alphabet to work! Turn a shared resource on a remote computer into a drive letter. (See? That's the relationship.) When you assign a drive letter to (or, in other words, map) a shared resource on a remote computer, your life gets easier (well, your life as a computer user gets easier; the rest of your life is your problem, not mine). Here are some of the benefits of mapping:

✔ Every object on your computer that has a drive letter is displayed in Windows Explorer in a logical list, so you don't have to open Network Neighborhood in Windows Explorer to find a mapped share.

✔ Every object on your computer that has a drive letter is displayed in My Computer. You can double-click the My Computer icon and then open a local drive or a remote share with equal ease.

✔ You can use an MS-DOS command session and MS-DOS commands to work with any remote storage object (drive or folder) that has a drive letter. For example, if you want to copy documents from a remote folder that you've mapped to drive G: to your documents folder, you can type **copy g:*.doc c:\documents**.

When you open the hard drive of a remote computer, you can use any folder on that drive. However, if a folder isn't configured specifically as a shared resource, you can't map it. Ask the person who uses that computer to create a shared resource for that folder. Or go to the computer and do it yourself.

The easiest and fastest way to do anything with the remote computers on your network is with Network Neighborhood, because it's dedicated to network resources. Follow these steps to map a network drive using Network Neighborhood:

1. **Double-click the Network Neighborhood icon.**

   The Network Neighborhood window opens and displays the computers on the network.

2. **Double-click the icon for the remote computer that you want to use.**

   All the shared resources on the remote computer appear in the window (see Figure 11-3).

3. **Right-click the share that you want to map as a network drive.**

   The shortcut menu for the share appears.

4. **Choose <u>M</u>ap Network Drive from the shortcut menu.**

   The Map Network Drive dialog box opens, as shown in Figure 11-4.

5. **Se<u>l</u>ect Reconnect at Logon if you want to map this drive automatically every time you start this computer.**

   This feature can become a bit complicated; see "Reconnecting mapped drives," later in this chapter, for more information.

6. **Click OK.**

You can open a file and go to work, or map another network drive by repeating these steps.

Figure 11-3:
This remote computer has shares for the hard drive and a few folders.

You can also map a network drive in Windows Explorer. Just click the Network Neighborhood icon in the left pane, click the icon for the appropriate computer in the right pane, right-click the share you want to map, and choose Map Network Drive.

Figure 11-4: Windows uses the next available drive letter for your first network drive.

You can tell Windows to connect to this network drive every time you start this computer.

The path for this share appears as a UNC statement.

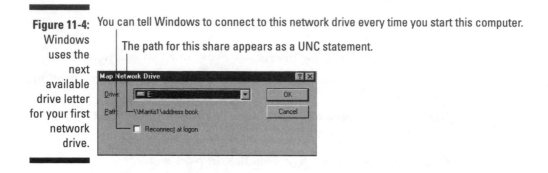

Viewing and using mapped drives

After you map a shared resource as a drive, you can move easily to that share using one of these techniques:

✔ **Double-click the My Computer icon to open the My Computer window.** All the drives on your computer, including remote shares that are mapped to a drive letter, appear in the My Computer window (see Figure 11-5). Just open the drive and go to work.

✔ **Double-click the Windows Explorer icon to open the Windows Explorer window.** All the drives on your computer appear in the left pane, including every remote share that is mapped to a drive letter. Click the minus sign next to drive C: to get rid of the folder display so you can see all your drives more easily. Open any drive to use it.

Even though you added new drive letters, you didn't add any new physical drives to the computer. These are *virtual drives.* Going back to the example of Eve and Adam (if you haven't yet met Eve and Adam, see "Understanding drive letters," earlier in the chapter), you can see how this works.

Figure 11-6 shows Eve after a network drive (drive E:) was mapped to the share named \\adam\legal. You can see that the new drive letter isn't connected to a physical drive.

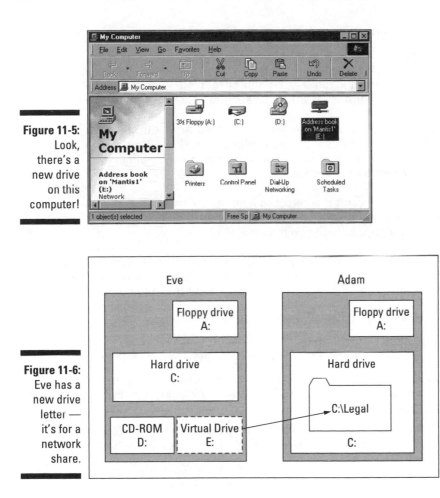

Figure 11-5:
Look,
there's a
new drive
on this
computer!

Figure 11-6:
Eve has a
new drive
letter —
it's for a
network
share.

Reconnecting mapped drives

When you're mapping a remote resource to a drive letter, you can select
the Reconnect on Logon option. This means that every time you log on,
Windows verifies the network drive — or, in other words, it peers down the
network cable to make sure that the shared resource that's mapped to the
drive is there. This slows down the logon process, but you probably won't
notice a big difference.

Incidentally, the reason that the option is Reconnect on Logon instead of
Reconnect on Startup is that the mapped drives you create are part of your
personalized profile. If multiple users share a computer, the mapped drives
that appear are those created by the user who is logged on. The jargon for
these mapped drives is *persistent connections*. Persistent connections are
linked to a user (a logon name), not to a computer. See Chapter 6 to find out
about personalizing a computer with user profiles.

Remapping when reconnection fails

You can easily imagine that a problem may arise if you have two computers on your network and both have mapped network drives that are configured for reconnection on logon. The computer that runs the logon procedure first loses, and the computer that logs on second wins!

When the first computer looks for the mapped drive during logon, the second computer isn't yet up and running. The share doesn't exist, so the mapping function fails. Windows displays a message telling you that the mapped drive isn't connected.

If your computer can't reconnect to a mapped drive at logon, it's no big deal. The logon process works, and everything's fine, except that the mapped drive doesn't appear until you map it again.

You can make remapping a drive easier by placing a button for mapping network drives on the toolbar in the Network Neighborhood window. Follow these steps to configure Network Neighborhood for easy remapping:

1. **Double-click the Network Neighborhood icon.**

   When the Network Neighborhood window opens, a toolbar should appear in the window. If the toolbar is there, move to Step 3.

2. **Add the toolbar to the Network Neighborhood window in Windows 98 by choosing View➪Toolbars➪Standard Buttons; add it in Windows 95 by choosing View➪Toolbar.**

   In Windows 98, you can alternatively choose View➪Toolbars➪ Text Labels if you want text instead of buttons on the toolbar.

   Skip the remaining steps if you're running Windows 95 — Windows 95 puts a Map Network Drive button on the toolbar.

3. **Choose View➪Folder Options.**

   The Folder Options dialog box for Windows 98 opens.

4. **Click the View tab of the Folder Options dialog box.**

   The Advanced Settings box shows the current settings for this folder (see Figure 11-7).

5. **Select the option Show Map Network Drive Button in Toolbar.**

6. **Click OK.**

Now you see a button for mapping drives on your Network Neighborhood toolbar. In fact, you also have a button for disconnecting mapped drives; the two buttons travel as a pair.

You can add the Map Network Drive button to your Explorer window also. Use the same steps (except start with Windows Explorer, of course).

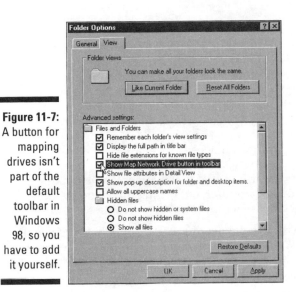

Figure 11-7:
A button for mapping drives isn't part of the default toolbar in Windows 98, so you have to add it yourself.

When the Map Network Drive button appears on your toolbar, remapping is much easier. Follow these steps to remap a drive that you previously mapped:

1. **Click the Map Network Drive button on the toolbar.**

   The Map Network Drive dialog box opens with the next available drive letter selected.

2. **Click the arrow to the right of the Path text box.**

   A list appears that shows the network shares that you recently connected to, not just the shares that you previously mapped (see Figure 11-8). Choose the share you want to use for this drive letter.

Figure 11-8:
Windows tracks the shared resources that you've accessed recently.

Configuring reconnection options

You can configure Windows to wait until you need to use the drive before the network resource is checked. If the computer that contains the shared resource isn't ready, you won't suffer any delay during the logon process (Windows keeps searching for several seconds before giving up). On the other hand, when you use the network drive, Windows checks its availability first, delaying access to the network share for a few seconds.

Here are the available configuration choices:

- ✔ **Quick Logon.** The network drives that you mapped are listed in Windows Explorer and My Computer, but during the logon process Windows doesn't check to see if they're really available.

  Your computer doesn't try to connect until you actually try to use the drive, which is when Windows checks to make sure that the remote share is available. This speeds up the logon process by a few seconds, but it delays the connection process by the same few seconds.

- ✔ **Logon and Restore Network Connections.** Your computer connects to the remote resources for the mapped drives during the logon process.

  This delays the logon process, but you know immediately if a problem exists with any of your mapped drives.

Follow these steps to configure the way you want mapped drive reconnections to work:

1. **Choose Start⇨Settings⇨Control Panel.**

   The Control Panel opens.

2. **Double-click the Network icon.**

   The Network dialog box opens with the Configuration tab in the foreground.

3. **Select the component named Client for Microsoft Networks to highlight it.**

4. **Click the Properties button.**

   The Client for Microsoft Networks Properties dialog box opens, as shown in Figure 11-9.

5. **Select either Quick Logon or Logon and Restore Network Connections.**

6. **Click OK twice.**

Windows displays a message telling you to restart the computer to put this change into effect. In fact, the message dialog box offers to restart Windows for you. Because you don't particularly need to make the change right now, and it's only important the next time you log on, you can just click No.

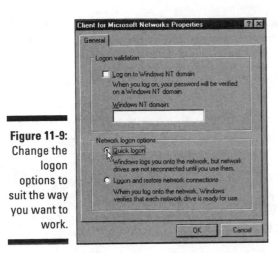

Figure 11-9:
Change the
logon
options to
suit the way
you want to
work.

Quick Tricks for Working with Remote Resources

If you map network drives for the remote shares you use, you have a lot of shortcuts and quick tricks available. Most of the work you do on the remote computer is easier if a mapped drive is available.

Working with mapped drives in Windows Explorer

The first thing you notice when you map drives for all the network resources you use often is that you save a whole lot of time in Windows Explorer. If you want to copy or move a file, everything you need is right in front of you in the Explorer window. The mapped drive is listed in the left pane of the Explorer window, along with all the folders on your local hard drive and all the other drives on your computer. You don't have to expand Network Neighborhood; expand the computer that has the share that you want to use, and then click the share.

If you have a long list of folders on your hard drive and you have to scroll through them to see the other drives on your computer (including mapped drives), save yourself the trouble. Enter the letter of the drive that you want to access in the Windows Explorer address bar.

In Windows 95, which doesn't have an address bar, you can move to the mapped drive quickly by using either of two methods:

- Choose Tools⇨Go To from the Windows Explorer menu bar. Enter the drive letter for the mapped drive in the Go to Folder dialog box, and press Enter (or click OK).

- Click the arrow to the right of the Folder list box on the Windows Explorer toolbar and select the mapped drive.

Both the address bar and the Go To dialog box also accept UNC statements. You can enter the UNC for a remote share to display its contents in Windows Explorer. This is handy if you haven't mapped a drive for a remote resource.

Working with mapped drives at the command line

If you're comfortable working with MS-DOS commands, you can use those commands on a mapped drive just as if you were working on a local drive.

In a couple of situations, I find that the command line is faster and easier than Windows Explorer. For example, if I need to rename a group of files that have similar file names (all the files start with abc), I can accomplish that in one command (ren abc*.* xyz*.*). In Windows Explorer, I'd have to rename each file separately.

All you have to do is open a command prompt window (choose Start⇨ Programs⇨MS-DOS Prompt) and enter the drive letter followed by a colon. You're working on the remote computer, and you can perform any command line tasks.

You can even map a drive with a command prompt. Windows has a command named Net Use. The syntax for creating a mapped drive with the Net Use command is: **net use x: UNC**, where x is the drive letter you want to use and UNC is the UNC statement for the shared resource.

For example, if you want to map G: to the shared resource named letters on the computer named Adam, enter **net use g: \\adam\letters** and wait for the response "The Command Completed Successfully." Now drive G: is mapped, and it will show up in Windows Explorer and My Computer.

Using the Run command to access remote shares

Another quick way to open a remote share is to use the Run command that's on your Start menu. Follow these steps to use the Run command for remote shares:

1. **Choose Start⇨Run.**

   The Run dialog box opens, as shown in Figure 11-10.

2. **If the share is mapped, enter the drive letter (don't forget the colon).**

3. **If the share is not mapped, enter the UNC statement.**

4. **Click OK.**

   The remote share opens in a window on your screen.

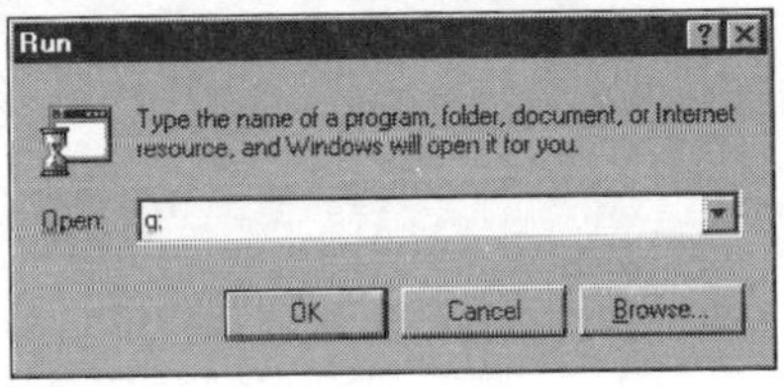

Figure 11-10:
"Run" to a
remote
share (don't
you hate
puns? — it's
okay to
groan).

Creating shortcuts for remote resources

If you use a particular remote folder or drive frequently, create a Desktop shortcut for it. Then all you have to do to reach the remote resource is click the shortcut. Follow these steps to create a Desktop shortcut:

1. **Choose Start⇨Programs⇨Windows Explorer.**

   The Explorer window opens.

2. **If the resource is mapped to a drive, right-drag the drive object from the left Explorer pane to the Desktop.**

   If the resource isn't mapped, double-click the Network Neighborhood icon and then double-click the icon for the remote computer. Right-drag the shared object to the Desktop.

3. **Choose Create Shortcut(s) Here from the menu that appears when you release the right mouse button.**

   The shortcut is on your Desktop. Click it when you want to use the remote resource.

Part V
Sharing Hardware

The 5th Wave — By Rich Tennant

"I think Doreen is trying to send me a message. She set up the vacuum cleaner for sharing."

In this part . . .

These chapters show you how to save time, energy, and — most important — money by sharing printers, peripheral drives, and a modem.

Set up a printer for sharing, and you can send documents to that printer from any computer on the network, even if the printer is attached to a computer on another floor of the house. And if you have more than one printer, you can put envelopes in one printer and your company letterhead in another and then send your documents to the appropriate printer.

Set up a CD-ROM drive for sharing, and you can use your favorite recipe CD on the kitchen computer even if the CD is in the den computer's CD-ROM drive.

Share a modem on your network and put an end to Internet access squabbles. With a shared modem and the right software, everyone can surf the Net at the same time using a single Internet connection — no waiting, no arguments.

Chapter 12

Sharing Printers

• •

In This Chapter

▶ Setting up shared printers

▶ Installing a network printer

▶ Understanding spooling

▶ Manipulating the printer and the documents that are printing

▶ Simplifying network printing with troubleshooting tricks and timesaving tips

• •

*O*ne terrific side effect of installing a computer network in your home is the ability to share a printer. Households without networks face some difficulties when it comes to printing. Network-deficient households (that seems to be a politically correct term, don't you think?) have had to rely on some less-than-perfect solutions.

One solution is to buy a printer every time you buy a computer. I can think of lots of other ways to spend that money, and I bet you can, too.

Another solution is to buy one printer. Anyone who uses a computer that doesn't have a printer has to copy files to a floppy disk, go to the other computer, load the same software that created the files (the same software has to be installed on both computers), open each file from the floppy disk, and print. I guess all this walking comes under the heading of "healthy exercise," especially if the computers are on different floors of the house, but this setup isn't exactly a model of efficiency.

Neither of these scenarios is acceptable once you understand how easy it is to share printers over a network.

Setting Up Shared Printers

If you want all the computers on your network to be able to access a single printer, you have to set up the Windows printer-sharing feature. Then you have to set up the printer itself for sharing. You perform these tasks at the computer to which the printer is connected.

The most difficult part of setting up network printing is deciding which computer gets the printer. Here are some common guidelines:

- ✔ **Location.** If you have room for a table at the computer location (and some storage space for paper), that's the computer to choose.

- ✔ **Usage patterns.** If one computer on the network is used far more often than any other computer, that's the computer to select.

Some households have more than one printer. You may have a monochrome printer (which prints in black and grayscale) and also a color printer. When you enable printer sharing, each user can choose a printer every time he or she wants to print.

You can attach two printers to one computer if that's more convenient, but you have to add a second printer port to the computer. Printer ports are inexpensive (usually less than $10) and are easy to install. (Just read the directions that come with the hardware.) The port is a card that fits in a slot on the computer's motherboard. Chapter 1 tells you how to buy the right type of card for your computer.

Enabling printer sharing

The first thing you have to do is tell Windows that the printer attached to the computer should be shared with other users on the network. Follow these steps to accomplish this simple task:

1. **Choose Start➪Settings➪Control Panel.**

   The Control Panel opens.

2. **Double-click the Network icon in the Control Panel.**

   The Network dialog box opens.

3. **Click the File and Print Sharing button.**

   The File and Print Sharing dialog box opens. (See Figure 12-1.)

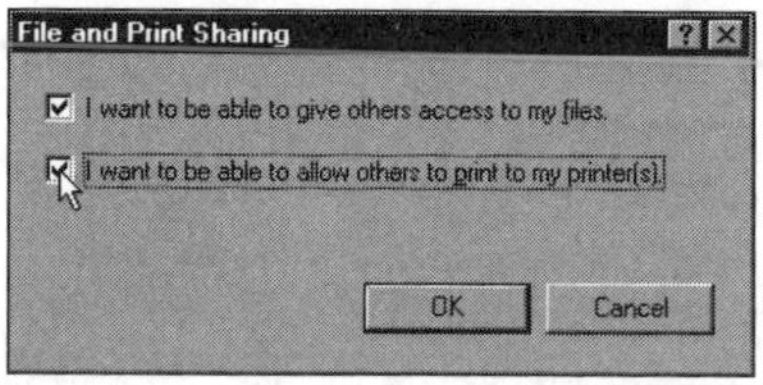

Figure 12-1:
A simple click of the mouse turns your computer into a network print server.

4. **Click the I Want to Be Able to Allow Others to Print to My Printer(s) check box.**

5. **Click OK.**

   You return to the Network dialog box.

6. **Click OK again.**

Windows displays the Systems Settings Change dialog box, which informs you that you must restart the computer in order to put your new setting into effect. Click Yes to restart the system now.

Installing a printer

You have to *install* a printer, which means setting up the files Windows needs to communicate with the printer. Those files are called *printer drivers*. Then you must tell Windows that this printer is going to be shared with other users on the network. Well, of course, *installing* also means the physical installation of the printer, but that's quite simple and the documentation that comes with your printer explains all the steps.

If you already installed a printer for this computer, you can skip this task and move ahead to the section "Sharing the Printer," later in this chapter.

Using Windows files to install a printer

You need your Windows CD to install a printer because the printer driver files are on the disk. If your printer came with its own CD or floppy disk, read the section "Using manufacturer disks to install a printer," later in this chapter.

Put the Windows CD in the CD-ROM drive. Hold the Shift key so the CD doesn't open automatically. If it does open, just click the X in the upper-right corner of the window to close it. Then follow these steps to install your printer:

1. **Double-click the My Computer icon.**

   The My Computer window appears.

2. **Double-click the Printers folder in the My Computer window.**

   The Printers window opens. If this is the first printer you're installing on this computer, the only icon in the folder is the one named Add Printer. (If you installed faxing services, you also have an icon for Microsoft Fax.)

3. **Double-click the Add Printer icon.**

   The Add Printer Wizard window opens. The first window explains that the wizard helps install a printer. Click Next.

4. **Select Local Printer.**

The wizard wants to know whether this printer is a *local printer* (attached to the computer) or a *network printer* (attached to another computer). (Information on installing a network printer is in the section "Installing a Network Printer," later in this chapter.)

Click Next after you make your selection.

5. **Select the manufacturer and model for the printer.**

Scroll through the Manufacturers list in the left pane (see Figure 12-2) to find the company that made your printer. When you select it, the Printers pane on the right displays all the printers from that manufacturer. Scroll through the list to find the right printer model. Then click Next.

If you can't find the exact printer model, read the documentation that came with your printer. Look for the section on printer emulation and see which model matches your printer.

6. **Select the port to which you've attached your printer.**

It's probably LPT1:, but if this is the second printer you're attaching to this computer and you've installed another printer port, choose LPT2:, which doesn't appear unless you have installed a second printer port. Click Next after you select the port.

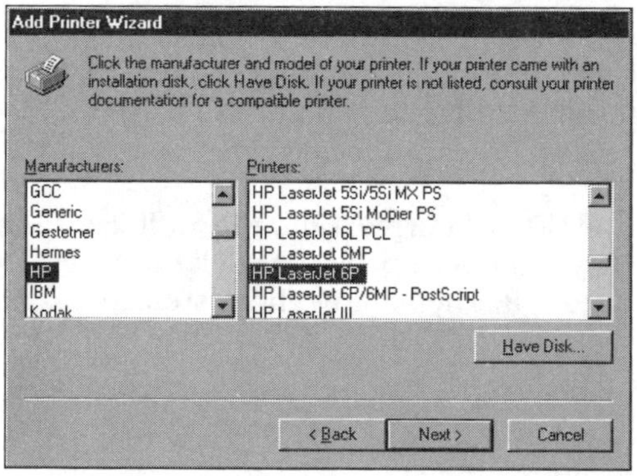

Figure 12-2:
The wizard lists a slew of manufacturers and models, so you shouldn't have a problem finding your printer.

Add Printer Wizard

Click the manufacturer and model of your printer. If your printer came with an installation disk, click Have Disk. If your printer is not listed, consult your printer documentation for a compatible printer.

Manufacturers:
GCC
Generic
Gestetner
Hermes
HP
IBM
Kodak

Printers:
HP LaserJet 5Si/5Si MX PS
HP LaserJet 5Si Mopier PS
HP LaserJet 6L PCL
HP LaserJet 6MP
HP LaserJet 6P
HP LaserJet 6P/6MP - PostScript
HP LaserJet III

Have Disk...

< Back   Next >   Cancel

7. **Name the printer and specify whether it is the default printer. (See Figure 12-3.)**

Enter a name for this printer in the Printer Name text box. By default, the wizard inserts the model name for the printer, which is usually perfectly acceptable.

You also have to tell Windows whether or not this is the default printer for Windows software. Select Yes if this is the printer you expect to use when you print from your software programs. Of course, if this is the first printer you're installing, it has to be the default printer.

The default printer is the printer that is automatically selected when you print from software. If you have other printers, you can use the software Print dialog box to change to another printer. More important, for those occasions when you don't have a choice of printers, the default printer delivers your print job. Examples of not having a choice include printing by clicking the Print icon on a toolbar, printing from Notepad, and printing from many DOS programs.

Click Next to move on.

8. Select Yes to print a test page.

The wizard gives you a choice, but it's foolish not to test the printer.

Click Finish because this is the last wizard window, although you're not quite done.

The files that Windows needs are transferred from the CD to your hard drive. Then the test page is sent to the printer. Look at the test page. (It congratulates you on setting up a printer successfully and prints all sorts of technical information about the printer drivers that were installed.)

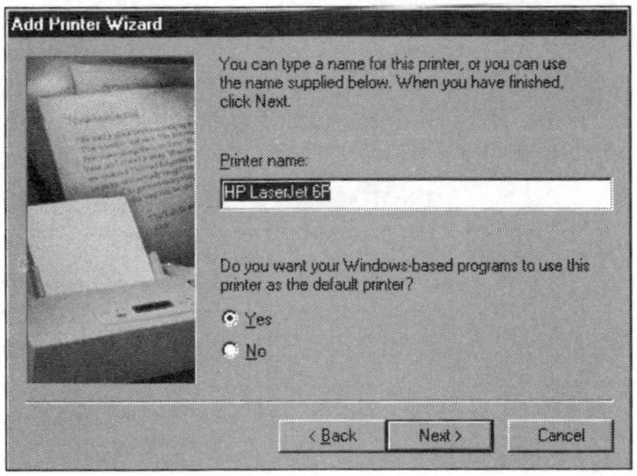

Figure 12-3:
That's as good a name for a printer as any I could invent.

9. Tell Windows whether the test page printed correctly.

If the test page printed successfully, you're finished. If not, Windows opens a Print Troubleshooter. (See Figure 12-4.)

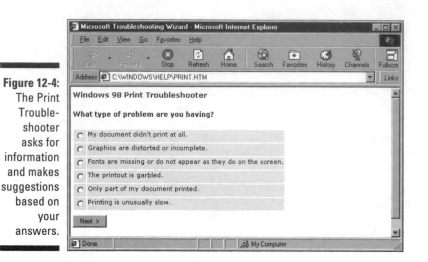

Figure 12-4:
The Print
Trouble-
shooter
asks for
information
and makes
suggestions
based on
your
answers.

Select the appropriate choices, and the troubleshooter will make suggestions. Keep going until you solve the problem. If the problem isn't solved by the time the troubleshooter runs out of suggestions, you're advised to call the printer manufacturer for more help.

Using manufacturer disks to install a printer

Windows supports most printers, which means that the printer drivers are on your Windows CD. However, Windows doesn't support some printers, in which case you must use the drivers supplied by the manufacturer. Those drivers probably came with the printer (either on a CD or floppy disk), but if not, you can call the company or visit its Web site to get the files.

In addition, some printers come with software that works with the manufacturer's drivers to enhance your ability to control and manipulate the printer's features.

If you are using the manufacturer's disks, read the directions to find out which of the following two methods you should use:

 ✔ Use a setup program on the disk to install the software.

 ✔ Use the Printer wizard and choose Have Disk when the wizard presents a window listing printer manufacturers and models.

If you're instructed to use a setup program, the software can usually be launched automatically by placing the CD in the CD-ROM drive. If the CD-ROM doesn't start by itself, follow these steps to begin setup manually:

 1. **Double-Click the My Computer icon.**

    The My Computer window opens, displaying the drives on the computer.

2. **Double-click the CD-ROM drive icon.**

   The opening window of the CD-ROM drive varies, depending on the manufacturer. Usually a menu appears, sometimes in icon form. Choose the installation item. If the installation procedure isn't evident on the opening screen, read the documentation that came with the printer to find out how to install the software.

If you're instructed to use the Windows Printer wizard, follow these steps to install the printer:

1. **Follow the first four steps in the "Installing a printer" section.**

2. **At Step 5, choose Have Disk instead of choosing a manufacturer and model.**

3. **Supply any information and follow any instructions that appear on your screen.**

Sharing a printer

After your printer is installed, you can begin using it on your computer. But the household members who are using the other computer(s) on your network want to print, too. You have to share this printer with them. If you don't, they'll just keep bothering you to insert a floppy disk, load software, and print the documents they've created. To save yourself all that aggravation, follow these steps to share the printer with the rest of the network:

1. **Choose Start⇨Settings⇨Printers.**

   The Printers folder opens, displaying an icon for the printer you installed on this computer.

2. **Right-click the icon for the printer you want to share and choose Sharing from the shortcut menu that appears.**

   The printer's Properties dialog box opens, and the Sharing tab appears in the foreground. The Not Shared option is selected, and all the other fields on the dialog box are grayed out.

3. **Select Shared As.**

   The text boxes on the dialog box are now accessible. (See Figure 12-5.)

4. **Enter a name for the printer in the Share Name text box.**

   You can accept the name Windows automatically enters, which is usually a shortened form of the printer model. Or you can use a name of your own choice.

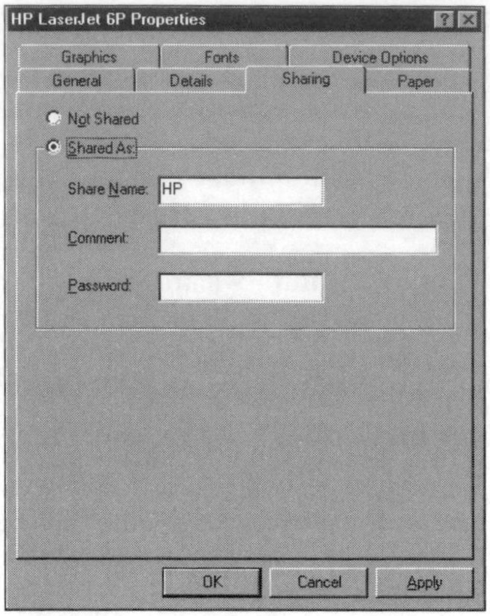

Figure 12-5:
Configure
this printer
for sharing
so that
everybody
else in the
household
can use it.

5. Optionally, enter a description in the Comment text box.

Large companies with large networks and lots of printers use the Comments text box to help users identify the printers. For example, "laser printer next to the cafeteria" might be a good identifier for a corporate printer, while "Den printer" might work well for home use. Users only see the comment text if they select the Details view in Network Neighborhood when they double-click the icon for the computer that is directly connected to the printer.

6. Optionally, enter a password for the printer.

If you choose to require a password, users who don't have the password won't be able to use the printer. On a home network, there's rarely a reason to use this option. Companies with printers that hold checks use passwords for those printers. If you do enter a password, you're asked to confirm the password by entering it again. You won't see the actual password as you're typing because Windows substitutes asterisks for your characters.

7. Click OK.

You return to the Printers folder, and your printer icon has a hand under it, indicating that this printer is a shared resource.

Installing a Network Printer

Put on your running shoes! After you configure a printer for sharing, it's time to run to the other computers on the network and install that same printer.

Of course, you're not going to perform a physical installation; the printer is staying right where it is. Installing a printer on a computer that has no physically attached printer means you're installing a *network printer*.

Choosing an installation method

Two approaches are available to you for installing a network printer:

▸ **Use Network Neighborhood.** Double-click the Network Neighborhood icon. In the Network Neighborhood window, double-click the icon for the computer that has the printer. Right-click the printer icon and choose Install from the shortcut menu that appears.

▸ **Use the Printers Folder.** Double-click the Printers folder and then double-click the Add Printer icon.

Either method launches the Add Printer wizard. Both methods require the installation of software drivers for the printer, so you need to have your Windows CD or disks from the printer manufacturer.

Running the installation procedure

For this example, I use the Add Printer icon in the Printers folder. This method makes the example slightly longer, but it provides a complete explanation for installing network printers. (My job is to be as thorough as possible.) If you use the printer icon in Network Neighborhood, you can jump to Step 4, where you can find the information about the printer location already filled in.

Be sure that the printer software CD or disk is in the appropriate drive and then follow these steps:

1. **Choose Start⇨Settings⇨Printers.**

   The Printers folder opens.

2. **Double-click the Add Printer icon.**

   The Add Printer wizard opens with a welcoming message. Click Next to get started.

3. **Select Network Printer and click Next.**

4. **Click the Browse button to search the network for shared printers.**

   This wizard window has two parts: the location of the network printer and a question about printing from MS-DOS software.

Clicking the Browse button opens a window in which you can search the network, but if you know the location of the network printer, you can enter it directly in the Network Path or Queue Name text box. The location is a UNC (Universal Naming Convention) statement in the form of *computername**printername*. Find out about using UNC statements in Chapter 11.

5. **When the Browse for Printer dialog box opens (see Figure 12-6), click the plus sign next to the computer that has the printer.**

   The listing in the Browse for Printer dialog box expands to display any shared printers that are connected to that computer.

6. **Select the printer and click OK.**

   The printer's location (in the form of a UNC statement) is entered in the Network Path or Queue Name text box.

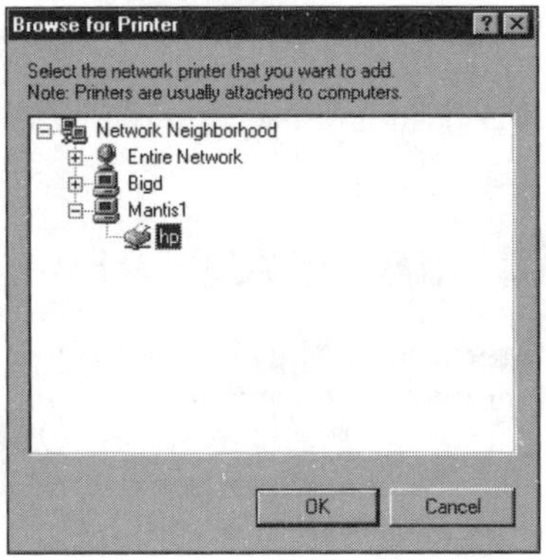

Figure 12-6:
Click a
network
computer's
icon to see
the printer
attached
to that
computer.

7. **Specify whether you print from MS-DOS-based programs. Then choose Next.**

   MS-DOS software can't handle network printing, so Windows uses a special feature called *capture*. The print job is captured when it's sent to the printer port and is then redirected to the network printer. The software thinks that the printer is connected to your computer.

   If you say Yes to MS-DOS printing, the next window explains that your software needs to have a port associated with the printer. Click the Capture Printer Port button, select LPT1 as the device, and click OK. You return to the previous wizard window.

   Click Next.

8. **Select** <u>Y</u>**es to send a test page to the remote printer and then click Finish.**

The printer files are copied to your hard drive, and a test page is sent to the printer. If the test page prints correctly, select Yes in the dialog box that asks about the test. If the test page does not print properly or doesn't print at all, select No. Then use the printer troubleshooter to try to resolve the problem. See the section "Installing a printer," earlier in this chapter, for information about the Print Troubleshooter.

An icon for the printer appears in your Printers folder. Whenever you print, the print job is sent to this remote printer.

Renaming network printers

After you install a network printer, you can change its name to something that reminds you where it is or what it does. This changes the printer name on only your computer; it doesn't change anything on the computer to which the printer is attached. Follow these steps to give the network printer its own personalized name:

1. **Choose Start⇨**<u>S</u>**ettings⇨Printers.**

The Printers folder opens.

2. **Right-click the icon for the network printer and choose Rena**<u>m</u>**e from the shortcut menu that appears.**

The icon title is selected (highlighted), which means you're in edit mode.

3. **Enter a new name and press Enter.**

Choose a name that describes the printer for you. For example, "HP in Den" is a good descriptive name.

Using both local and network printers

If you have two printers in the house, you can attach them to separate computers. Just follow the steps explained earlier in this chapter for installing local printers and then follow the steps to install each printer as a remote printer.

You can switch between printers when you want to print by using the Print feature of your Windows software. All Windows software works in the same fashion, so you can count on being able to use these steps to switch printers:

1. **Choose File➪Print from the menu bar of your software program.**

   The Print dialog box opens. The appearance of this dialog box differs depending on the particular software you're using, but the essential features are the same.

2. **Click the arrow to the right of the printer Name text box.**

   A list of installed printers (both local and network) appears in the drop-down list, as shown in Figure 12-7.

If you click the Print button on the toolbar of your Windows software or you print from Notepad, the currently selected printer receives the print job. No dialog box opens to afford you the chance to choose a printer.

Using password-protected printers

It's highly unusual to password-protect printers in a home network environment, but you may have some reason to do so. When you want to use a remote printer that's password-protected, you're asked to supply the password. (See Figure 12-8.)

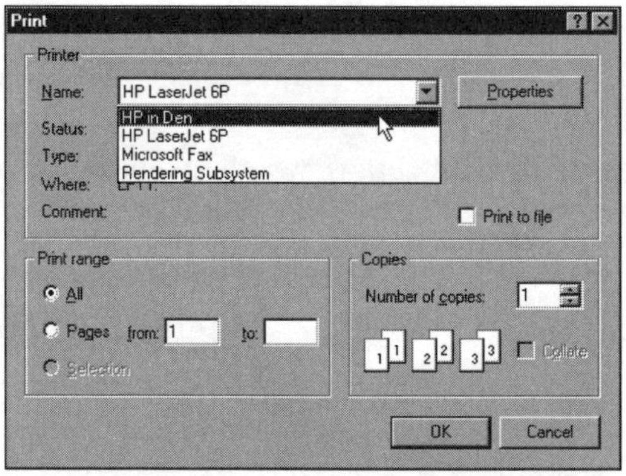

Figure 12-7: The Print dialog box for every Windows software program has a drop-down list of the printers you've installed.

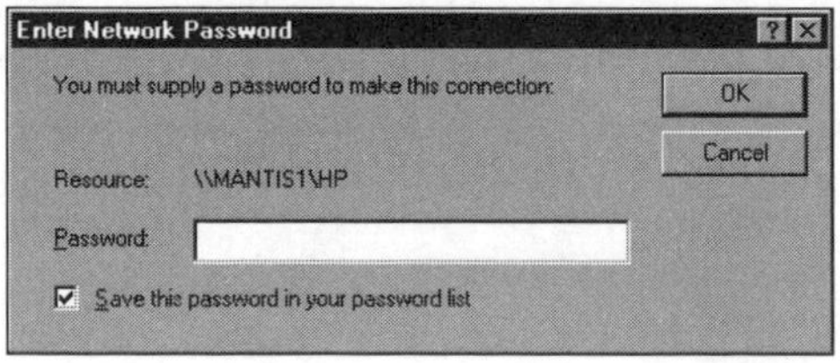

Figure 12-8: If you don't know the password, you can't print.

The first time you use the printer, select Save This Password in Your Password List. You won't have to enter the password again (unless it changes). See Chapter 7 for more information about saved passwords and your password list file.

Devising schemes for using multiple printers

You can design all sorts of arrangements to take advantage of having multiple printers on your network, with each printer attached to a different computer. When you devise a method to manage your printers, your decisions should be based on the types of printers you own. Here are some suggestions:

✔ **Make the local printer the default printer.**

This works well if all the printers are the same type of printer, or at least similar — for example, they're all monochrome inkjet printers (print in black and shades of gray), laser printers, or color inkjet printers.

With this scheme, you don't need the network printer unless something happens to the local printer. If the local printer stops working or the cartridge goes dry and you don't have a spare handy (or you're in a hurry and decide to worry about replacing the cartridge later), you can switch to the network printer quickly. Using the local printer for most print jobs saves you the annoyance of getting up and walking to the network printer every time you print (although, if you need the exercise, you might want to reverse the scheme).

✔ **Configure the printers for different features.**

If your printers have the capability of holding different paper sizes, make one of them the letter-size printer and make the other the legal-size printer. Or put inexpensive paper in one printer and good bond in the other. Or use one printer for paper and the other for envelopes. Then just switch printers to use the paper you need.

If you use accounting software and print checks, leave the checks in one printer and put paper in the other printer. This setup saves you the time and aggravation of loading and unloading checks every time you have to pay your bills.

If both printers are color, use one for color and the other for black-and-white printing. To make this work automatically, you can configure the printer you want to use for black-and-white printing so it prints only in black, white, and gray. Right-click the printer's icon in the Printers folder and choose Properties. Then use the appropriate tab and options to tell the printer to print in grayscale instead of color. This is a great way to save money on color cartridges. Even when a print job doesn't really have to be in color, most users send it to the printer without changing the settings to grayscale, which is a silly waste of color cartridge ink.

✔ **Use each printer for its best feature.**

If you have a dot-matrix printer and an inkjet or laser printer, use the inkjet or laser printer for stuff that has to look good (for example, your resume or a letter to your senator). Use the dot-matrix printer for everything else.

If one printer is an inkjet and one is a laser printer, use the laser for multiple page print jobs (lasers usually print faster) or for print jobs with a lot of graphics (most laser printers have more memory than most inkjet printers).

If one printer is color and the other is black and white, use the printer that's appropriate for the job.

Some of these schemes are important for more than convenience; they actually lower the cost of using printers. The business term for this is *TCO* (total cost of ownership), and it's a significant consideration when you buy and use any type of equipment.

After you design your scheme, you have to do two things in order to make sure that the plan is implemented successfully:

✔ Rename the printers using names that reflect their intended uses.

✔ Explain the plan to all the members of the household. This works best if you use a threatening tone or some other means of making everyone take you seriously.

Renaming network printers is simple; just change the name under the icon by following the instructions in the section "Renaming network printers," earlier in this chapter.

Renaming the local shared printer, however, is a bit more complicated. If you rename the icon, it doesn't change the name of the shared resource. In fact, if you rename the icon, the printer is no longer shared. (Windows considers it a new and different printer after a name change.) Follow the steps to create a shared printer (again) if you rename a local shared printer.

Managing Network Printing

Keeping the printing process on an error-free even keel is slightly more complicated with network printing than it is for a one-computer-one-printer environment. However, it's not overly complex, and printer problems aren't all that common.

Understanding the spooler

When you send a file to a printer, Windows does some work on the file with the help of those files (drivers) you copy to your hard drive when you install the printer. Windows checks the file to make sure that everything is sent to the printer in a format the printer understands. The work that Windows performs is saved in a file, and that file is placed in the folder \Windows\Spool\ Printers. The file is called a *spool file,* and it's named *filename*.spl, where *filename* is the name of the document you sent to the printer.

The process of taking your print job and turning it into a file is called *spooling.* The folder into which the file is placed is called the *spooler.* It all happens behind the scenes; you don't see any messages or other indications that anything is going on. This invisibility is why we say that printing is a *background process.*

In addition to the spool file, Windows creates a second file for each print job. That file holds other information about the print job, such as the name of the user who sent the job to the printer, the data format type of the print job, and other technical information. This file is called a *shadow file.* The shadow file is also placed in the spooler, and it is named with the format *XXXXXX*.shd, where the *X*s represent a numbering system (starting with 000001).

The two files sit in the spooler, waiting for their turn at the printer. Documents are sent to the printer in a first-come, first-served order (unless you interrupt that order using a process I discuss in the next section, "Manipulating print jobs"). This lineup of documents waiting to go to the printer is called the *queue.*

All of this occurs on the computer that sent the file to the printer — it doesn't matter whether the actual printer is attached to that computer or is a remote printer.

After the document prints, the spool file is deleted from the spooler. The shadow file stays in the spooler. It is deleted when you restart the computer. I have no idea why Windows keeps this file on the hard drive — there's absolutely no use for it after the document has printed. But it isn't deleted when the spool file is deleted. The problem is, if you print a lot of documents and you don't reboot your computer every day, you end up with a lot of shadow files taking up disk space. You can go to the spooler (\Windows\Spool\Printers) and delete all the files with an extension of .shd. Don't do this if there are files waiting to print. (You can tell because you'll see files with the extension .spl.)

The spooler is one reason to make sure that you keep free space on your hard drive.

Manipulating print jobs

You can control individual print jobs that are sent to the printer, but you have to move fast, because everything happens very rapidly.

Printing controls are available in the printer's dialog box, which you can open with these steps:

1. **Choose Start➪Settings➪Printers.**

   The Printers folder opens.

2. **Double-click the icon for the printer.**

   The printer's dialog box opens, displaying any print jobs that are currently in the queue.

You can pause, delete, and move the print jobs that are in the queue, but which print jobs you see depends upon these factors:

   ✔ If you open the dialog box for a remote printer, you see the jobs that you sent to the printer.

   ✔ If you open the dialog box for a local printer, you see all the jobs that the local and remote users have sent to that printer. (See Figure 12-9.)

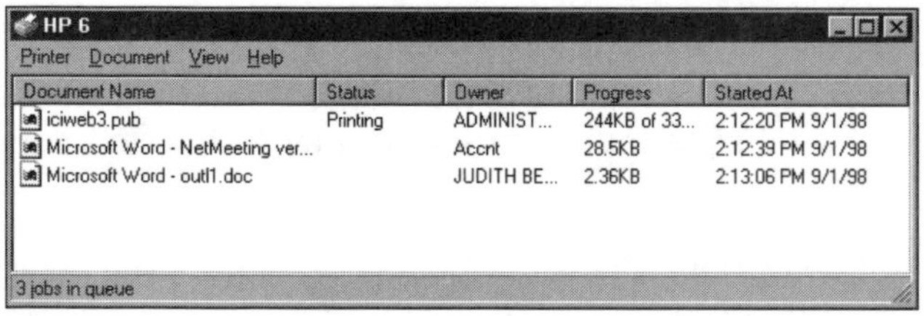

Figure 12-9:
The printer
attached to
this
computer
has jobs
from three
different
users on
three
different
computers.

HP 6				_ □ ✕
Printer Document View Help				
Document Name	Status	Owner	Progress	Started At
iciweb3.pub	Printing	ADMINIST...	244KB of 33...	2:12:20 PM 9/1/98
Microsoft Word - NetMeeting ver...		Accnt	28.5KB	2:12:39 PM 9/1/98
Microsoft Word - outl1.doc		JUDITH BE...	2.36KB	2:13:06 PM 9/1/98
3 jobs in queue				

You can manipulate each job, or the printer itself, with the commands available in this dialog box. Here are the things you can do to change the way documents print:

✔ **Pause a print job.** Right-click the listing for the print job and choose Pause Printing from the shortcut menu that appears.

A check mark appears next to the Pause Printing command to indicate that the job status has changed to paused. The print job is temporarily stopped, and the next job in line starts printing.

This is a quick way to let an important print job jump ahead of the job in front of it.

✔ **Resume a print job.** Right-click a paused print job and choose Pause Printing again from the shortcut menu that appears to remove the check mark.

The job status changes to Printing.

✔ **Pause the printer.** Choose Printer➪Pause Printing from the menu bar in the Printer dialog box.

All the print jobs are paused. Most of the time you use this command to clear a paper jam in the printer or to change paper.

✔ **Cancel a print job.** Right-click a print job listing and choose Cancel Printing from the shortcut menu that appears.

The document will not print.

✔ **Cancel all the print jobs.** Choose Printer➪Purge Print Documents from the menu bar of the printer dialog box.

All print jobs are cancelled.

When you pause or cancel a print job, the printer itself usually keeps printing. This is because any data that has been sent to the printer is in the printer's memory and continues to print.

You can also drag print jobs around to change the order of printing. Select the job you want to move and drag it up higher in the queue if it's important or down to the bottom of the queue if it's unimportant. There are two restrictions to dragging print jobs:

✔ You can't move any print job ahead of the job that is currently printing.

✔ You can't move the job that is currently printing — it's too late.

Making Network Printing Easier

Very little goes wrong with the printing processes in Windows, even across a network. However, you should know a few tricks that can make network printing easier. This section covers those tips.

Troubleshooting remote printing

Sometimes when you're printing to a remote printer, you see an error message telling you that there was a problem printing to the port (the *port* is the path to the remote computer that has the printer attached). Before you panic, thinking that something awful has happened to your network printing services, check the condition of all the hardware.

Check the print server

Computers that have printers attached (called *print servers*) have to be turned on if you want to print from a remote computer. If the computer is turned off, turn it on.

It doesn't matter whether you know the logon password for the user name that appears during the logon process because you don't have to complete the logon process. Nobody has to be logged onto a computer in order to use its shared printer. The Windows operating system on that computer simply must be started. That's a really nifty way to design network printing!

Check the printer

If the computer is turned on and you still get error messages when you try to print, check the printer. Make sure that it's turned on. Check any buttons, indicator lights, or message windows that might be trying to tell you that something is amiss.

Most printers have a "ready light," a button that lights up to say that everything is cool and the printer is ready to do your bidding. If the ready light isn't on, follow the instructions in the printer manual to investigate the problem. The most common problems are that the printer is out of paper, there's a paper jam, or the cartridge is out of toner (or ink).

Check the network cable

If the computer is on and the printer is fine, check the network cable. Cable that isn't connected properly can't send data.

Using a printer shortcut on the Desktop

Most of the time you print from a software program. You create a document, and then you print it. But sometimes you just need a printed copy of an existing document and you don't want to open the software, open the document, and use the commands required to print the document.

If you put a shortcut to the printer on your Desktop, you can drag documents to the shortcut icon to print them effortlessly. Here's how to create a printer shortcut on your Desktop:

1. **Choose Start⇨Settings⇨Printers.**

   The Printers folder opens.

2. **Right-drag the printer icon to the Desktop.**

   When you release the right mouse button, a shortcut menu appears.

3. **Choose Create Shortcut(s) Here from the shortcut menu.**

   A printer shortcut appears on your Desktop.

A good place to put the printer shortcut is at the edge of your Desktop, preferably near a corner of your screen. That way it won't be hidden by an open window.

Using the printer shortcut is easy and time-saving. You can use it whenever you have any folder or window open (such as Windows Explorer, My Computer, or My Documents) that contains document files. Just drag a document file to the printer shortcut on the Desktop. That's all you have to do — Windows does the rest. You can leave the room or sit and watch as the following events take place:

1. **The software that was used to create the file opens.**

2. **The file is opened in the software window.**

3. **The software sends the file to the printer.**

4. **The software closes.**

Cool!

If you right-click a document file instead of dragging it to a Desktop shortcut, you can choose Print from the shortcut menu that appears. The same automatic printing events occur.

Using separator pages to identify users

When multiple users print to a single printer on the network, the out-tray on the printer can get crowded. People don't always rush to the printer to pick up their documents — they frequently wait. Sometimes they wait a long time if it isn't urgent to mail or file the document.

Eventually, one user wanders over to the printer to pick up his print jobs. Lots of other print jobs are in the tray. This user picks up the first piece of paper and reads it — it isn't his print job so he tosses it aside (hopefully it lands on a tabletop instead of the floor). He continues to shuffle through the papers, taking his own documents and tossing the others helter-skelter.

It's less messy if each job comes out of the printer with a form that displays the name of the owner. Luckily, such a form exists in Windows, and it's called a *separator page*.

A *separator page* (sometimes called a *banner*) prints ahead of the first page of each document. You just have to look for your name on a separator page and take all the pieces of paper that are between it and the next separator page. Don't toss any paper around; just go through the stack looking for your name on a separator page.

The nifty thing about separator pages is that you don't have to do anything to force them to print. They print automatically after you enable the separator page feature. Go to the computer that has the printer attached and follow these steps to turn on separator pages:

1. **Choose Start⇨Settings⇨Printers.**

   The Printers folder opens.

2. **Right-click the appropriate printer icon and choose Properties from the shortcut menu that appears.**

   The printer Properties dialog box opens, with the General tab in the foreground.

3. **Click the arrow to the right of the Separator Page list box and choose a Separator Page type. (See Figure 12-10.)**

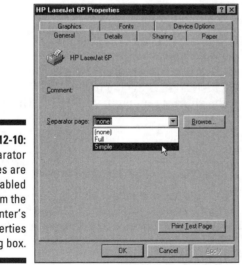

Figure 12-10:
Separator
pages are
enabled
from the
printer's
Properties
dialog box.

The Separator Page choices are None, Full, and Simple. Both the Full and Simple separator pages contain the document name, the user name, and the date and time the document was printed. The difference is that the Full separator page uses large, bold type, and the Simple separator page uses the Courier typeface that's built into the printer.

4. **Click OK.**

Chapter 13

Sharing Peripheral Drives

● ●

In This Chapter

▶ Sharing CD-ROM drives

▶ Sharing removable drives

● ●

*E*ver since computers became commonplace at work and home, a new law of nature has been added to all the other laws of nature. Besides the sun rising in the morning and rain falling after you wash the car, you now have to deal with the law that says your need for software and document files continues to grow as you add hard-drive space.

You'll never have enough file storage space. No matter how large a hard drive you purchase, it won't be long before you run out of space. Luckily, you can choose from a wide assortment of removable drives to augment the fixed hard drive in your computer.

A real advantage of a home network is that you don't have to duplicate additional storage drives on every computer you buy. Most of the equipment that's on one computer can be shared by users at all the other computers on the network. This chapter covers the ways you can configure and use these drives on a network.

Working with CD-ROM Drives

If you've shopped for a home computer within the last couple of years, chances are you've seen a lot of computers called *multimedia PCs*. By definition, a multimedia computer contains a CD-ROM drive, a sound card, and speakers.

Some people consider sound an "extra," but nobody could call a CD-ROM drive anything but a necessity today. Software comes on CDs, and even though you can purchase software on floppy disks, you usually have to call the manufacturer and place a special order. When the order arrives, you're overwhelmed by the number of disks it takes to install the software. If you've ever installed a large software program from floppy disks, you'll never do it again! Spending most of the day inserting and removing disks is even more boring than weeding the garden or ironing.

Many home networks link a new PC with one or more older PCs. The new machine probably has a CD-ROM drive (buying a computer without one these days is hard), and networking means that you don't have to upgrade the older machine because one CD-ROM drive on the network is all you need.

Setting up shared CD-ROM drives

You can share a CD-ROM drive with all the other computers on your network. However, you have to configure the CD-ROM drive to enable sharing before the other computers can access the drive. Follow these steps to share a CD-ROM drive with the other computers on the network:

1. **Double-click the My Computer icon.**

   The My Computer window opens.

2. **Right-click the icon for your CD-ROM drive and choose Sharing from the shortcut menu that appears.**

   The CD-ROM Properties dialog box opens, with the Sharing tab in the foreground. The Not Shared option is selected by default, which means that all the other fields in the dialog box are grayed out and inaccessible.

3. **Select Shared As to make all the sections of the dialog box accessible (see Figure 13-1).**

4. **Enter a name for the CD-ROM drive in the Share Name text box.**

   By default, Windows inserts the drive letter assigned to the CD-ROM as the name of the drive. You should change that name to something a bit more descriptive, such as KitchenCD or MomCD.

5. **Optionally, enter a descriptive phrase in the Comment text box.**

   The contents of the Comment text box are displayed in the Details view in Network Neighborhood on the other network computers. (By default, Network Neighborhood uses the Icon view.)

6. **Select an access type by clicking the appropriate option button.**

   The access type that you select determines what network users can do when they access this shared resource. By default, Read-Only is selected, which is just fine for a CD-ROM drive (most CDs are read-only anyway).

7. **If you want to restrict access to the CD-ROM drive, enter a password in the Read-Only Password text box.**

   If you enter a password, only those users who know the password can use the shared CD-ROM drive.

   When you enter the password, you won't see the characters you type because each character is represented by an asterisk.

8. **Click OK.**

   You're returned to the My Computer window, and the icon for the CD-ROM drive has a hand under it, indicating that it's a shared resource.

   If you entered a password, the Password Confirmation dialog box opens. Enter the same password again to confirm it (asterisks replace your characters again). Then click OK.

The shared resource is the drive, not a disc that happens to be in the drive when you enable sharing. In fact, you can enable sharing even if the drive is empty.

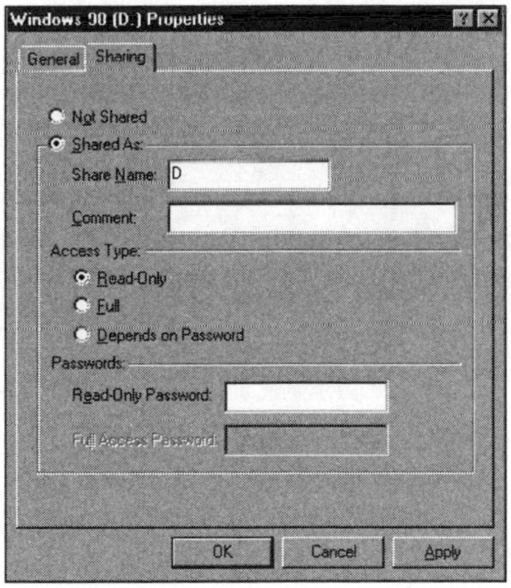

Figure 13-1:
You don't
have to
fill out
everything
in the
Sharing
dialog box;
a name is
sufficient to
enable
sharing.

TIP

Disabling AutoPlay

There you are, working furiously at your computer, which has a CD-ROM drive. Another household member calls to you from another room, "Hey, would you please put the Widget Software disc in? I want to install the software." This person is working at a computer that has no CD-ROM drive, and she wants to use your shared drive.

You find the disc and insert it in the CD-ROM drive. The opening window for the Widget Software disc opens on your screen. It's loaded with graphics, so it takes many seconds to finish drawing the window. Finally, the window displays, and you can click the X in the upper-right corner to close the window. Now you can finally resume your work.

If you regularly use the computer that has the shared CD-ROM drive, this scenario is going to repeat itself constantly. To save time and your sanity, you can turn off the AutoPlay feature that automatically starts the CD. Follow these steps to eliminate the aggravation of automatic startup of CDs:

1. **Right-click the My Computer icon and choose Properties from the shortcut menu that appears.**

   The System Properties dialog box opens.

2. **Click the Device Manager tab.**

   The Device Manager dialog box opens.

3. **Click the plus sign next to the CD-ROM listing to see the CD-ROM drive(s) attached to this computer.**

   Your installed CD-ROM drive is listed. If you have more than one CD-ROM drive, all are listed.

4. **Select the CD-ROM that you want to configure, and click the Properties button.**

The Properties dialog box for your CD-ROM drive appears on your screen.

5. **Click the Settings tab of the CD-ROM Properties dialog box.**

   The configuration settings for the CD-ROM appear, as shown in the following figure.

6. **Click the Auto Insert Notification check box to remove the check mark.**

7. **Click OK.**

From now on, when you insert a CD in the CD-ROM drive, the AutoRun program on the disc won't launch. If you want to launch the automatic startup for a CD (because you're the one using it instead of a remote user), right-click the CD-ROM drive icon and choose AutoPlay from the shortcut menu that appears. This forces the AutoPlay feature for this CD to launch.

Accessing a shared CD-ROM drive

If your computer doesn't have a CD-ROM drive, you can use the CD-ROM drive on another computer on the network as long as that drive has been configured for sharing. See the section "Setting up shared CD-ROM drives," earlier in this chapter.

The computer that has the drive must be turned on, and Windows must be running. It doesn't matter if nobody has logged on (the logon dialog box is sitting on the screen waiting for a user to log on); you can still access the shared CD-ROM drive.

Finding the drive

A shared CD-ROM drive icon appears in Network Neighborhood or Windows Explorer when you double-click the icon for the computer to which it is attached (see Figure 13-2).

Incidentally, when you look for a remote CD-ROM, you understand why naming the shared resource correctly is important. If you use the name supplied by Windows, which is the drive letter for the CD-ROM, recognizing the device when you're trying to use it is difficult. Looking at a device named "D" isn't a clear indication of the type of device — it could be a second hard drive.

When you double-click the My Computer icon on the computer that has the CD-ROM drive, the icon for the CD-ROM drive usually displays the name of the disc in the drive. That information isn't available when you view a CD-ROM drive from a remote computer. In fact, you can't tell whether or not a disc is in the drive until you double-click the icon for the drive. If there's no disc, you see an error message telling you that the drive is not ready.

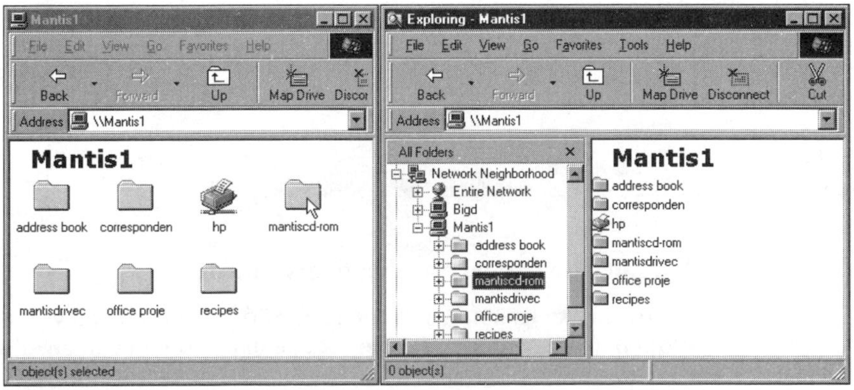

Figure 13-2:
Use
Network
Neighborhood
or Windows
Explorer to
locate a
shared
CD-ROM
drive on
another
computer.

Using a remote CD-ROM drive

The problem with a remote CD-ROM drive is that you have to walk to the computer that contains the drive to insert the disc you want to use. Or you can ask the person working at that computer to insert the disc for you (hopefully, he or she is within shouting distance, or you have a home intercom system).

When the correct disc is in the CD-ROM drive, you can use it by following these steps:

1. **Double-click the Network Neighborhood icon.**

   The Network Neighborhood window opens.

2. **Double-click the icon for the computer that has the CD-ROM drive that you want to use.**

   A window opens, displaying the shared resources attached to that remote computer.

3. **Double-click the CD-ROM icon.**

   A window opens, displaying the contents of the CD-ROM drive (see Figure 13-3).

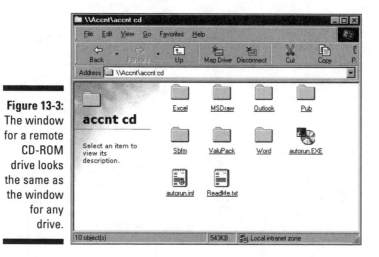

Figure 13-3:
The window for a remote CD-ROM drive looks the same as the window for any drive.

4. **Open the file named autorun.exe, if it exists.**

   If autorun.exe exists, it's in the root folder (that means you don't have to open a folder to see the file) of the disc, so you can see it in the window that you opened.

When autorun.exe launches, you see the opening window of the CD, just as if it were in a CD-ROM drive in your own computer. Then follow the instructions in the documentation or on the screen (or both) to use the disc.

5. **If autorun.exe doesn't exist, refer to the documentation that came with the disc to find out which file you should open.**

Follow the instructions in the documentation or on the screen (or both) to complete the task you needed the disk for.

Using a password-protected CD-ROM drive

If the CD-ROM drive has been protected by a password, you're asked to supply the password when you try to access the drive (see Figure 13-4).

Enter the password and click OK. If you want Windows to remember the password (the operating system keeps a file of your passwords on your computer), select the Save This Password in Your Password List check box. Then, the next time you access this drive you won't be asked for the password (unless it changes, at which point you repeat this task). You can find lots of information about the way passwords work in Chapter 7.

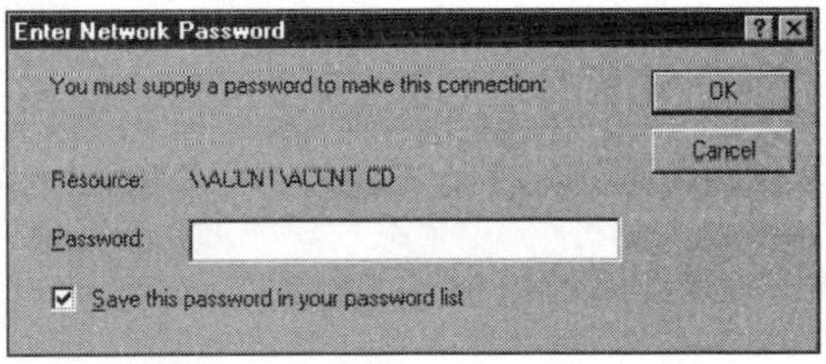

Figure 13-4:
No password, no access — sorry.

Tricks and tips for using remote CD-ROM drives

If you're using a remote CD-ROM, you should know about some important "gotchas."

✔ Playing CD-ROM games that have large, complicated graphics or viewing animated video files can be annoying. CD-ROM drives aren't all that speedy to begin with, but even if you have a super-fast CD-ROM drive, sending the data over network cable can slow everything down even more.

✔ Don't forget that if you want to play a CD-ROM game, many games require you to go through an installation process. Some files (not all the files) are transferred to your hard drive, and the game is put on your Programs menu. When you select the game from your Programs menu, Windows knows where to look for the CD-ROM drive to find the game files you need to start playing (the operating system keeps track of this stuff). The same thing is true for encyclopedias and other large reference discs. If two remote CD-ROM drives are available on your network, be sure you always use the one you originally used when you installed the software.

✔ If you're installing software, such as a word processor or spreadsheet program, Windows keeps track of the remote CD-ROM drive that you used as the source drive. Every time you want to add a component or access a file that isn't transferred to the hard drive (for example, clip art), you must use the same remote CD-ROM drive.

✔ If you have lots of space available on your hard drive, you may want to transfer files that you continuously access on the CD to your own computer. It can save you the walk to the remote computer, and it also speeds up file access times.

Using Shared Removable Drives

Removable drives that give you additional storage space are becoming extremely popular, and their prices are getting lower (I've noticed that those things usually go together).

The most popular are Jaz and Zip drives, which are made by a number of companies, and a variety of drives from SyQuest. You insert cartridges into the drives, and the cartridges act like additional hard drives. Jaz cartridges are available in 1GB and 2GB configurations; Zip drives hold 100MB; and SyQuest cartridges range from 230MB to 4.7GB capacity. You can install removable drives internally or attach them to your computer's parallel port. If you use the latter configuration, don't worry — there's a connection at the back of the removable drive so that you can attach your printer cable. The parallel port works for both devices.

Configuring removable drives for sharing

Removable drives are assigned drive letters when they're installed on your computer, which means, like all drives, they appear in the My Computer window. That's the place to start when you want to configure the drive for sharing. Follow these steps to create a shared resource for your removable drive:

1. **Double-click the My Computer icon.**

   The My Computer window opens, displaying all the drives in your system.

2. **Right-click the icon for your removable drive and choose S̲haring from the shortcut menu that appears.**

   The Properties dialog box for the drive opens, with the Sharing tab in the foreground. By default, Not Shared is selected and all the other fields in the dialog box are grayed out and inaccessible.

3. **Select the Shared As button.**

   The other options in the dialog box become accessible (see Figure 13-5).

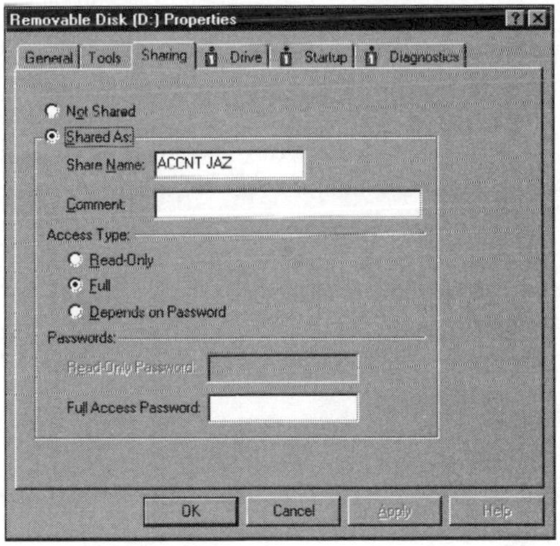

Figure 13-5: The dialog box for your removable drive may look different, depending on the brand and type of drive you have.

4. **Enter a name for the shared resource in the Share N̲ame text box.**

   Use a name that's descriptive of the drive or the computer it's attached to.

5. **Optionally, enter a description in the C̲omment text box.**

   The information in the Comment text box is visible if remote users choose the Details view in Network Neighborhood. By default, Network Neighborhood presents the Icon view.

6. **Choose an access type.**

   The access type enables you to decide what remote users can do when they use the drive. For a full explanation of each access type, see Chapter 7.

7. **Optionally, enter a password for access to this drive.**

    You can give the password to those users you want to permit access to the drive.

8. **Choose OK.**

    You return to the My Computer window, and the icon for the removable drive has a hand under it, indicating that it's a shared resource.

    If you entered a password to access the drive, reenter the password in the Password Confirmation dialog box and then click OK.

Accessing a shared removable drive

If another computer on the network has a removable drive that has been configured for sharing, you can use it to provide additional storage space for your documents or to back up your documents. Because most of the work you do with a removable drive involves copying or moving files, using Windows Explorer is easier than using Network Neighborhood or My Computer. Follow these steps to access a shared removable drive on a remote computer:

1. **Go to the computer that has the removable drive and insert the cartridge that you want to use.**

2. **Go back to your computer and choose Start⇨Programs⇨ Windows Explorer.**

    The Explorer window opens.

3. **Click the plus sign to the left of the Network Neighborhood icon in the left Explorer pane.**

    All the computers on the network appear in the left Explorer pane, below the Network Neighborhood listing.

4. **Click the plus sign to the left of the listing for the computer that has the removable drive.**

    All the shared resources on that computer are displayed in the left Explorer pane.

5. **Select the removable drive that you want to use.**

    All the contents of the removable drive are displayed in the right Explorer pane. If the removable drive has folders, a plus sign appears to the left of its icon. Click the plus sign to display the folders in the left pane, and then click the folder that you want to use.

You can use Windows Explorer to select files you want to copy or move between the removable drive and your hard drive. You can also create folders on the removable drive and perform all the tasks you perform on your hard drive.

For more information about copying and moving files, read *Windows 95 For Dummies,* 2nd Edition, or *Windows 98 For Dummies,* both written by Andy Rathbone and published by IDG Books Worldwide, Inc.

Accessing a password-protected removable drive

If the removable drive is password-protected, you see the Enter Network Password dialog box when you select the drive (see Figure 13-6).

Enter the password and click OK. If you want Windows to remember the password (the operating system keeps a file of your passwords on your computer), select the Save This Password in Your Password List check box. Then, the next time you access this drive you won't be asked for the password. You can find information about the way your password file works in Chapter 7.

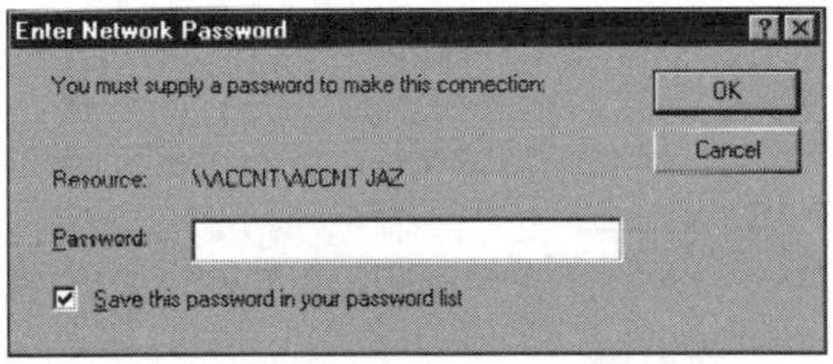

Figure 13-6:
If you don't
know the
password,
you can't
use the
drive.

Tricks and tips for using removable drives

When a removable drive is shared among multiple computers, devising a scheme that suits everybody's needs can be difficult. You're going to find that purchasing extra cartridges is a necessity, by the way. Here are some suggestions for using cartridges:

  ✔ **Give each user his own cartridge.** Put a label on the cartridge and keep all the cartridges near the computer that has the removable drive. Some users may want to tuck their cartridges away in some secret place instead. Removable media provides absolute privacy and security.

  ✔ **Create a cartridge for specific file types.** You might want to have a cartridge for correspondence, another for work you bring home from the office, and so on. Create a folder on the cartridge for each user. You can also create a cartridge for software files that you download from the Internet so you have a backup copy of the software.

Speaking of backups, one excellent use of cartridges is for system backups. You can devise lots of backup plans and use removable cartridges as the target media (instead of tape drives or floppy disks). See Chapter 15 for information about backing up computers.

Chapter 14

Sharing a Modem

Modem-sharing software is a miracle of modern software engineering that enables all computers on a network to access the Internet simultaneously through the modem attached to one computer. This means that you don't need to buy a modem for each computer on the network.

In fact, even if you had a modem on each computer, how would everyone get onto the Internet at the same time? Do you have a separate telephone line for each computer? Does each person have his or her own Internet service provider (ISP) account? Probably not.

The bad news (you didn't actually think you were going to get away with nothing but good news, did you?) is that you may have to do a little work for all this economy, and your connection speed will suffer to some degree because you have to divide the single connection between all the machines that log on at the same time.

The benefits that you enjoy by sharing a modem are worth the work, though, so read on to find out everything you need to know to set up modem sharing on your network.

Preparing for Modem Sharing

Before you can use modem-sharing software, you must install a few things: a modem, a Dial-Up Networking (DUN) connection, and TCP/IP.

Because these items are also required for Internet access of any kind, you can skip this section if you already have Internet access on the computer you plan to use as the server. If, on the other hand, you don't yet have Internet access on that computer, you must first ensure that you have a working modem, a DUN connection, and TCP/IP before proceeding.

Choosing a modem type

Because a wide variety of modem types and brands is available, providing instructions for installing any particular modem is beyond the scope of this book. However, you should consider two important things when selecting the modem to use for modem sharing, whether you're buying a new modem specifically for this purpose or trying to choose among modems already installed in your computers: modem type and modem speed. The following descriptions discuss some of the pros and cons of each modem type.

Standard modem

If you're using a standard modem, make sure that it's rated for 33.6 Kbps at the very least — 56 Kbps is better. (A *kilobyte* is a thousand bytes.)

ISDN modem

ISDN modems (ISDN stands for Integrated Services Digital Network, in case you were wondering) offer faster transmission speeds. The drawback with ISDN modems is that they require a special ISDN phone line (which is more expensive than a standard phone line) and are generally more expensive than standard modems. In addition, connect time beyond an initial base number of hours (200 hours in my area) is usually charged on a per-minute basis.

Cable modem

Check with your local cable television company to see whether it offers cable modems in your area. Cable modems are significantly faster than standard modems but aren't yet available everywhere. These modems connect to your cable television company's cable lines (but they don't interfere with the television transmission). Their speeds are measured in millions of bytes per second rather than in thousands of bytes per second like standard modems.

ADSL modem

An emerging technology is ADSL, which stands for Asymmetric Digital Subscriber Line. This technology uses your standard telephone lines to produce incredibly fast connections to the Internet. You need a special ADSL modem and a telephone company that maintains ADSL modems that can connect to your modem. The telephone company takes you to the Internet using special technology. Check with your local phone company to see when your neighborhood can take advantage of this speed-demon Internet connection.

Installing TCP/IP

Although TCP/IP is the acronym for Transmission Control Protocol/Internet Protocol, you may find a number of folks who claim it really stands for Terribly Confusing Proposition/Irritating and Perplexing. I say pay them no mind. They're just a little cranky because they haven't yet found a simple, straightforward explanation of TCP/IP. To ensure that you don't join their ranks, let me quickly explain what TCP/IP is.

Think about the fact that you can send a letter to someone in Paris, London, Tokyo, or Sydney and be reasonably sure that they'll get it (as long as you address it properly). That's actually a pretty amazing feat when you realize that each country has its own language, its own customs, and its own unique postal system. The reason your letter makes it to its destination is simply that there's a standardized set of rules for the manner in which mail is transmitted.

That, in a nutshell, is what *TCP/IP* is — a set of standardized rules for transmitting information. In the case of TCP/IP, the information is in electronic rather than paper form, and the medium is the Internet rather than the various post offices. TCP/IP enables Macintosh, IBM, UNIX, and other dissimilar computers to jump on the Internet and communicate with one another as long as each computer uses TCP/IP.

E-mail, Web pages, files, and other data are transmitted over the Internet in *packets,* which are nothing more than small electronic parcels of information. The computer doing the transmitting takes a large amount of information and breaks it up into small, manageable individual packets to send it across the Internet. The receiving computer collects each of the packets and puts them all back together to reconstitute the original piece of information. Both computers follow the rules built into TCP/IP to know how to break up and reconstitute the data.

You must install TCP/IP if you want to access the Internet. If you haven't already installed it, do it now. In reality, installing TCP/IP is a piece of cake. If you don't believe me, try it yourself by following the instructions below. (By the way, you're going to need your Windows CD before you're finished, so you may want to find it and have it handy before starting.)

1. **Choose Start⇨Settings⇨Control Panel.**

   The Control Panel opens.

2. **In the Control Panel, double-click the Network icon.**

   The Network dialog box opens, with the Configuration tab in the foreground.

3. **Click the Add button in the Network dialog box.**

   The Select Network Component Type dialog box appears.

4. **In the Select Network Component Type dialog box, select Protocol and click Add.**

   The Select Network Protocol dialog box appears.

5. **Choose Microsoft from the list of manufacturers in the left pane of the Select Network Protocol dialog box.**

   A list of available Microsoft network protocols appears in the right pane.

6. **Select TCP/IP and click OK.**

   The Network dialog box appears.

7. **Click OK in the Network dialog box.**

The necessary files are transferred to your hard drive, and a message appears to tell you that the settings won't be used by your computer until you restart Windows. Click Yes to restart your computer.

Installing a Dial-Up Networking connection

Dial-Up Networking (DUN) is a feature in Windows 98 and Windows 95 that enables your modem to dial out and connect to the Internet through an *Internet service provider* (ISP). You can have as many DUN connections as you need (one for each ISP you use). Most people have only one ISP, but some families have both an ISP and an AOL account, for example. Additionally, some people have accounts through their employers.

You install a DUN connection on the computer that acts as the host or server for your modem-sharing software.

Setting up a Dial-Up Networking (DUN) connection is actually quite simple. Before you start, be sure you have the following information at your fingertips (it's all provided by your ISP):

✔ The local phone number that you dial to log onto your Internet service provider (ISP).

✔ Your online account user name. (You choose this name yourself, and you must give it to the ISP when you sign up.)

✔ Your online account password. (Some ISPs give you a password; others let you choose the password yourself, and you must give it to the ISP when you sign up.)

✔ Any TCP/IP settings needed to reach your ISP.

With that information handy, follow these steps to create a Dial-Up Networking (DUN) connection:

1. **Double-click the My Computer icon.**

   The My Computer window opens.

2. **Double-click the Dial-Up Networking folder in the My Computer window.**

   In the Dial-Up Networking folder, you should see the Make New Connection icon. If any other objects are in the folder, you have already created a Dial-Up Networking connection.

3. **Double-click the Make New Connection icon.**

   The Dial-Up Networking wizard launches and walks you through the process of installing your Internet connection.

4. **Click Next on the Welcome wizard page to start the process and move to the Make New Connection screen.**

   This wizard screen shows the name of your modem. If you haven't told Windows about your modem yet, you can accomplish that from the wizard. In fact, the wizard will automatically go into "install a modem" mode if it doesn't detect a modem.

   (However, I'm assuming you've already installed your modem. To learn all about setting up modems, read *Windows 95 For Dummies,* 2nd Edition, or *Windows 98 For Dummies,* both written by Andy Rathbone and published by IDG Books Worldwide, Inc.)

5. **Enter a name for this Dial-Up Networking (DUN) connection.**

   It's a good idea to give the connection a name that makes it easily identifiable — the name of your ISP is usually a good choice.

6. **Continue to fill in information about your ISP, clicking Next to move through the wizard screens.**

7. **Click Finish on the last wizard screen to save the new Dial-Up Networking connection and return to Windows.**

Now when you open the Dial-Up Networking folder in the My Computer window, an icon for your connection is waiting for you. Click the icon to connect to your ISP.

Installing Modem-Sharing Software

Quite a number of modem-sharing applications are available, with installation difficulty levels ranging from "fairly difficult" to "plan to spend a long time figuring this out."

Because the installation and configuration process differs from one program to another, I can't give you specific step-by-step information. However, I can tell you what those steps usually entail.

Configuring servers and clients

The computer that has the modem is called the *host* or *server*. All the other computers that access the host to use the modem are called the *clients*. The client computers find the server across the network through the use of special addresses called IP addresses. *IP addresses* are numbers (see the next section, which covers assigning IP addresses). Some modem-sharing software also includes a feature that translates the IP address into computer names.

When you install modem-sharing software, you must always begin the installation on the server before installing the software on the client computers. That's because the client installation procedure asks the question "Where's the modem?" The answer isn't "Next to the blue chair" — the answer is the address of the server computer.

Assigning an IP address to the server

Part of the installation process for modem-sharing software is the assignment of an IP address for the server. Most of the software is explicit — it tells you what address to use. For private networks (networks communicating over cable), you should use a specific range of IP addresses. Your modem-sharing software probably assigns IP addresses in the range 192.168.0.0 to 192.168.255.255. The addresses within that range are not used on the Internet; they're only used in private networks, such as the home network you're setting up.

Configuring a proxy server

Modem-sharing technology works because the server (the computer with the modem) acts as a *proxy server* in addition to providing the modem. This is a computer term that means the same thing it seems to mean in English — proxy means "in the place of." The server acts in place of the client computer as each client computer accesses the Internet. For example, the functions of a Web browser are all performed on the proxy server, which acts for the individual computers.

Some modem-sharing software requires that you to set up the proxy server configuration in your browsers. Other modem-sharing software builds proxy-sharing features into the software so that you don't have to go through all the work of configuring your browsers.

One modem-sharing software application that is quite easy to install and configure and doesn't require you to set up your browsers for a proxy server is called WinGate, and a demo version is on the CD that accompanies this book.

Part VI
Keeping Your Network Working

The 5th Wave   By Rich Tennant

"Oh no— Phillip was too smart to waste money on surge protectors. Now, this is all that's left of the network after last night's storm."

In this part . . .

In this part, I tell you how to back up all the computers on your network, how to clean up your hard drives, and how to prevent power surge damage so that your network works for a long, long time.

Chapter 15

Backing Up

● ●

In This Chapter

▶ Planning for backups

▶ Setting up Microsoft Backup

▶ Using floppy disks for backups

▶ Using removable drive cartridges for backups

▶ Using tapes for backups

▶ Using remote computers for backups

● ●

Computers die. Sometimes only one part of a computer dies, but it's usually one of the important parts, like the hard drive. You have to approach the use of computers with the attitude that your machine could go to la-la land, or your hard drive could go to hard-drive heaven, tomorrow.

If you don't plan for a sudden demise of your equipment, the computer fairies figure it out — they notice that you're complacent (they call it smug) and they break something. It must be fairies — nothing else explains the fact that most computers bite the dust the day after the user has finished writing the greatest novel in the history of literature or an important report for the boss that's sure to mean a promotion, and no backup files exist.

Making a backup doesn't prevent the death of your computer. And there's no proof that skipping a backup invites a serious problem — it just seems to happen that way. But just in case, backing up important files every single day is imperative.

You need to back up your data files religiously. If you have a tape backup system or a large removable disk, such as a Jaz drive, you can back up everything on the computer. In this chapter, I walk you through the backup process.

Ensuring Safe and Easy Backups

If you take the time to establish a plan of attack, you can fight back when disaster strikes. For computers, the best plan of attack is a well-designed backup plan. Your plan must provide protection for important files and must be so easy to implement that you won't be tempted to skip backing up.

Configuring your computer for easy backups

If something bad happens to your computer and you haven't backed up, you can reinstall the operating system and all your software (assuming you saved all the installation disks), but you can kiss that letter to grandma and that promotion-earning PowerPoint presentation goodbye. Say "so long" to that fat inheritance check and that office with a view.

The easier it is to back up your data files, the more likely it is that you'll actually perform the task every day. It's like keeping the vacuum cleaner in the hall closet — your house stays cleaner than it would if you kept the vacuum cleaner in the attic. Convenience is an invaluable assistant.

Store all your data files in the My Documents folder. If you like to organize your files by type, either by software application or by some other scheme (perhaps separating letters from other documents), create subfolders for each type. When you copy the My Documents folder, you copy all of its subfolders.

Some software applications (for example, Quicken) have a backup routine built into the software. If the software backs up your data files to a floppy disk, that's fine. If, however, the software backs up your data files to a separate backup directory on your hard drive, redirect that backup to a subfolder under your My Documents folder. Otherwise, you have to take the time to back up that separate folder in addition to your My Documents folder.

Safeguarding software CDs and disks

If your hard drive dies, you have to install Windows on the new drive. Then, if you have a total backup of your entire drive, including the Registry, you can restore that backup and put everything back the way it was before the demise of your equipment. You usually have to do a bit of tweaking, but essentially, the move to the new drive goes pretty smoothly.

If you don't have a total backup of your drive, all isn't lost. As long as you backed up your data files, you can reinstall the operating system, reinstall your software, and then restore the data files that you backed up.

This plan works only if your original software CD or disks are available. Storing the original disks for Windows and the software that you purchased in a safe place is important. I recommend that you use one of those fireproof boxes that you can buy in office supply stores.

If you have software that you downloaded from the Internet, put that software on a disk and store it with the other software disks. If you have a removable disk drive on your system, dedicate one cartridge to downloaded software programs (many downloaded programs won't fit on a floppy disk).

Safeguarding backup media

Whatever backup media you choose — whether it be floppy disks, Zip or Jaz cartridges, or backup tapes — make sure that you have more than one disk, cartridge, or tape on hand. Don't back up on the same disk, cartridge, or tape that holds your last backup — if something goes wrong during the backup, you not only don't get a good backup this time, but you also destroy your previous backup.

The ideal situation is to have a disk, cartridge, or tape for each day of the week. If that seems too difficult or too expensive (in the case of cartridges and tapes), create one set of disks, cartridges, or tapes marked Odd (for odd days) and another set marked Even (for even days).

Once a week, take your backup media out of the house. If a fire, flood, or any other catastrophe strikes, then after you clean up the mess you can replace the computers. You can replace and reinstall software, but you have no way to restore all those important documents, accounting information, and other data that you created on your computer unless you have a backup stored out of harm's way.

Store your backup media — floppy disks, tapes, or removable cartridges — in the same safe container that you use for your original software disks.

Take the media to a neighbor, to work, or to your vacation home. Don't forget to bring it back the following week so that you can put a current backup on the media and take it away again. You'll probably be able to find a neighbor with a computer and backup media who wants to do the same thing, so just trade disks.

Using Microsoft Backup

Microsoft provides backup software with Windows 98 and Windows 95, and since I operate on the theory "if it's free and it works, why not use it?" I find Microsoft Backup to be an excellent choice for safeguarding my files. In this section, I walk you through using Microsoft Backup to ensure a safe computing environment.

Installing Microsoft Backup

Microsoft Backup is not installed during a typical installation of Windows. Unless you perform a customized installation and install the backup software at that time, it won't be available.

Here's how to install Microsoft Backup:

1. **With your Windows CD in the CD-ROM drive, choose Start⇨Settings⇨Control Panel.**

   The Control Panel opens.

2. **Double-click the Add/Remove Programs icon and click the Windows Setup Tab in the Add/Remove Programs Properties dialog box that appears.**

3. **Click the System Tools listing and then click the Details button.**

4. **Select Backup from the list of components, and then click OK.**

When you want to run the program, simply choose Start⇨Programs⇨ Accessories⇨System Tools⇨Backup.

Configuring Microsoft Backup

Microsoft Backup for Windows 98 and Windows 95 uses floppy drives, network drives, removable drives, and tape drives as the target media when you make a backup. The *target media* is the drive onto which the backup is copied. When you use Microsoft Backup for the first time, you need to create a backup job (a set of instructions to tell Microsoft Backup which files to back up and when they should be backed up). You have three configuration options in a backup job:

- The folders and files that you want to back up
- Whether you want to back up all the files you've selected or only those that have changed since the last backup
- The target media

After you configure the backup options, you can give the backup job a name. For example, if you select a full backup, you might name it *full,* while you might name a backup of your My Documents folder *docs*. Thereafter, when you start the backup software, you can select an existing job or create another job with a different configuration.

Backups are not like copies. You can't retrieve the individual files from the target media, because the entire backup is one big file. The backup software makes a catalog that it displays if you need to restore any files. You must select the individual files from the catalog — you won't see the file names on the media.

For full explanations of backing up and restoring your computer, read *Windows 95 For Dummies*, 2nd Edition, and *Windows 98 For Dummies,* both written by Andy Rathbone and published by IDG Books Worldwide, Inc.

Backing Up Data on Floppy Disks

You can back up your data files to floppy disks. You have a couple of methods to choose from for getting your files on the disks.

Using Microsoft Backup with floppy disks

You can configure the backup software that's available with Windows 98 and Windows 95 to back up to floppy disks. Just select your floppy drive as the backup target when you're configuring your backup.

Using Send To with floppy disks

You can copy files to a floppy disk to create a backup. Select all the files that you want to back up and right-click on any file. Choose Send To from the shortcut menu that appears, and then choose the floppy drive. When the disk is filled to capacity, an error message appears to tell you that the disk has no more room on it. Put another formatted, empty floppy disk in the drive, and then click Retry.

Send To doesn't really *send* the file; it copies it. The original file stays where it was.

Backing Up Data on Removable Drive Cartridges

Removable drives are terrific backup targets! You can use them with Microsoft Backup or with the Send To command (or by clicking your way through the files and folders in Windows Explorer if you like to do things the long way).

You can use a removable drive for backing up whether or not it's attached to your computer. Remote drives (drives attached to another computer on your network) work just fine.

Using Microsoft Backup with removable drives

Microsoft Backup works beautifully with removable cartridges. If you're using a Jaz drive or another large capacity drive, you can probably back up everything on your computer. If you're using a Zip drive, you probably have to be more selective about the files you're backing up because you have less space. Make sure that you back up all your data files, and if any room is left after that, you can back up some of your software folders, which is especially useful for software you've configured, tweaked, and manipulated until it's just perfect.

You can do a full backup on a cartridge that's smaller than the amount of hard drive space you're using as long as you have extra cartridges. The backup software tells you when it's time to put another cartridge in the drive.

Using Send To with removable drives

You can use the Send To command that appears when you right-click on a folder or file to copy that folder or file to a removable drive. Oops, you just looked at the Send To choices and you don't see a removable drive as one of the options? Okay, you're right, it's not on the Send To submenu. Wouldn't it be handy if it were? Well, go ahead and put it there! It's not hard to add a removable drive to the Send To submenu.

First, create a Desktop shortcut for the removable drive. If the drive is on your computer, double-click the My Computer icon to see the drive's icon. If the drive is on a remote computer, double-click the Network Neighborhood icon and then double-click the icon for the computer that holds the drive in order to see the icon for the removable drive.

Now that you can see the removable drive, right-drag its icon to the Desktop. Choose Create Shortcut(s) Here from the menu that appears when you release the right mouse button. Drag the shortcut to one side of your Desktop, because you need to see it after you open the SendTo folder window.

Open the SendTo folder window by choosing Start⇨Run and typing **sendto** in the Open text box. Click OK. The SendTo folder appears on your screen. Left-drag the shortcut from the Desktop to the SendTo folder. That's it! The removable drive is on your Send To command list. Cool!

The title under the icon in the SendTo folder is the command that appears on the Send To submenu. If you want to change the title (and therefore the command), click the icon and press F2. Then enter a new name. I do this because I think it's tacky to see *shortcut to Mom Jaz* (if that's the name of the shared resource) and prefer to see something like *Remote Jaz Drive* on the menu.

Now you can select folders or groups of files and use the Send To command to copy them (back them up) to the removable drive.

Backing Up Data on Tapes

Zip and Jaz drives may be all the rage right now, but the capacity of tapes is usually much larger than any removable drive cartridge. Besides that, the software that comes with tape systems can compress files so that you can transfer many gigabytes of data to a single tape.

You can also use Microsoft Backup to back up to a tape drive if your tape drive is supported by Microsoft Backup. Check the documentation that came with your tape drive.

One disadvantage of using tapes is that they wear out. The edges fray, the tension disappears, and an assortment of other problems can show up. Tapes are not as durable as the cartridges for removable drives. Keep tapes in sealed boxes, away from moisture and direct sunlight.

If you purchase a backup tape system, it comes with software. Not all backup programs perform exactly the same way, so I can't tell you exactly how to configure and use your particular software. In this section, I give you some basic guidelines for getting the most out of your tape backup system.

Pay attention to the configuration options available in your backup software. Remember that you're likely to need the tape to restore files after your hard drive dies. Therefore, if the software presents an option to put a copy of the catalog on the tape, select that option. (The *catalog* is the list of folders and files that you backed up.) The catalog on the hard drive will die with the drive.

Always include the Registry in your backup files, so that if you have to restore everything, you also restore the Registry. The *Registry* is a database that keeps track of the configuration options, software, hardware, and other important elements of your Windows system.

Select the option to verify the backup, which means that the software makes sure that the copy of the file on the tape matches the copy on your hard drive.

Many backup software programs keep copies of every catalog. These copies take up a lot of hard-drive space, so do some hard-drive housekeeping and get rid of the catalogs that you no longer need. When you tape over a previous catalog, you can get rid of the original one.

Backing Up on Remote Computers

One easy way to back up your data files is to use another computer on the network. If your network has two computers, each computer uses the other as the place to store backups. If your network has more than two computers, you can pick one of the other computers. In fact, you can back up your data to every remote computer in a frenzy of cautiousness.

This technique works if you operate on the theory that it is highly unlikely that all the computers on the network could die at the same time. The fact is that a fire, flood, or power surge from lightning could very well destroy every computer on your network. If you use remote computers for backing up, you should also back up on some sort of media, whether it be floppy disks, removable-drive cartridges, or tapes, on a weekly or monthly basis.

Start the backup by creating a folder for yourself on the remote computer. Make it a shared resource and call it Fred (unless your name isn't Fred). To find out about creating shared resources, refer to Chapter 9.

Then, every day, perform these steps:

1. **Double-click the Windows Explorer icon (on your own computer) and copy your document files to your folder on the remote computer.**

2. **Right-click on your My Documents folder and choose Copy from the shortcut menu that appears.**

3. **Click the plus sign to expand the Network Neighborhood listing in Windows Explorer and also expand the computer that has your folder.**

4. **Right-click on your personal folder and choose Paste from the shortcut menu that appears.**

If you're making another backup on another remote computer for safety's sake, repeat the preceding steps.

Chapter 16

Working with Windows Tools

*W*indows has a virtual toolbox built into the operating system. This toolbox features a bunch of handy programs you can use to perform maintenance and repair tasks on the computers in your network.

The equipment you find in your toolbox differs depending on the choices you made when you installed the operating system. If you chose a typical installation and didn't specifically select the components you wanted to install, you don't have a lot of tools in your toolbox.

For information about the Windows installation procedure, read *Windows 95 For Dummies*, 2nd Edition, or *Windows 98 For Dummies,* both written by Andy Rathbone and published by IDG Books Worldwide, Inc.

By default, the Disk Defragmenter and ScanDisk are installed with the operating system. Those tools are discussed in this chapter, as are a number of other tools that are not installed automatically.

Defragging Your Hard Drive

Disk Defragmenter is a program that takes fragments of files and puts them together so that every file on your drive has its entire contents in the same place. This makes opening files a faster process.

Before I discuss the Disk Defragmenter tool, it's important to understand a piece of jargon. Nobody who is hip (well, as hip as a computer geek can be) uses the term "Disk Defragmenter." In fact, nobody uses the terms "fragmented" or "defragmented." Instead, when your disk is "fragged," you "run the defragger to defrag" it.

Installing additional Windows tools

After you read this chapter, you'll probably want to install some of the nifty tools that are discussed. Here are the easy steps to follow when you want to install more Windows tools:

1. **Put the Windows CD in the CD-ROM drive.**

   Hold down the Shift key to prevent the CD from launching its opening screen automatically.

   If your computer came with Windows pre-installed, you may not have a CD because the files have already been placed on your hard drive. Proceed to Step 2.

2. **Choose Start⇨Settings⇨Control Panel.**

   The Control Panel opens.

3. **Double-click the Add/Remove Programs icon.**

   The Add/Remove Programs Properties dialog box opens.

4. **Click the Windows Setup tab.**

   Windows checks your system to see which components are installed, and a list of components is displayed in the dialog box.

5. **In Windows 98, select the System Tools listing. In Windows 95, select the**
Accessories listing. Then click the De-tails button.

A list of specific components appears. A check mark appears next to each tool that is already installed on your system.

In Windows 95, two disk tools, Backup and Disk Compression, are found in the Disk Tools listing. The other tools appear in the Accessories listing.

6. **Click the check box of any uninstalled tool you want to add to your system.**

   A check mark appears in the check box. If you change your mind, click the check box again to remove the check mark (it's a toggle).

7. **Click OK twice.**

   The necessary files are transferred to your hard drive. Depending on the tools you select, you may be told to restart the oper-ating system to have the changes take effect.

Now you can use your Windows tools by choosing Start⇨Programs⇨Accessories⇨ System Tools and then choosing the appropri-ate tool from the menu.

Files get fragmented get (oops, I meant fragged) as a matter of course; the fragging (there — I've redeemed myself) isn't caused by anything you do or any problem with your computer. The more a drive fills up with files, the more likely it is to become fragmented.

Here's what happens: After you've used your computer for a while, your hard drive starts to fill up. One day, you launch your word processor and open a document that's on your hard drive. That document is 50,000 bytes in size. You add more text to the document, and when you save the document, it's 75,000 bytes. The particular section of the drive where it was originally stored has room for 50,000 bytes, so the operating system puts 50,000 bytes of your new version back where it was and finds another spot on the drive to lay down the remaining 25,000 bytes.

Windowrø9akes a note about that file, and the note says something like, "I stuck the first 50K here and put the next 25K there." The note isn't a note, though; it's an entry in a part of the operating system that's called the *File Allocation Table,* which acts like an index or a table of contents. (It's from that component that we get the acronym FAT for the file system used in Windows.)

Later you open that file again, and the operating system fetches all those fragments, in the right order, after checking the FAT to see where the pieces of the file ard\‡You add even more information to the file. The operating system puts the first two sections back where they were and then finds another spot for the additional bytes. The next day, you add more to the file, so more sections of the disk are used to hold the pieces of the file. Each time you load the file, its fragments must be fetched from more and more separate locations. The same thing happens to the files you create and save in all your software programs.

After a while, your system seems slower: It takes a long time to load a document and save a document. That's because your operating system must do all this legwork to fetch and lay down the file parts.

Eventually, you need to tell the operating system to pick up all the parts and put them together, making all the parts of every file contiguous. This is what the Disk Defragmenter does. To accomplish this, the Disk Defragmenter juggles file parts, holding some in memory while it finds room for them, moving some stuff on the drive out of the way to make room for the stuff in memory.

Follow these steps to defrag your drive:

1. **Choose Start➪Programs➪Accessories➪System Tools➪ Disk Defragmenter.**

   The Select Drive dialog box opens.

2. **Select the drive you want to defrag (usually C:). Then click OK.**

   In Windows 98, the program begins defragging the drive immediately. In Windows 95, the program checks the current state of the drive, and if the drive isn't badly fragmented, a message appears telling you that the drive doesn't really need defragging. You can opt to run the program anyway, if you want to.

   During the defragging process, the program displays a progress report so that you can see how much work remains to be done.

3. **Click the Show <u>D</u>etails button to see a full-color representation of your hard drive and its fragmented files.**

You can watch the pieces of files being put together as the defragging proceeds.

Technically, you can do work on your computer during the defragging operations, but things go very slowly (because the computer and the hard drive are very busy), and the defragmenter program itself is slowed by your actions. Go grab a bowl of cereal and watch a few commercials instead.

If you absolutely must perform some task at the computer during this procedure, click the Pause button on the Disk Defragmenter dialog box. After you finish your work, click Resume. You can also click Stop to end the process.

If you pause or stop the Disk Defragmenter, the response isn't immediate. The program finishes the file it's currently working on and updates the FAT information. Then it responds to your selection.

A message lets you know when the defragging is complete. After the defragging, you should notice a much peppier response when you load or save files. Of course, you're going to continue to open and save files, so the fragging starts all over again, and eventually your system will slow down, and you'll have to defrag again.

Checking Your Hard Drive for Damage with ScanDisk

ScanDisk is a program that checks the condition of your hard drive, looking for two specific problems:

- ✔ Damaged sections of the drive.
- ✔ Pieces of files that don't seem to belong anywhere (or the operating system can't figure out where they belong).

If a damaged section is identified, ScanDisk takes files off the damaged section and moves them to a good spot on the drive. Then the program marks the damaged section as bad so that the operating system won't use it to store files again.

If pieces of files are found and ScanDisk can't figure out where they belong, the software puts the pieces into files that you can look at to see whether you can identify them. However, there's usually nothing you can do with them except delete them. Those files are placed in the root folder (right on the hard drive, not in any folder) of your hard drive, and they're named FILE0000.CHK, FILE0001.CHK, and so on. You could try to read them, but even if they're readable (most of the time they're not text, so you can't decipher them), there isn't anything you can do with them. Delete them.

I bet you're wondering how you get pieces of files floating on your drive. As I explain in the previous section about using Disk Defragmenter, Windows keeps track of the location of a file on the hard drive every time you save it. The information about file locations appears in the File Allocation Table (FAT).

However, if your computer unexpectedly shuts down while files are open, the operating system has no opportunity to tell the FAT where all the files or parts of files were placed on the hard drive. The data is on the drive, but there's no reference in the FAT for them. This means you may lose parts of any open files, both data and software, because Windows doesn't know where they're located on your drive.

Unexpected shutdowns aren't limited to sudden power failures. If you shut off your computer without going through the Shut Down dialog box, that counts as an unexpected shutdown and can do just as much damage to your file system as a power failure. In fact, after an unexpected shutdown, ScanDisk usually runs automatically the next time you start your computer.

Launch ScanDisk from the System Tools submenu by choosing Start⇨Programs⇨Accessories⇨System Tools⇨ScanDisk. Select the drive you want to check when the ScanDisk dialog box opens. You can choose one of the following types of tests to run:

✔ **Standard.** This test checks the files and folders on your hard drive.

Most of the time the Standard test is sufficient, because the files and folders are where most system errors are found.

✔ **Thorough.** This test examines the surface of your drive, looking for physical errors (bad spots).

This test takes much longer. It isn't necessary to select a Thorough test unless you've seen some peculiar behavior, such as messages that say there's an error trying to read or write from the drive. However, it probably doesn't hurt to run a Thorough test as a preventive measure once in a while, in case a bad spot has developed on your hard drive.

Physical hard drive problems are serious

If there's a physical problem with your hard drive, you'll probably see one of these messages (substitute the letter of your hard drive for X):

- Serious Disk Error Writing Drive X
- Data Error Reading Drive X
- Error Reading Drive X
- I/O Error
- Seek Error — Sector not found

If you get any of these error messages, your hard drive may have a serious health problem that could even be fatal.

Perform a backup immediately, as explained in Chapter 15 (although there may be some files that cannot be read from the drive and won't be backed up). If the backup program doesn't work without producing error messages, manually back up as many important data files as you can.

Then take your computer to a computer store to see whether your hard drive can be fixed or you need to buy a new drive.

Select the Automatically Fix Errors check box. After all, there's no point in running a test if you don't fix any problems that are found. If you don't select this check box, the errors are reported to you, and then you have to tell ScanDisk to fix them. Why do twice the work?

If you want to, you can click the Advanced button to see the ScanDisk Advanced Options dialog box, where you can specify the test procedures more precisely (see Figure 16-1).

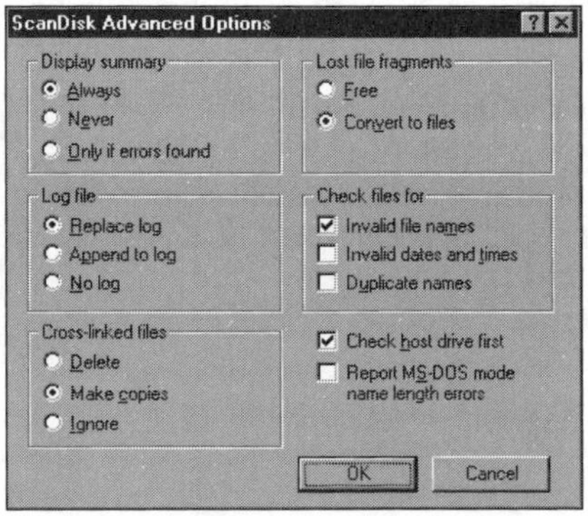

Figure 16-1:
You can decide for yourself what you want ScanDisk to check.

If you enabled power management features for your monitor and your screen goes dark while ScanDisk is running, do not press the spacebar or the Enter key to bring the display back. Pressing either of those keys stops ScanDisk. If you want to watch the ScanDisk progress and your monitor goes dark after the specified amount of time of inactivity, use any key except the spacebar or Enter to bring the monitor back.

ScanDisk runs automatically when you restart your computer after you shut down improperly (when you forget to use the Shut Down command on the Start menu or a power failure occurs). You must let ScanDisk scan the entire disk under these circumstances. Do not click Stop to stop the process. If you don't complete the process, ScanDisk will probably run the next time you start the computer, even if you perform a valid shut down procedure this time.

There's a reason you must let ScanDisk complete an entire scan if it runs automatically after a bad shutdown. A file on your computer (MSDOS.SYS) tracks whether there was a clean shutdown and also whether ScanDisk completed its job. ScanDisk doesn't update the information in that file until the scanning procedure is finished. If the information isn't updated, every time you start your computer, the operating system thinks you're recovering from a bad shutdown.

Managing Devices with Device Manager

The Windows Device Manager is a powerful tool. You can use it to view all sorts of information about the hardware in your computer. You can also use it to make changes to the way hardware is configured or the way it behaves.

To use the Device Manager, right-click the My Computer icon and choose Properties from the shortcut menu that appears. When the System Properties dialog box opens, click the Device Manager tab. All the hardware categories that exist in your computer are displayed, as shown in Figure 16-2.

Viewing a specific device

The first list that appears is a list of hardware types, not the actual hardware that's installed in your computer. Click the plus sign to the left of a device type to see the specific hardware in your system. You'll usually see an exact description, sometimes including a brand name and model.

Select the specific device and click Properties to see information about the device and the way it's configured. The information in the Properties dialog box differs according to the type of device you're examining.

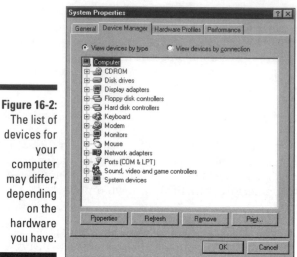

Figure 16-2:
The list of
devices for
your
computer
may differ,
depending
on the
hardware
you have.

You can change the configuration for some devices right in the Properties dialog box. Just select the setting that needs changed and enter a new setting.

Managing device problems

If there's a problem with any device, the specific device listing already appears. An icon appears in the listing, indicating the type of problem. The icon may be a red *X*, a yellow exclamation point, or something else.

Select the device and choose Properties to see a message explaining the problem. Sometimes, the problem isn't so serious, and the device continues to operate. Other times, you may have to reinstall or reconfigure the device. The Properties dialog box usually provides enough information to guide you to a resolution.

Printing a report about devices

It's a good idea to have a list of all the devices in your system and the re-sources they use. I've found that such a list is handy in a couple of situations:

✔ If you have to reinstall everything when you replace a hard drive, all the configuration information for each device is available in your list.

✔ If you want to install additional devices, you know which resources on your computer are available by viewing your list.

To print a report on all the devices in your system, click the Print button in the Device Manager dialog box.

Determining Who's On Your Computer

Net Watcher is a handy tool that you can use to keep an eye on visitors — that is, those users working on other computers on the network who are accessing your computer. Net Watcher gives you all kinds of who, what, and where information.

Choose Start⇨Programs⇨Accessories⇨System Tools⇨Net Watcher. The window that opens displays a list of visitors, if any other users are accessing your computer. By default, the window displays a User view, which provides the following information about each visitor:

- ✔ The user name
- ✔ The name of the remote computer
- ✔ The number of shares in use
- ✔ The number of open files
- ✔ The length of time the visitor has been connected to your computer

You can select a specific user and see which shared folder that user is accessing (the information appears in the right pane of the Net Watcher window).

The Shared Folders view displays all the shared folders on your computer. You can double-click any folder to see the name of the user accessing the folder. This view is not named correctly because it doesn't just display shared folders — it also lists all the shared resources on your computer (printers, removable drives, and so on).

The Show Files view lists all the open files in use by visitors. Incidentally, only software program files are tracked, not data files. In addition to the name of each open file, the name of its shared folder is listed, as are the name of the remote user and the type of access (Read-only or Full).

In addition to viewing all this information, you can perform a number of tasks in the Net Watcher window, including the following:

- ✔ Close a file that's in use.
- ✔ Add a new shared folder to your computer.
- ✔ Stop sharing a folder that's currently shared.

> ✔ Change the properties of a shared folder (such as passwords and access options).
>
> ✔ Disconnect a user.

Some of these options sound like dirty tricks — I mean, after all, disconnecting a user? But if you think of Net Watcher as a security measure, you'll understand why this tool can be important. Suppose that your son and his friend are using a computer and decide to open the family budget or personal letters. If you use Net Watcher, and as a result, learn that remote users are accessing files and folders you'd prefer to keep private, you can adjust the way you configured your shared resources. (See Chapter 9 for more information about configuring shared folders.)

Cleaning Up Files

Using the Disk Cleanup tool (available only for Windows 98) is like bringing in a housekeeper to clean up all that junk you never use — the stuff that's been lying around taking up space.

In your house, that stuff could be old magazines, newspapers, or clothing you haven't been able to fit into for years.

On your computer, that stuff is files you don't use and probably don't even realize are stored on your drive. Those are the files that Disk Cleanup looks for and offers to sweep out.

Use either one of these methods to open the Disk Cleanup program:

> ✔ Double-click the My Computer icon and right-click the drive you want to clean. Choose Properties from the shortcut menu that appears and click the Disk Cleanup button on the General tab of the Properties dialog box.
>
> ✔ Choose Start⇨Programs⇨Accessories⇨System Tools⇨Disk Cleanup. Then choose the drive you want to clean.

The Disk Cleanup dialog box opens. File types that are candidates for safe removal are already selected (see Figure 16-3).

Scroll through the list of file types in the Files to Delete box and select any additional file types you want to remove. Click on each file type listing to see more information in the Description box.

The last item in the Files to Delete box is Non Critical Files. If you select this file type, the cleanup is not automatic. Instead, the files are displayed so that you can decide which of them you want to delete.

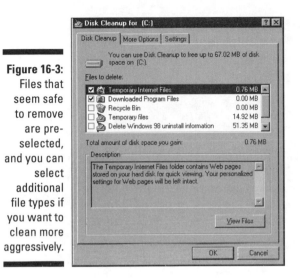

Figure 16-3:
Files that
seem safe
to remove
are pre-
selected,
and you can
select
additional
file types if
you want to
clean more
aggressively.

When you're ready to clean out all this stuff, click OK. Disk Cleanup asks if you're sure you want to delete these files. Click Yes to proceed, or click No if you suddenly panic.

Working with System Information

The System Information tool (available only in Windows 98) is misnamed, because it's not a tool — it's an entire toolbox. It starts off looking like a nifty, handy-dandy tool, but then you discover a menu item named Tools that leads you to more cool tools. In this section, I cover the System Information tool and then follow up with sections for some of the embedded tools in its toolbox.

The primary focus of SI (short for the System Information tool) is to gather information and diagnose problems. Just choose Start➪Programs➪ Accessories➪System Tools➪System Information. When the SI window opens (see Figure 16-4), categories appear in the left pane, and information about the selected category appears in the right pane.

General System Information

The System Information category presents general information about your computer, the operating system, the current user, and drives that are local to the computer or mapped to a remote computer. You can't do anything with this information — it's purely informative.

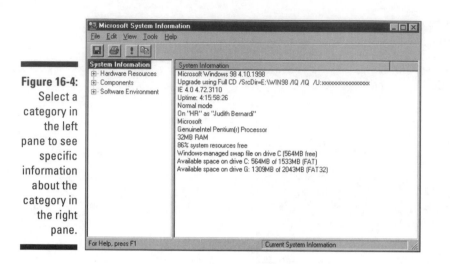

Figure 16-4:
Select a
category in
the left
pane to see
specific
information
about the
category in
the right
pane.

Hardware Resources

Click the plus sign to the left of the Hardware Resources category and select a subcategory to view information in the right pane. Here are the subcategories for Hardware Resources:

- ✔ **Conflicts/Sharing.** This subcategory lists any resource conflicts. It also identifies resources that are being shared by Peripheral Component Interconnect (PCI) devices. This information can be helpful when you are trying to discover whether a hardware conflict is to blame for a device problem.

- ✔ **Forced Hardware.** Select this subcategory to see a list of devices that have user-specified resources instead of resources assigned by the system. Sometimes this information is helpful when you're having trouble installing a Plug and Play device that should have been easy to install.

- ✔ **I/O.** Selecting this subcategory produces a list of all the I/O addresses (parts of memory assigned to a device) currently in use. The devices that occupy each address range are also displayed. You can use this information to avoid the occupied addresses when you're configuring a new device.

- ✔ **IRQs.** Select this subcategory to see a display of the IRQs in use, along with the device that is using each IRQ. (An IRQ is a channel of communication that a device occupies.) There's also a list of unused IRQs, which is handy when you're configuring a new device.

- ✔ **Memory.** This subcategory displays a list of memory address ranges being used by devices. Most of the time this information is used when you're troubleshooting a device, especially if you call the manufacturer's customer support line. It's not unusual for a support technician to ask for this information.

Components

The Components category contains all sorts of information about your Windows 98 configuration, including information about the status of device drivers as well as a history of all the drivers you've installed (it's not unusual to upgrade drivers when they become available from manufacturers or from Microsoft). Information about your network and multimedia components is available. There's also a summary of devices that the System Information tool suspects are not working properly.

Table 16-1 lists descriptions of the subcategories in the Components list.

Table 16-1	Components Category Descriptions
Subcategory	*Description*
Multimedia	Information about sound cards and joysticks. Additional subcategories provide specific information about audio, video, and CD-ROM configuration.
Display	Video card and monitor information.
Infrared	Information about any Infrared devices you've installed.
Input	Keyboard and mouse information.
Miscellaneous	Information about any miscellaneous components, such as printers you've installed (both local printers and network printers).
Modems	Technical information about your modem.
Network	Information about your network adapter, as well as the client services and protocols you've installed.
Ports	Technical information about the serial and parallel ports in your computer.
Storage	Information about storage devices (hard disks, floppy drives, and removable media).
Printing	A list of installed printers and printer drivers.
Problem Devices	A list of devices with problems, including information about the status of the device.
USB	Information about any Universal Serial Bus (USB) controllers and drivers that are installed.
History	A history of drivers that have been installed, including updates and changes. This is a good way to see the changes you've made to your system when something goes wrong.
System	Information about your computer's Basic Input/Output System (BIOS), motherboard, and other built-in devices.

You can change the view in the right pane in order to change the level of information. The choices are Basic Information, Advanced Information, or History (for device drivers).

Software Environment

The Software Environment category covers information about the software that's loaded in your computer's memory. Included are drivers, software programs, tasks that are currently running, and all sorts of technical data that's hard to understand. However, the information can be useful to support desk personnel if you're calling for help.

Saving System Information to a file

You can save all the information that the SI tool provides in a file and then use that file as a reference when you configure new devices or call a support desk. To send the data to a file, choose File⇨Export from the System Information menu bar. A Save As dialog box opens so you can name the file and select the folder in which to save it. The file is a text file, so you can open it and print it in WordPad (it's usually too large to use Notepad).

Checking Your System Files

Windows 98 provides a tool called the System File Checker that you can use to, well, check your system files. *System files* are the files that Windows 98 installs to make the operating system run. All the files for all the Windows components you install are transferred to your hard drive during the installation process. Most of the files end up in the Windows folder or one of the subfolders under the Windows folder.

Sometimes a system file gets corrupted or disappears. The System File Checker verifies the files on your hard drive, and if any of them are corrupt or missing, they're replaced from the original Windows 98 disc.

Incidentally, if a system file disappears, you can bet that it wasn't an accident, and somebody probably deleted it. It's very dangerous to open Windows Explorer and delete files from the Windows folder or one of the subfolders. In fact, when you select the Windows folder in the left pane of Explorer, you don't see a file listing in the right pane. Instead, the left pane displays a message warning you that modifying the contents of the folder can be dangerous. You have to click Show Files to force Explorer to display the contents of the Windows folder.

Follow these steps to run the System File Checker:

1. **Choose Start⇨Programs⇨Accessories⇨System Tools. Then choose Tools⇨System File Checker from the System Information menu bar.**

   When the System File Checker dialog box opens, the Scan For Altered Files option is already selected.

2. **Click Start to have the System File Checker go through your hard drive(s) and check all the Windows system files.**

   The process takes a couple of minutes.

   If any files have been altered, you're prompted to restore the original file from the Windows CD (or the Windows 98 files folder if your computer came with the operating system preinstalled).

   If you're a control freak, you might want to click the Settings button so that you can configure the way the System File Checker works. The available options are self-explanatory, and if you're not sure about an option, you can right-click it and get information from the What's This? dialog box that opens.

Automating Maintenance Tasks

The Maintenance Wizard, available only in Windows 98, is a nifty way to make sure that important maintenance tasks are performed regularly and automatically. In addition, you can schedule these chores so they take place at times that won't interfere with your work.

Choose Start⇨Programs⇨Accessories⇨System Tools⇨Maintenance Wizard. Each wizard window presents a question to answer or an option to select. Click Next to move to the next window.

The opening window offers these two configuration options:

- ✔ **Express,** which automatically configures the wizard for the most common maintenance settings
- ✔ **Custom,** which allows you to select your own settings

The common maintenance settings differ according to the software and Windows features you've installed in your system. However, the following programs usually run (each of which is discussed in this chapter):

- ✔ ScanDisk
- ✔ Disk Cleanup
- ✔ Disk Defragmenter

If you installed additional utilities — especially if you installed the Windows 98 Plus! add-on — additional programs may be selected for the Express option.

No matter which option you select, you can choose the time at which the Maintenance Wizard performs its tasks. The process usually takes about three hours to complete, and the computer must be running for the Maintenance Wizard to perform its tasks.

The schedule options are as follows:

- ✔ **Start at Midnight,** which is convenient because it probably won't interfere with your work

- ✔ **Start at Noon,** which is handy for households with folks who work or go to school during the day

- ✔ **Start at 8:00 PM,** which may be convenient if the members of your household don't work at the computers after dinner

Chapter 17

Practicing Preventive Maintenance

● ●

In This Chapter

▶ Preventing electrical damage

▶ Checking network hardware

▶ Caring for monitors

▶ Safeguarding printers

● ●

*S*ometimes, things go wrong with the computer itself — the physical parts of a computer. You can avoid many problems with a little preventive maintenance.

The important consideration, now that you're a network administrator, is that you're protecting your network in addition to protecting each individual computer.

Network computers are connected — they talk to each other, and they interact with each other. Each computer on the network has a physical relationship with the other computers on the network. The computers can pass problems around the network neighborhood through the cable.

In this chapter, I tell you how to care for your hardware so you don't have an epidemic of sick computers.

Avoiding Electricity-Related Computer Catastrophes

You know that electricity is dangerous, so you probably avoid sticking your fingers into live lightbulb sockets and electrical outlets (at least, I hope you do). Your computers may not have fingers, but they're very sensitive to electricity, too, and it's up to you to protect them from a variety of electrical dangers.

Protecting against electrical surges

An *electrical surge* is a sudden spate of very high voltage that travels from the electric lines to your house, and ultimately to your computer. Computers are particularly sensitive to surges, and a real surge can fry your computer. The chips burn up, and your computer becomes a doorstop.

Most of the time, surges occur as a result of a lightning strike, but the danger of a surge also exists if there's a brief blackout followed by a return of electricity. During the return of power, the voltage can spike. (See the section "Protecting against lightning hits," later in this chapter.)

You can safeguard against spikes by plugging your computer into a *surge protector*. The surge protectors that are commonly used look like electrical power strips, usually with four or five outlets. Read the specifications before you buy a surge protector to make sure that it's rated for real surge protection. (Voltage can rise by 10 volts or hundreds of volts, so make sure that the surge protector you buy can handle these extreme surges.)

Surge protectors work by committing suicide to protect your computer. They absorb the surge so it doesn't travel to your equipment. (Some surge protectors have reset buttons that bring the strip back to life.)

If a power surge hits any piece of equipment that is attached to your computer by cable, the surge can travel to your computer. Therefore, plugging the computer into the surge protector isn't quite enough; you also have to use the surge protector to power the accessories connected to your computer.

Because any surge received by a single computer can travel over the network cable to the other computers on your network, make sure that all of the following equipment for each of your computers is plugged into surge protectors.

- Monitors
- External modems

✔ External removable drives

✔ Speakers

Notice that I didn't list a printer. Never plug a printer into the same surge protector as your computer. (In fact, if you have a laser printer, you should *never* plug it into the same circuit as your computer.) See the section "Protecting Printers," later in this chapter, for more information.

Protecting against telephone line surges

I've seen several large networks destroyed during a lightning storm, and in each case, the surge came through the telephone lines, not the electrical lines. Here's what happens: Lightning hits the telephone line; the surge comes through the telephone jack in the wall; it travels along the telephone cable from the wall to the modem; it travels from the modem to the computer's motherboard; it travels from the motherboard to the rest of the computer parts, including the network interface card (NIC); the NIC sends the surge out to the network cable; the cable sends the surge back to every NIC on the network; and each NIC sends the surge to its computer's motherboard. Every computer on the network is fried.

In most communities, the power company installs lightning arresters, which help diffuse the effects of a direct lightning hit on the electric lines. However, I know of no telephone company that protects its phone lines against lightning. When a lightning storm is close, unplug your modem telephone cable at the wall jack and then unplug the computers.

If your telephone company has fiber-optic lines, you don't have to worry about lightning hits because those lines don't conduct electricity. Ask your telephone company what type of lines are connected to your home.

Protecting against lightning hits

If lightning hits your power lines or your house, your surge protector may not be able to protect your equipment against the resulting surge. Thousands or tens of thousands of volts — sometimes more — result from a lightning strike. A surge protector can provide only so much protection, and a direct lightning hit exceeds that limit.

The only protection against lightning strikes is to unplug your computers and all your computer equipment. Stop working. Then walk around the house and unplug other equipment with chips that could fry during a lightning storm (like your microwave oven).

Saving your computer when power fails

When you're running Windows 98 or Windows 95, you can't just turn off your computer. You must initiate a shutdown procedure to shut down all your files in an orderly manner. Otherwise, you may have a problem starting your computer, or you may run into mysterious problems when you try to use software and Windows features after a power failure.

The electric company doesn't know and doesn't care about the need for an orderly shutdown, and if the folks there did know or care, they couldn't do much about it. Sometimes the power just shuts down.

You can keep your computers running long enough to complete an orderly shutdown of all your software and the operating system if you have an *uninterruptible power supply* (UPS). A UPS is a mega-battery that you plug into the wall, and you then use the UPS outlets to connect your computer and monitor. If your power fails, your computer draws power from the battery, giving you enough time to shut down everything.

UPS units come in a variety of power configurations (measured in watts). Some have line conditioning (see the section "Fixing low voltage problems") in addition to the battery feature. Some have software that performs the orderly shutdown for you. (The UPS unit connects to your computer through a serial port in order to communicate.) This is a nice feature if your power dies while you're away from the computer.

Fixing low-voltage problems

Sometimes, the electrical voltage drops, which is called a *brownout*. Computers — especially their hard drives — are extremely sensitive to brownouts. Well before you see the lights flicker, your hard drive can react to a brownout. Most of the time, that reaction destroys the part of the drive being accessed. Your drive develops bad spots, which means that part of the drive can't be written to or read from. You can mark the bad spots to prevent the operating system from using those spots to hold data, but if the spots that go bad already have data on them, that data goes bad, too. (See Chapter 16 for a discussion of the Windows tools that can help you find and mark bad spots on your hard drive.)

You can prevent most of these problems, and you can overcome those that you can't prevent by purchasing a *voltage regulator*. This clever device sells for about $50 to $100 (depending on how many devices you want to plug into it). It constantly measures the voltage coming out of the wall and brings it up to an acceptable minimum. Several companies make these devices (try TrippLite), and some uninterruptible power supplies have voltage regulation built in. See the sidebar "Saving your computer when power fails."

Here are some of the causes of low voltage, along with possible fixes:

- ✔ **Too many appliances are plugged into the same circuit as your computer.**

  This is something you can fix. Move stuff around, buy some very long heavy-duty extension cords to get to an outlet on another circuit, or call an electrician and get more outlets connected to empty breakers.

- ✔ **An appliance that's a voltage pig (central air conditioning, electric heating systems) kicks on, disrupting voltage throughout the house.**

  Plug your computer into a voltage regulator.

- ✔ **Your laser printer (or powerful inkjet color printer) is plugged into the same circuit as your computer. See the section "Protecting Printers," later in this chapter.**

  You shouldn't plug these printers into the same circuit as your computer. If you have no choice, plug the computer into a voltage regulator. Do not plug the printer into the voltage regulator.

- ✔ **The electric company is sending low voltage into your home.**

  Sometimes, the electric company just can't keep up with demand, and it delivers lower-than-normal voltage to your home. When the voltage really drops, the electric company calls it a brownout. This frequently occurs during very hot weather, when air conditioners in your area are running constantly and working hard.

  The solution? Plug your computer into a voltage regulator.

Preventing static electricity damage

Static electricity is responsible for more damaged computers than most people realize. One day, when some hardware component mysteriously dies, you may not realize that you zapped it yourself.

Static electricity charges that zap your computer come from you. You pick up static electricity, carry it with you, and pass it along when you touch any part of the computer. Usually, the keyboard receives your first touch, and even though it's connected to your computer, it doesn't always pass the electricity along to the computer.

However, if you touch the monitor or the computer box, you can pass a serious or fatal amount of electricity to the motherboard (fatal to the computer, not to you) or to any component in your computer (including chips).

You must discharge the electricity from your body before you touch the computer. Touch anything metal (except an electric appliance such as a computer or a lamp). A filing cabinet is good if one is handy. If nothing metal is within reach, attach a metal bar to the desk or table that your computer sits on.

Computers and carpeting create the ideal atmosphere for zapping. New carpeting is really dangerous, followed by carpeting with a thick pile. If you can't pull the carpeting up, go to an office supply store and buy one of those big plastic mats that goes under the desk and your chair. If you don't, each time you move your feet, you'll collect static electricity and eventually pass it to the computer.

Caring for Network Hardware

If you receive an error message while trying to move files between computers or when you open the Network Neighborhood window, it's time to check your network hardware.

The network hardware, connectors, cable, and NICs may require some maintenance. In the following sections, I list the hardware components in the order in which they usually cause problems. Connector problems are the most common, then cable problems, and finally bad NICs.

Checking connectors

Cable connectors are the weakest link in the network hardware chain. Because of this, you should check the connectors first when your computers can't communicate.

Here's what to check if you wired your network with 10BaseT (twisted-pair) cable:

✔ Make sure that the connectors are properly inserted in the NICs.

✔ Make sure that the connectors are properly inserted in the concentrator.

✔ Make sure that the concentrator is plugged in. (There's usually no on/ off switch on a concentrator — if it's plugged in, it should be working.)

For coaxial cable networks, check these items:

✔ Make sure that the connector at both ends of the crossbar of every T-connector is tight.

✔ Make sure that the end of the cable that goes into the connector isn't loose or jiggling in the little sleeve at the bottom of the connector.

✔ Make sure that the straight leg of the T-connector is firmly attached to the NIC.

✔ Make sure that there are terminators at the first and last positions of the cable run.

Here's what to check if you're using your household telephone line for your network:

✔ Make sure that the connectors are firmly seated in both the NICs and the wall jack.

✔ If you're using a splitter (also called a *modular duplex jack*) to plug in both a telephone and the network cable, make sure that the splitter is firmly positioned in the jack.

Splitters weigh more than the fraction of an ounce that the connector on the end of a phone cord weighs, and sometimes this extra weight pulls the splitter out of the jack just a bit. Frequently, you don't notice this problem when you look at the connection, but if you push on the connector, you do notice that it isn't all the way in the phone jack. This may happen in these situations:

  • The cable between the splitter and whatever the other end of the cable plugs into (either the telephone jack or the NIC) is taut.

  • The telephone is moved, because either it's placed somewhere else or a person using the telephone walks around while chatting.

Checking terminators in coaxial cable networks

In a coax network system, terminators are the most likely culprits when you have a communications problem between computers. Unfortunately, you can't just look at a terminator to determine whether it's working properly.

If you can't find a bad connection on your system, replace one terminator. If that doesn't restore communications, put the original terminator back and then replace the other terminator. If that doesn't work, keep the spare terminator handy for the future and look elsewhere for the problem.

Checking cables

Make sure that the cables aren't pinched or bent to the point that they can't handle data. Have you ever sharply bent a water hose? The water stops flowing. The same thing can happen to cable.

If you have excess cable, don't twist it into a knot to avoid having it spill on the floor. Gently roll the cable into a circle and use a twist tie to keep it together. (Don't tie it tightly.)

I pounded thin nails into the backs of the tables that hold my computers, and I hang coils of excess cable on those nails to keep the cable off the floor.

Checking NICs

It's unusual for a NIC to give up, roll over, and die (unless you've had a power surge or did something dumb like stick a bobby pin in the connector).

However, sometimes NICs — like all hardware — just stop working. If your NIC has a light on the back panel near the connector, it should glow green. (All of today's 10BaseT NICs have little lights, and some Coax NICs do.) If no light is glowing and you've checked the connectors and the cable, the only way to check the NIC is to replace it. If the new NIC works, the old NIC was bad. If the new NIC doesn't work, recheck your connectors and cable. Take the new NIC back to the store and get a credit.

If your NIC has two little lightbulbs and the red one is glowing, your NIC is working but isn't receiving or sending data. You can be fairly sure that you have a connector or cable problem.

Monitoring Monitors

Monitors require some special attention, and too many people maul and mishandle them. By no coincidence at all, those are the same people who have to buy new monitors more frequently than should be necessary.

A monitor's screen attracts and collects dust — it actually sucks it out of the air. You can't avoid monitor dust. Remove the dust by wiping the screen with a soft, dry cloth. It's best to do this with the monitor turned off. (Static electricity, which is responsible for attracting the dust, can build up to explosive levels when you rub the screen.)

Learning to love canned air

Office supply stores sell cans of air. It's not just air; it's air that comes out of the can with enough pressure to push dust out of places it shouldn't be. The cans come with little straw-like tubes that you can attach to the sprayer so that you can get inside your removable drives and between the keys of your keyboard.

Spray every opening, pore, and vent in your computer frequently. Built-up dust can interfere with the operation of your computer.

CD-ROM drives and floppy drives that stop reading files usually have nothing wrong with them except dust. (Don't tilt the can when you're spraying air — if the can isn't upright, you won't get the power blast you need.)

I use canned air everywhere. It's the handiest cleaning tool I have in my house. I spray all the openings on my CD player, television set, radio, and cable box. It works great on the ridges that hold my storm windows and screens, too.

If you're a person who points to the screen when you show somebody a beautiful sentence you've just composed or a mind-blowing graphic you just created, you probably have fingerprints on your monitor. Fingerprints are oily and don't always disappear with a dry cloth. Office supply stores sell premoistened towelettes for cleaning monitors. You just pull one out and wipe the screen. (Remember to close the container's lid to keep the remaining towelettes moist. They're like the towelettes you use on infants when you change diapers, although I assume that the moistening agent is different and isn't so gentle on baby's bottom.)

If you want to use the bottle of window cleaner that you keep around the house, spray it on a cloth, not on the monitor; the monitor isn't sealed properly to avoid leaks. Then wipe the moistened cloth across the screen.

You can also use a cloth moistened with window cleaner on the keyboard and mouse (the other collection points for fingerprints).

Protecting Printers

You should perform a few maintenance chores regularly to make sure that your printed documents look terrific and your printers perform without errors:

✔ Don't overfill paper trays — doing so results in printer jams.

✔ If you have to clean up a printer jam, unplug the printer. Never yank on the jammed paper. Pull it steadily and gently.

✔ Always clean a laser printer when you change toner cartridges, following the directions that come with the cartridge.

✔ Dust is the printer's biggest enemy. Keep printers covered when they aren't in use.

✔ Don't put label sheets back into the printer for a second pass. If you only used a couple of labels on the sheet, throw away the sheet. The chemicals on the sheet can damage the internal mechanisms of the printer.

✔ Use paper that's compatible with your printer. (Check the documentation that came with your printer.)

✔ When you use heavy paper stock, labels, transparencies, or envelopes in a laser printer, open the back door to let the paper go through the printer in a straight path. That way, the stock doesn't have to bend around the rollers.

✔ Use the features in the software that came with your color inkjet printer to check the alignment of the color cartridge. (No alignment maintenance is required for monochrome cartridges — you simply replace the cartridges when they run out of ink or dry up.)

Besides protecting your printer, you also need to protect your computer from your printer, especially if you use a laser printer or a powerful color inkjet printer. These printers use a lot of power, and if they're on the same circuit as your computer, you're probably causing minor brownouts for the computer, which can harm your hard drive and your data.

Part VII
The Part of Tens

The 5th Wave   By Rich Tennant

NERD MOMS

Okay young man, it's time to wash your hands, brush your teeth, and back up the network files.

Awwww, Mom.

In this part . . .

The two chapters in this part offer some motivation for setting up a network. I give you 10 reasons why you'd be crazy to not set up a network, and I show you some nifty ways you can use your network more efficiently and amaze your friends.

Chapter 18

Ten Good Reasons to Set Up a Home PC Network

● ●

*O*kay, I know that you're interested in creating a network for your home computers — otherwise, you probably wouldn't have purchased this book. But perhaps you're having second thoughts about diving into this project (don't worry, it's easy). Or maybe you're a procrastinator, and nothing you plan to do is actually accomplished in a timely fashion. This chapter gives you plenty of reasons to set aside the excuses and set up your network — today.

Avoid Cyberspace Squabbles

I bet that if therapists did some research on family arguments, they'd create a special category for households that share one computer and one modem. When you have multiple family members who want to travel in cyberspace at the same time, you have arguments.

Until recently, Internet access was a one-at-a-time activity no matter how many computers were in the house. Even if you tried to avoid arguments by putting a modem in each computer and installing a second phone line, when the second person in the family tried to dial out, your Internet Service Provider responded with, "Sorry, your account is already in use."

Technology now permits multiple users working at separate computers to go online at the same time. There are only two rules for creating this environment: The computers must be connected by a network, and you must have software that supports simultaneous multiple-user Internet access. Luckily, you bought this book, which teaches you how to build a household network and provides the necessary software (WinGate) on the accompanying CD.

Save Time and Money by Sharing a Printer

There's nothing more annoying than having to save a file on a floppy disk, carry the floppy disk to a computer that has a printer, open the software, open the file in the software, print the file, close the software, take the floppy disk back to the first computer, and start the whole routine over again for the next document.

Wait — I take that back. There is something more annoying than that: buying a printer for every computer in the house.

A network makes printing easy, even if there's no printer attached to the computer you're using. Click the print button, and the network takes care of sending the document to the printer that's connected to another computer.

Before you tell me that you already have two printers, I'll tell you I know that's possible — lots of households with two computers have two printers. Think about the advantages of sharing the printers across the network, though. If one printer is *monochrome* (prints in black and grayscale) and the other printer is color, you can print to either printer from any computer. If both printers are color (or both printers are monochrome), you can load different paper types in each printer and then print on the appropriate printer. For example, you may want to put good bond paper or letterhead in one printer and plain paper in another. Or you could load large paper (legal size) in one printer and letter-size paper in another.

Collaborate on Document Files

Suppose that your son wants your help on a homework project. Or suppose that you want input from your spouse as you prepare your resume or write a letter of complaint to your local elected official.

If you don't have a network, you have to print the document, give the printout to your "editor" for feedback, read her handwritten comments, and then make the changes in your original document.

With a network, you can copy the file to another computer and ask another family member to suggest changes. After he makes the changes, you can bring the document back to your own computer and then use simple editing procedures to accept or reject the changes.

Share a CD-ROM Drive

Even if every computer in your household has a CD-ROM drive, there are real advantages to having a network that lets each computer access every CD-ROM drive. Put a game in the CD-ROM drive of the computer in the den and put a CD filled with graphics in another computer. Then just access the CD-ROM drive that holds the CD you need. It doesn't matter which computer the CD-ROM drive is attached to.

Start a Document on One PC; Finish It on Another

Last week you were working on the computer in the den, creating the greatest novel ever written (or maybe just updating the family budget). Tonight you want to continue your work, but your daughter is using that computer and can't be interrupted because she's working on a lengthy book report that's due tomorrow.

If you have a network, you don't need to ask, "Excuse me — can you stop what you're doing for a moment and copy a file to a floppy disk?" (A good reason to avoid asking that question is the fact that kids have an incredible ability to rattle off an answer that consists of telling you why the interruption is an imposition, how you're interrupting a chain of thought, how you're interfering with a deadline, how you don't understand how mean the teacher can be if assignments are handed in late, and how if she fails this course it's your fault.)

After you finish reminding her that you've reminded her for the past three nights that this report was coming due (which is an exercise in futility, trust me), mosey over to the computer in the bedroom. You won't interrupt your daughter by locating your file on the den computer, moving it over to the bedroom computer, and working on it.

What Else Can You Do with All of that Coaxial Cable You Stole from Work?

You can't wrap presents with it — it's too thick. Stretch it between two trees in the backyard and use it as a clothesline. Give it to the kids to use as a jump rope, but remove the connectors first as a safety measure. If enough cable is left after you tie tree seedlings to sticks and rig up a festive maypole, why not set up a home PC network, just for the fun of it? That will give you a good reason to read this book instead of using it as a doorstop, too.

Play Games across the Network

In my house, we play Hearts across the network for several reasons:

- ✔ We don't have to search the house for a deck of cards.
- ✔ We don't have to clean off the kitchen table to make room for playing cards.
- ✔ We don't argue about whose turn it is to keep score.
- ✔ We don't have to search for a pencil and paper to keep score.
- ✔ We don't argue about the score because computers don't make math errors.
- ✔ We don't have to argue about who should put the cards away.

(Because just about any reason is a good reason to play games, I put a bunch of network games — including Hearts — on the CD that comes with this book.)

Simplify File Backups

Everybody knows that backing up computer files is important. Everybody knows that if you don't back up your important files regularly, you'll regret it. Everybody knows that having a recent backup is like having insurance on your home and its contents, and you'd be crazy not to have it.

But everybody fails to back up.

Home users are the worst offenders — they don't back up regularly. In fact, they back up so irregularly that their backed-up documents are no longer important.

The truth is, people inadvertently delete important files, hard drives develop bad spots just where important files are stored, hard drives die, computers die, and all sorts of other horrible things happen.

A network makes backing up easier, and — more importantly — gives you a way to make backing up a family chore. You can split the task, assigning individuals responsibility for certain days. (If anyone complains, make him take out the trash for the next month.)

With a network, you can back up every household member's documents to one computer and then back up that computer using a Zip, Jaz, or tape drive.

Amaze Your Friends with Your Networking Know-How

Imagine going to dinner parties and throwing around terms like Interrupt Request Levels, 10BaseT, coax, data packet throughput, and mapping drives.

People will think you're a geek and will have new respect for your brain. They'll look at you and think, "Wow, she's a person on the cutting edge of technology."

Of course, the downside is that whenever those people have computer questions, they'll ask you because they'll think you're an expert. (That happens to me all the time, especially at parties.)

When your friends with multiple computers (but no network) complain about all the fighting in their households as their kids battle for Internet access, you can say, "We don't have those arguments in our house." Everyone will think that you have unbelievable parenting skills.

Start a Whole New Career

Do you have any idea how many two-computer households there are? Lots and lots. That's why I wrote this book. Find out who didn't buy this book and offer to install home networks for those people. Develop a business installing home networks now that you know how.

You can start it as a part-time endeavor, but home networks make so much sense that you'll soon have a booming business.

If you don't want to be bothered with constant support calls and questions after you install the networks, buy extra copies of this book and give them to your customers after you receive your payment.

Chapter 19

(Almost) Ten Cool Ways to Use One Computer as a Server

• •

*1*n a corporate environment, some computers are set up to act as servers. The *servers* provide all kinds of services for the users on the network. This is an efficient way to run a large network because the files, printing services, logon services, and other functions are easier to control.

For example, at work you may have a server for your e-mail program, a server for the company accounting software, and a server that makes sure that your logon password is correct.

In a home network of only two or three computers, keeping track of users, files, and software is pretty simple — a little too basic to support the need for a server.

However, some of the specific functions that servers provide in a corporate setting are just as handy on a home network, so you may want to extend those functions to all the users in the household.

You don't have to set up real servers or configure a complicated network environment to take advantage of these functions. You just need to set up the stuff that seems interesting and useful for your own home network. This chapter explains some quasi-server features that are worthwhile to people who run small networks. Some or all of them may be useful at your house.

Because the computer you designate as a server isn't technically fulfilling the role of a true server, one of my clients calls his designated server a *functional server*. I think that's a fine description, so I'm just going to steal the terminology from him.

In this chapter, I suggest nine ways to use a functional server to get the most out of your network. (I bet that because this is a Part of Tens chapter, you were expecting me to list ten functional server roles here, weren't you? I decided to give you nine just to see whether you're paying attention.)

No matter which role or roles you choose for your functional server, you must back up this computer regularly (see Chapter 15 for help creating a backup plan). You have too much to lose if you don't.

Selecting the server

When choosing a computer to act as the functional server, think about the functions that you want to assign to the server. If both, or all, of the computers on your network have similar power, throw a dart to make the decision.

If, on the other hand, your computers differ when it comes to features and power, consider the following characteristics of each computer when making your decision:

Computer speed: The speed of the computer's main chip (measured in MHz) isn't the primary factor. Don't select a computer as a functional server because it has a faster chip. The speed of the computer that's doing the work is the speed at which the work is done. If you're working at a slower computer and you access files from a remote computer that's faster, you aren't going to get your work done at the speed of the remote computer. Sorry, but the computer you're using is doing all the work.

In addition, the speed at which information transmits over network cable does have an upper limit. That limit usually acts as an equalizer between computers of unequal speeds.

One place where speed counts is the hard drive. Manufacturers rate hard drives for the speed at which they access data — known as the *access rate.* Check the documentation that came with your computers for information about the access rates of the hard drives.

The reason that access rate counts is that most of the work you're going to perform with the functional server involves files. When the server is fetching files and saving files, the speed of the hard drive counts.

Memory: Now, here's a really important factor. The amount of random-access memory (RAM) is critical, especially for a home network. When remote users access the functional computer within your home, they're joining the user who's sitting in front of that computer. (In a corporate environment, on the other hand, the server is only used for administrative tasks or maintenance.) Having two users accessing folders and files on a single computer simultaneously is serious multitasking!

Hard-drive space: You're likely to use your functional server to store files that all the users on the network want to use. In that case, the size of the hard drive makes a difference.

Peripherals: If you're planning to use your server for functions that involve peripherals, the available peripherals become the criteria to use to make the decision. For example, if the primary function you require is backing up, the computer with a backup tape drive or a removable drive is the best choice for your functional server.

Of course, if your peripheral device is external (for example, attached to the parallel port), you can move the device to the computer with the RAM and storage space.

Set Up a Household Message Center

One nifty trick that you can perform if you have a functional server is to create a household message center. An electronic communications hub is more reliable than hand-scrawled notes left on the blackboard in the kitchen: You're less likely to run out of room, and even more importantly, you don't have to decipher handwriting.

You can create a shared folder named *messages* and use it to hold all the messages. However, the file names for the messages must indicate both the recipient and the subject matter. For example, Sandra Please Call Mark is a good candidate for a filename that contains a message telling Sandra when Mark called, what he said, and so on. If you just use the recipient's name for the file name — in this example, Sandra — the second message to Sandra would overwrite the first one. (Remember, if you save a file with a file name that already exists, Windows asks if you want to replace the original file with the new one.)

You can create a folder for each member of the household, making it less of a pain to name files. Separate folders make life easier for everybody if you share those folders so that they show up in Windows Explorer and Network Neighborhood without having to expand other folders. (Chapter 9 explains how to create shared folders.)

If everyone in the household uses the same word processor application, you can use it for writing messages. If only a couple of people are comfortable with word processors, use Notepad instead.

Establish Graphics Headquarters

A lot of software comes with graphics that you can use to enhance your documents. Word processors, desktop publishers, and presentation software all have goo-gobs of clip art, pictures, cartoons, and other graphics. Because software installation often skips these files, you have to rely on the software CD when you want to put a graphic in a document.

If you don't always work at the same computer, using the CD may present a problem. If you're like me, no matter which computer you're using, the CD you need is always near another computer, and one of the kids' game CDs is in the computer you're working on. Even though running upstairs to fetch the CD does provide healthy exercise, the required trip is annoying. Besides, roller blading or swimming is more fun.

If one of the computers on your network has a great deal of hard-drive space, use that computer as a functional server to hold all the graphics files that remain on the software CD.

You can't just copy the files to the functional server after you install the software because the software continues to look at the CD-ROM drive for the files. Use the original software CD and re-run the setup program. This time, choose the option to copy the graphics files so that the software knows where they are when you need them. Then create a shared resource for the folder that holds the graphics files.

When you work at the other computer, you can map a drive letter to the folder on the functional server that has the graphics. That means you can tell your computer that a new drive exists. (Your computer already has drives A and C and perhaps more drives if you have a CD-ROM or a Zip drive.) The new drive isn't really a physical drive — it's a folder on another computer. Read Chapter 11 to find out how to perform this nifty trick.

Put Together an Archive Library

As you use software, the number of documents you amass becomes large, or perhaps enormous. Even if you have plenty of disk space, scrolling through all those files when you want to find a file is time-consuming.

Lots of the files you create can, and should, be deleted. You know which files they are, and you know there's no reason to keep them. We're all lazy about cleaning out useless documents that we'll never need again.

However, you keep lots of files because you want to, or you feel a compelling reason to hang on to the information they contain. Even if you don't expect to ever edit or update a certain file, you may have a perfectly sound reason you want to keep that file. Letters to government agencies and letters involved with legal issues are prime examples. If you print each important document and file it, you still may need to produce another copy somewhere down the road (and you probably don't have a copy machine).

Use your functional server to archive documents that are important. You can create a master folder for your archive library and then create subfolders for each archive category. Make sure that you back up this folder when you back up your functional server.

Set Up Budget Central

Setting up a budget center on a home network is a clever idea, especially for finance-conscious families. A budget center not only gives you a way to see the latest and greatest version of the household budget, but it also helps kids learn to manage their own money.

You can prepare your budgets using several types of software. Most word processors have a feature called Tables that you can use to create lists and columns of numbers, and the software adds up those numbers for you. Spreadsheet programs are designed for budget-type documents.

Some bookkeeping software programs provide budget modules or budget features, and the budget files are independent of the other data files. You may not be able to separate the budget file from the other data files, but you can usually discover a way to export the budget, which enables you to maintain copies of each year's budget. (Some bookkeeping software replaces the previous budget year with the current budget year.) You can discover a lot about where your money goes by keeping budgets year after year.

After you put the budget in your budget center folder, you can copy it and play "what if" games, which means you change figures to see the results. What if you put $100 a month into a mutual fund and reduce other budget categories to make up for that expenditure? You figure out quickly whether the investment is possible.

The real budget — the one that you use to run the household — must have a column in which you can enter the actual numbers. Be sure to password-protect that document so that only authorized family members (usually parents) can use it. Your software program has a way to save a file with a password (check the Help files).

You can also create other specialized budgets, such as a savings plan for a vacation, a new car, or college tuition. Budget regular contributions and then update the document each time you make a deposit.

The budget center is also the place to track your investments. And, if you track investments online, you can save financial updates that you download from the Internet in your budget center folder.

You can also use your budget center as an educational tool. Kids can explore the software and discover how to budget their dollars and cents. Show the kids how to password-protect their documents so that they can keep their stuff private. Of course, when it comes to your offspring's trust funds, investment funds, and the millions they make by starting computer companies in the garage, you'll probably want access to the files.

Collaborate on Documents

You can set up a shared folder on a functional server to hold collaborative documents (documents that have contributions from multiple users). Creating a collaborative document is not the same thing as giving someone a document and asking that person to contribute comments and changes. In that case, if you make your own adjustments to the document on your computer while the other person is editing a copy of it on another computer, you must later manually input your changes in your editor's copy of the document. Your edits don't magically appear in the copy that your editor is working with.

By comparison, a centrally located collaborative document is the only existing copy of that document. Each user's changes automatically appear in the document, creating a single, collective document.

Collaborative documents are appropriate for lots of occasions. When you have to write a letter of complaint to the tax examiner or you need to update your resume, you can invite input from other household members. Think of the open forum as a kind of insurance, especially against the possibility of making a fool of yourself.

On a less serious scale, you can set up the family budget as a collaborative spreadsheet, welcoming each member to enter his or her own income and expense figures. A letter from the whole family to relatives and friends is another good candidate for a collaborative document.

Create a shared folder for collaborative documents on the functional server, and when you use software, open and save all your collaborative documents in that folder. See Chapter 10 to find out all about opening documents on remote computers when you're using software.

Most Windows software has a feature that enables you to see changes, additions, and deletions to a document on a user-by-user basis. A different color, automatically assigned to each user, makes it easy to identify who made which changes.

Download Internet Files to One Location

When you download files from the Internet, putting everything in one location is a good idea, and a shared folder on a functional server can fulfill this role. Two good reasons to set up a central repository for downloaded files are:

✔ You can make sure that virus-checking software is set up and avoid problems for other computers on the network.

✔ The downloaded files are available to any user in the household.

When you download a file, a Save dialog box opens because you're actually saving the file on your local drive. Downloading requires saving. That dialog box usually has default selections for the folder that accepts the downloaded file, as well as the file name. Use the tools in the Save dialog box to change the destination folder to the downloaded files folder on your functional server. (Don't change the filename.) Then run your virus-checking software on the downloaded file.

Centralize Software Documents

If one of your computers is bigger, better, stronger, and altogether nicer than the other computers on your network, why not use it as the repository for everybody's documents? This decision has a number of advantages, including the following:

✔ You don't have to worry about disk space on your other, weaker, smaller, less modern computers.

✔ No matter which computer anyone uses, you have no problem getting to your documents.

✔ Because all the documents are on one computer, backing up that computer takes care of everyone's documents.

Set up a shared folder for each user in the household. If password protection is preferred, each person can set up his or her own shared folder (see Chapter 9 for details about the process).

Run Software from a Server

If your functional server is a lot bigger and stronger than the other computers on your network, you may want to run your software from the server.

You can install and configure most software to run from a server. Some software programs install a small number of files on the user computers, in addition to the software files that install on the server. Each user launches the software from the server.

Follow the instructions in the software documentation to install the program as a network application.

Create a Backup Server

Here's some wisdom from my personal experience: You'll be sorry if you don't back up regularly — in fact, you should back up every day. As sad as it seems, your computer, or some important part of your computer (like the hard drive) will die. Computers don't last forever.

Here's some more wisdom from my experience: You know that I'm right, but you won't do regular backups if they're time-consuming or require any real effort.

In fact, statistics show that even if the backup process is an extremely easy task, you're still not likely to back up your documents on a regular basis. Statistics also indicate that you're bound to lose important data as a result of the two important facts I've stated: Computers die, and users don't back up regularly.

However, as a compulsive optimist, I suggest a way to make backing up easier, in the hope that you may actually do it.

Here's the plan: You select one computer as a backup server, everyone copies his data files to the server, and then you back up the files on the server. Then you only have to perform a backup procedure on one computer, and everyone's documents are backed up. This plan only works if the machine you select as the backup server has a tape backup system or a removable drive that can accept the backup (otherwise, you'd need a whole lot of floppy disks and you'd have to spend hours sitting in front of the computer putting the disks into the drive as each disk filled up).

Create a separate shared folder on the functional server for each user. You don't need to create subfolders, even if all the users are putting documents into subfolders on their own machines. Users can copy their documents to the functional server in a way that creates subfolders automatically.

On the user side, you can easily copy your documents to the functional server for backup and duplicate any existing subfolders automatically. Here are some tips for setting up your computer to back up to a server:

- ✔ On your own computer, keep all your documents in one folder. (Use the My Documents folder that Windows creates for you automatically.)

- ✔ If you want to separate your documents by software type or by categories, create subfolders in the My Documents folder to accomplish that task.

Every day, open Windows Explorer and select your My Documents folder. Then press Ctrl+A to select everything in the folder (including the subfolders). Right-click on any object in the right pane and choose Copy from the shortcut menu that appears.

Scroll down the left Explorer pane to find the Network Neighborhood icon. Expand the Network Neighborhood listing to find your backup folder on the server. Right-click your backup folder and choose Paste from the shortcut menu that appears.

Your My Documents folder and any subfolders copy to your backup folder on the server. With every subsequent copy, you see a message announcing that some of the files already exist in the target folder, and asking whether you want to copy existing files anyway. Select the option to copy everything.

After every user performs this easy task, all you have to worry about is backing up the server. Use whatever backup scheme you prefer, employing a backup tape system or a large removable drive. Read Chapter 15 to check out all the different ways to back up a computer.

Part VIII
Appendixes

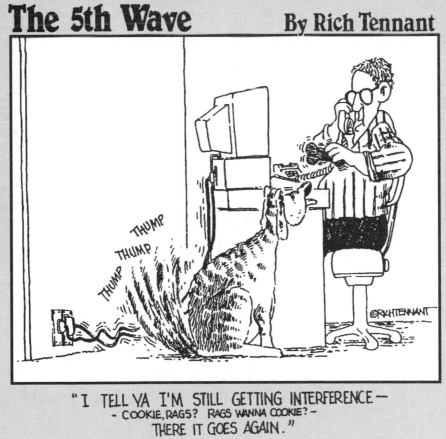

The 5th Wave   By Rich Tennant

"I TELL YA I'M STILL GETTING INTERFERENCE—
— COOKIE, RAGS? RAGS WANNA COOKIE? —
THERE IT GOES AGAIN."

In this part . . .

The first appendix in this part tells you about some networking techniques that I couldn't fit elsewhere in the book — stuff like adding a laptop computer or a Mac to your home PC network or networking without cables and wires. The second appendix tells you all about the cool stuff you'll find on the CD stuck inside the back cover of this book.

Appendix A
Other Networking Techniques

● ●

*Y*ou may need to use some additional networking schemes in order to connect all the computers in your household. For example, you may want to transfer files between your Windows PC and a Macintosh. Or you may find the notion of running network cable through your house daunting and would like an alternative.

In this appendix, I explain how to tackle these networking challenges and provide suggestions for where you can look for more information.

Networking with Windows NT 4.0

I don't specifically cover networking with Windows NT 4.0 in this book because it's not common practice to run this operating system at home. Still, for one reason or another, you may run Windows NT 4.0 on your home computer. (For example, some people use this operating system at home so that they can get familiar with Windows NT when employers deploy this corporate operating system.)

If you do run Windows NT 4.0, don't feel left out as you read this book. You can still do everything I discuss: You can participate in a home network; share printers, folders, and files; and access any computer you see in the Network Neighborhood window.

Some of the steps you follow to accomplish the tasks explained in this book may be slightly different if you're using Windows NT 4.0 rather than Windows 98 or Windows 95, but the Help files and dialog boxes in your operating system should clear up any confusion.

You can find out more about networking with Windows NT 4.0 in *Windows NT 4.0 Connectivity Guide,* written by Richard Grace and published by IDG Books Worldwide.

Adding a Mac to the Network

If you have a Mac in addition to a PC (or multiple PCs), you can add the Mac to your home network with the help of some special software.

Adding a Mac to your home PC network isn't as simple as adding a Mac to a NetWare network (a network environment that you may have at work), but it's not brain surgery either. Don't be daunted by the extra work.

Choosing Mac-enabling software

The people I know who have accomplished the feat of adding a Mac to a small network without suffering a nervous breakdown all used the same software program to do so. You may find other programs out there (Dave, from Thursby Systems, is quite popular — see the company's Web site at www.thursby.com), but I took my colleagues' advice and used PC MACLAN from Miramar Systems. For more information about PC MACLAN, point your browser to www.miramarsys.com, where you can also download a demo version of the software.

Installing Mac-enabling software

Here's the surprise — you install the software that enables you to add Macs to your network on the *PC,* not on the Mac (unless you're using Dave, discussed in the previous section — that program installs on the Mac). That's because Macs come from the factory in network-ready condition; they're "network eager."

Macs automatically talk to PCs across a network as soon as a PC can communicate with a Mac, and the PC needs software to do this. (PCs aren't built with networking capabilities installed and configured.)

The installation procedure should be the same for most software that provides Mac services for a network, so even if you're not using the same software I use, your first step should probably be to insert the software CD in the PC's CD-ROM drive. The setup program should automatically launch.

If the CD doesn't automatically launch the setup program, follow these steps to install the software:

1. **Double-click the My Computer icon.**

   The My Computer window opens, showing all the drives on your computer.

2. **Right-click the icon for the CD and choose Explore from the shortcut menu that appears.**

   The contents of the CD appear.

3. **Double-click on the file named setup.exe.**

   The setup program starts.

4. **Follow the setup program's instructions to install the software.**

   The steps are easy; you don't have to know all the technical stuff because the setup procedure handles all that automatically.

   The setup program installs all the files, protocols, and services that your PC needs to communicate with a Mac over the network. When the installation is completed, you must restart your computer.

If you download the demo version of the software, follow these steps to install it:

1. **Uncompress the demo file.**

   Follow the manufacturer's directions, which should include choosing a folder (or accepting the suggested folder) to unpack all the software files into one location. You can usually find the directions in a file called readme.txt or on the Web page that you downloaded the program from.

2. **Click setup.exe to start the setup procedure.**

   Check the manufacturer's instructions to find out the name of the setup file if you can't find setup.exe.

The setup procedure for downloaded demo software works the same way as the procedure for setting up software from a CD. However, you must purchase a real copy of the software within a stated amount of time (usually thirty days). The demo software stops working after that time period elapses.

Preparing the Mac to be networked

You need to follow a couple of easy steps to prepare your Mac to join your home network. You have to physically connect the Mac to the network, give the Mac a name, and enable sharing. I explain these tasks in the following sections.

Connecting the Mac to the network

Connect the Mac to the network by inserting the network cable in the Mac network port, which is built into the machine.

That's it! Move on to the next task.

Naming the Mac and turning on sharing

Your home network finds the computers on the network by name, so each computer must have a unique name. Naming a Mac is easy, and the dialog box that you use also includes the option for enabling the sharing of the files on the Mac. Name the Mac and set up file sharing by following these steps (commands that are different in Mac OS 8.5 are noted; otherwise, all these steps apply to Macs running OS 8.5 or earlier):

1. **Choose Apple Menu⇨Control Panels⇨Sharing Setup.**

   In Mac OS 8.5, choose Apple Menu⇨Control Panels⇨File Sharing.

   The Sharing Setup dialog box opens.

2. **Type your name in the Owner Name text box.**

3. **(Optional) Type a password in the Owner Password text box.**

4. **Type the Mac's network name in the Macintosh Name text box.**

   In Mac OS 8.5, type the Mac's network name in the Computer Name text box.

5. **Click Start in the File Sharing section of the dialog box to activate file sharing.**

   If you see a Stop button in the File Sharing section of the dialog box instead of a Start button, file sharing is already activated. Don't click Stop; you want to keep file sharing active.

6. **Close the Sharing Setup control panel.**

   In Mac OS 8.5, close the File Sharing control panel.

Sharing folders

After you turn on file sharing for your Mac, you must specifically share folders. (This is the same procedure you must go through on a PC.) Follow these steps to share a folder on a Mac:

1. **Click on the folder that you want to share.**

2. **Choose File⇨Sharing.**

   In Mac OS 8.5, choose File⇨GetInfo⇨Sharing.

   The folder dialog box appears.

3. **Select Share This Item and Its Contents.**

That's all you have to do to set up the Mac side of your network. Your Mac and your PCs are now network partners.

Adding a Laptop to the Network

If you have a laptop computer, you can add it to your home network. Almost everything about a laptop computer on a network is the same as a standard desktop PC on a network, except that the network interface card (NIC) is different.

Choosing a PCMCIA card

Laptop NICs are called PCMCIA cards or PC cards. (PCMCIA stands for Personal Computer Memory Card International Association.) You must purchase a PCMCIA card that matches the type of cable you're using on your network, either 10BascT or coax. Some PCMCIA cards are dual purpose and have both connector types available. Of course, if you're networking with telephone lines (see Chapters 4 and 5), look for a PCMCIA card that supports telephone cable.

You can also get external network adapters for laptops that connect to the parallel port of the laptop.

Installing a PCMCIA card

A PCMCIA card is about the size of a credit card. One end of the card has a device that provides a connection for the cable, and the other end has a row of holes. An arrow indicates which way to plug the PCMCIA card into the PCMCIA slot so that the holes meet the pins inside the slot.

Attach the cable to the external end of the PCMCIA card — the cable has a network connector at the other end.

When you turn on your laptop, Plug and Play should find the PCMCIA network adapter and install it automatically.

If Plug and Play fails to detect your laptop adapter, double-click the Control Panel icon to open the Control Panel, and make sure that PCMCIA services are installed. (If they are installed, a PCMCIA icon appears in the Control Panel.) If the services aren't installed, follow the laptop manufacturer's instructions to make your PCMCIA slot active.

If Plug and Play still fails to detect the adapter, you can double-click the Network icon in the Control Panel and install the adapter manually, using the method described in Chapter 3.

Networking with Electrical Lines

You can send data from one computer to another over the electrical wires in your home. The advantage to using electrical wires for networking is that you don't need to buy network interface cards, hubs, or cable. And you don't need to run cable through your house or open your computer to install the network interface cards, either.

The disadvantage is that the transfer of data between computers is much slower than the speed available with traditional network cables. Transferring large files, such as graphics, is agonizingly slow. However, if the transfer of files isn't mission critical and you don't mind waiting, you may want to opt for this inexpensive, easy-to-install network. Perhaps you always have some household chore to do, and you could complete it while waiting. And this networking scheme is still faster than a modem — you can transfer files between computers faster than you can download files from the Internet.

Several companies offer kits for networking over existing electrical wires, and you can check out the products at any computer supply store or large office supply store. The kit that I tested was configured for two PCs and a printer. The kit includes three adapters, each of which plugs into an electrical outlet. Two of the adapters are for PCs; the third is for a printer. The bottom of each adapter has a parallel port, and you connect the adapter to the PC (or the printer) with parallel cable. You can purchase additional adapters for additional computers (or printers).

The necessary software comes with the kit and works with Windows 98 and Windows 95. Installing the software provides the drivers that permit communication via the adapters.

I did have one mysterious misadventure during my use of this networking scheme. Everything worked perfectly well — albeit slowly — when both computers were in the same room. However, when I moved one of the computers to another room on a different floor, the network stopped working. When I moved the computer on the other floor to a different room on that floor (and therefore to a different electrical outlet), the network came back to life. Go figure.

The specifications say that the converter is shielded against interference, yet one outlet worked properly and another didn't. The outlet that caused the problem was working. (I plugged in a lamp to make sure.) I have no explanation for the problem.

Another issue with using electrical lines for networking is security. The software that comes with some of the kits includes features that secure your system. Without it, a neighbor who buys the same kit that you have can probably get into your computer files. If you're both getting electricity from the same transformer, you're really on the same network.

Networking without Wires

Your computers can communicate in a network environment without using any wires — that means no network cable, electrical wires, or telephone wires.

Wireless networking is an emerging technology, and you may be interested in participating if you can find a method that works for your household. You have two wireless technologies to choose from: Radio Frequency (RF) and Infrared (IR). Essentially, the two technologies operate the same way; they just have different data transmission methods. They both use electromagnetic airwaves to send data from one point to another without any physical connection between the two points. Here are the differences:

- **RF:** Data is transferred when one computer sends out a signal at a certain frequency. The receiving computer must be looking for that frequency.
- **IR:** One computer sends data via a beam of light, which is received by the other computer.

Both technologies require hardware on both computers in order to send and receive data. RF hardware includes transmitters and receivers; IR hardware includes IR ports. All this hardware is quite expensive when compared to standard network hardware, but if your goal is to be a cutting-edge computer geek, the cost may not matter to you.

At the moment, the technology is only useful if you have two computers that are in close proximity. In most cases, the distance between the computers can't exceed 100 feet.

RF signals should be able to travel through your household walls (unless you've built your house as a bunker or bomb shelter). IR signals can't penetrate any obstacles; the computers have to "see" each other.

Wireless technology is being used in businesses today as an add-on to standard network cabling. For example, it connects laptop computers to a network when a mobile user visits the main office. I've also seen wireless technology used with hand-held computers in hospitals, so that a doctor who's making rounds can view a lab report as soon as it's on the computer at the nurses' station.

If the concept interests you (even if you're not planning to use it for your home network), hold onto your hat; it's getting even more fascinating. A consortium of hardware companies has formed to make RF technology even more powerful.

The new technology, called Bluetooth, provides instant access as soon as a device realizes that an electromagnetic wave is available. No user action is required. A hand-held computer that's passing a server that holds e-mail messages will receive the messages. Look for mobile phones with Bluetooth technology any time now.

Appendix B

About the CD

● ●

*I*f you turn to the inside back cover of this book, you'll find a CD packed with a bunch of software goodies that can make your home network more efficient — and even more fun to use. This appendix tells you what programs are on the CD and explains how to install them. Enjoy!

System Requirements

Make sure that your computer meets the minimum system requirements listed below. If your computer doesn't match up to most of these requirements, you may have problems using the contents of the CD.

- ✔ A PC with a 486 or faster processor.
- ✔ Microsoft Windows 95 or Windows 98.
- ✔ At least 16MB of total RAM installed on your computer. For best performance, I recommend that Windows 98-equipped PCs have at least 32MB of RAM installed.
- ✔ At least 80MB of hard-drive space available to install all the software from this CD. (You need less space if you don't install every program.)
- ✔ A CD-ROM drive — double-speed (2x) or faster.
- ✔ A sound card.
- ✔ A monitor capable of displaying at least 256 colors or grayscale.
- ✔ A modem with a speed of at least 14,400 bps.

If you need more information on the basics, check out *PCs For Dummies,* 6th Edition, by Dan Gookin; *Windows 95 For Dummies,* 2nd Edition, by Andy Rathbone; or *Windows 98 For Dummies* by Andy Rathbone (all published by IDG Books Worldwide, Inc.).

Installing Programs from the CD

To install the items from the CD to your hard drive, follow these steps.

1. **Insert the CD in your computer's CD-ROM drive.**

2. **Choose Start⇨Run.**

3. **In the dialog box that appears, type** D:\SETUP.EXE.

   Replace *D* with the proper drive letter if your CD-ROM drive uses a different letter. (If you don't know the letter, see how your CD-ROM drive is listed in the My Computer window in Windows 95 or Windows 98.)

4. **Click OK.**

   A License Agreement window appears.

5. **Read through the license agreement, nod your head, and then click the Agree button if you want to use the CD — after you click Agree, you'll never be bothered by the License Agreement window again.**

   The CD interface Welcome screen appears.

   The interface is a little program that shows you what's on the CD and coordinates installing the programs and running the demos. The interface basically enables you to click a button or two to make things happen.

6. **Click anywhere on the Welcome screen to enter the interface.**

   Now you're getting to the action. This next screen lists categories for the software on the CD.

7. **To view the items within a category, just click the category's name.**

   A list of programs in the category appears.

8. **For more information about a program, click the program's name.**

   Be sure to read the information that appears. Sometimes a program has its own system requirements or requires you to do a few tricks on your computer before you can install or run the program, and this screen tells you what you need to do, if anything is necessary.

9. **If you don't want to install the program, click the Go Back button to return to the previous screen.**

   You can always return to the previous screen by clicking the Go Back button. This feature enables you to browse the different categories and products and decide what you want to install.

10. **To install a program, click the appropriate Install button.**

    The CD interface drops to the background while the CD installs the program you chose.

11. **To install additional programs, repeat Steps 7 through 10.**

12. **After you finish installing programs, click the Quit button to close the interface.**

    You can eject the CD now. Carefully place it back in the plastic jacket of the book for safekeeping.

What You'll Find

Each of the programs on the CD falls into one of the following categories: freeware, shareware, or evaluation (also called trial version or demo version).

Freeware is exactly what it sounds like. It's yours. It's free. Enjoy!

Shareware is software that you use under an honor system. If you try it and like it, you should pay for it. The software contains information about the amount required and the address to which you send your money. Most shareware software is less expensive than commercially distributed software, so it makes sense to support shareware developers by being honest and paying them for software that you continue to use.

Evaluation copies of software, also called *trial versions,* or *demo versions,* are specially programmed versions of commercial software. The special programming sometimes means that the software works fine for a period of time, then it stops working. Or, the special programming could mean that some features of the commercial version are missing from this CD version. In either case, if you like the software, you can find information on the CD about purchasing it.

Here's a summary of the software on this CD, arranged by category:

Games

Easy Bridge, from Steven Han

```
www.thegrid.net/shan/EasyBridge.htm
```

For Windows 95/98, freeware. Easy Bridge, awarded five stars by the ZD Software Library, introduces and teaches the game of bridge. You can play whenever you want to, without worrying about finding three other players. It contains instructions and playing tips that will have you playing like a pro in no time. You can save interesting games and go back and replay them and even print out interesting hands (take them with you when you play bridge with human beings so you can analyze the play).

Hi-Lo '95 3.01, from Green Gator Software

```
www.woohoo.com/members/greengator
```

For Windows 95/98, freeware. Do you have fond memories of the TV game show *Card Sharks?* Hi-Lo '95 lets you relive the excitement — without any commercial breaks or disappointing parting gifts.

Minute Math 3.1, from Green Gator Software

```
www.woohoo.com/members/greengator
```

For Windows 95/98, freeware. Two friendly alligators offer encouraging words as you test your math skills with this flash-card style program. Choose addition, subtraction, multiplication, and/or division problems; a time limit for answering questions; and a number range to test. (Young children can start with the 0-5 number range and basic addition or subtraction problems; older students will be challenged by the 0-20 number range and all four types of problems.) As you work, the gators keep a running total of your correct answers, wrong answers, percentage correct, and your grade. After you're done with a round, print out a record of all the problems you answered to see which skills need extra practice — or to share your impressive score with others.

MVP Hearts, from MVP Software

```
www.mvpsoft.com
```

For Windows 95/98, shareware. Here's a chance to play Hearts without finding a deck of cards or inviting people into your home (where you'd probably have to feed them or at least offer them something to drink). You can play other MVP Hearts participants across your network, or over the Internet.

Handy utilities

Acrobat Reader, from Adobe Systems

www.adobe.com

For Windows 95/98, freeware. Acrobat Reader is a free program that lets you view and print Portable Document Format (PDF) files. The PDF format is used by many programs you find on the Internet for storing documentation because it supports the use of such stylish elements as assorted fonts and colorful graphics. (For example, Eudora Light — also found on this CD — includes a manual in PDF format.)

Address Organizer, from PrimaSoft

www.primasoft.com

For Windows 95/98, shareware. This is an address book with lots of extra features. Besides the usual name and address information you need for friends, relatives, and business contacts, you can create your own categories and even store pictures. This organizer looks like a notebook with alphabetic tabs, so it's easy to get to the name you need quickly.

CleanSweep Deluxe, from Quarterdeck

www.qdeck.com

For Windows 95/98, trial version. CleanSweep is one of the leading disk cleanup programs available today. It's easy to use, fast, and efficient when you want to uninstall software. CleanSweep cleans up extraneous files you don't need anymore, after you've removed software with the standard Windows uninstall program. It also cleans out all those temporary Internet files that land on your hard drive while you're visiting Web sites. This software has won many awards for its speed and safety (it doesn't accidentally delete files you do need).

Drag And File, from Canyon Software

www.canyonsw.com

For Windows 95/98, evaluation. This handy utility provides all sorts of features you wish for when you use Windows Explorer. It works like Windows Explorer, but it has lots of useful enhancements. You can customize the way you want to be asked to confirm actions (like deleting files); you can look at two drives side-by-side at the same time; and you can compare the contents of folders. Also included is a file compression feature that lets you compress individual files so they're smaller or pack multiple files into one file. The compression makes sending files over the Internet faster and also makes it easier to archive old files to floppy disk.

FreeFive 2.0, from Green Gator Software

For Windows 95/98, freeware. With five different alarms to set, this program ensures that you'll never miss a meeting — or the rinse cycle — again. Choose from five attention-getting alarm sounds ("Neener" and "Woohoo" are particularly fun). If you're the sort of person who likes to watch the clock, you can set the alarm so that the running clock sits on top of your Windows Desktop, no matter what program you're using at the time.

Norton Utilities 3.0, from Symantec

```
www.symantec.com
```

For Windows 95/98, evaluation. Norton Utilities is a suite of programs that keep your Windows system running smoothly. If a program freezes and locks up your computer, Norton Utilities lets you thaw out the offending program without having to shut off the computer. A system doctor keeps an eye on what's happening on your computer, then helps you analyze and solve any problems. There are also utilities for making sure your shortcuts point to the right files, and your software has all the behind-the-scenes Windows files it needs.

NovaBack+ and NovaDisk+, from NovaStor

```
www.novastor.com
```

For Windows 95/98, evaluation. Back up your files and check for virus infection at the same time. You can back up to tape, removable disks (Zip, Jaz, et al), or floppy disks. If you have a disaster, the restore function helps you boot your computer in addition to copying back the files you backed up.

Three versions of this program are on the CD, for different types of backup storage media. Whether you back up to another hard drive (NovaDisk+) or to a tape drive, there's a version for you.

ThunderBYTE Anti-Virus, from Authentex

```
www.authentex.com/antivirus
```

For Windows 95/98, demo. ThunderBYTE finds and eliminates computer viruses. It even catches weird files that may be virus-infected, even if the virus is so new it hasn't yet been identified. The program comes with instructions for getting the latest virus lists and fixes.

WinZip 7.0, from Nico Mak Computing

```
www.winzip.com
```

For Windows 95/98, shareware. The CD includes the latest and greatest version of the most famous, most popular compression package available. Select a group of files and compress them into one file (makes it easier to exchange files across the Internet or on a floppy disk). Uncompress a zipped package of files you download from the Internet. The easy-to-use point and click technology makes it simple to use file compression technology.

Internet applications

Eudora Light, from Qualcomm

```
eudora.qualcomm.com/eudoralight
```

For Windows 95/98, freeware. A sophisticated and powerful e-mail software program, Eudora Light lets you dial into your Internet Service Provider and collect your mail. You can create folders and subfolders so you can sort your mail (both received mail and mail you've sent to others). You can also configure the software to open your ISP mailbox at regular intervals to collect your mail. Plenty of power for formatting messages with different fonts and font sizes. If you like Eudora Light, be sure to check out Eudora Pro, the even more sophisticated and powerful commercial version.

Net Nanny, from Net Nanny Software International

```
www.netnanny.com
```

For Windows 95/98, evaluation. Use Net Nanny to filter out offensive information from the Internet. You can prevent certain Web sites from presenting information on your screen or configure Net Nanny to avoid any content with words or phrases you find offensive. Another great feature is that you can turn off the ability to give your name, address, or e-mail address to any Web site that requests it. For households with kids, Net Nanny is invaluable.

SurfWatch, from SurfWatch Software

```
www.surfwatch.com
```

For Windows 95 only (Windows 98 version is planned), trial version. SurfWatch maintains a list of Web sites that you may find objectionable and blocks access to them. You can customize the type of Web site you want to avoid and report sites you think SurfWatch should add to the list. An easy-to-use method of keeping up to date on the site list is part of the software.

WinGate 2.1d, from Qbik New Zealand Ltd.

www.wingate.com

For Windows 95/98, evaluation. WinGate is an award winning modem-sharing application. Everyone on your network can be on the Internet at the same time. Easy to install and set up, the version on the CD is an evaluation copy that's good for 60 days.

If You Have Problems (Of the CD Kind)

I tried my best to compile programs that work on most computers with the minimum system requirements. Alas, your computer may differ, and some programs may not work properly for some reason.

The two likeliest problems are that you don't have enough memory (RAM) for the programs that you want to use, or you have other programs running that are interfering with the installation or running of a program. If you get error messages while using the CD or installing the software, try one or more of these methods and then run the software again:

- ✔ **Turn off any anti-virus software that you have on your computer.** Installers sometimes mimic virus activity and may make your computer incorrectly believe that it's being infected by a virus.

- ✔ **Close all running programs.** The more programs you're running, the less memory is available to other programs. Installers also typically update files and programs; if you keep other programs running, installation may not work properly.

- ✔ **In Windows, close the CD interface and run demos or installations directly from Windows Explorer.** The interface itself can tie up system memory or even conflict with certain kinds of interactive demos. Click the X in the upper-right corner of the CD interface window to close it. Then use Windows Explorer to browse the files on the CD and launch installers or demos.

- ✔ **Have your local computer store add more RAM to your computer.** This is, admittedly, a drastic and somewhat expensive step, but adding more memory can really help speed up your computer and enable more programs to run at the same time.

If you still have trouble installing the items from the CD, please call the IDG Books Worldwide Customer Service phone number: 800-762-2974 (outside the U.S.: 317-596-5430).

Glossary

10Base2: More commonly known as coaxial cable or thinnet cable. This network cable looks like a thin version of the cable that your cable television company uses. Today, 10Base2 isn't as popular as 10BaseT. Many companies are abandoning their 10Base2 systems in favor of 10BaseT. See *10BaseT.*

10BaseT: Also called twisted pair cable, 10BaseT is the current standard in network cable. 10BaseT looks like telephone cable, but it isn't the same thing — it's designed to transmit data rather than voice. The cable's wires are twisted along the length of cable — hence the name twisted pair cable. Two types of 10BaseT are available: unshielded twisted pair (UTP) and shielded twisted pair (STP). In STP, metal encases the cable wires, lessening the possibility of interference from other electrical devices, radar, radio waves, and so on. Using 10BaseT requires the purchase of a concentrator. Each network computer's NIC is connected to a length of 10BaseT, which is then connected to a concentrator. The concentrator disseminates data to the computers' NICs. See *concentrator, NIC, star topology.*

ADSL modem: ADSL stands for Asymmetric Digital Subscriber Line. This technology uses your standard telephone lines to produce incredibly fast connections to the Internet. You need a special ADSL modem, telephone lines that support the technology (coming soon to most cities), and an Internet host server that maintains ADSL modems that can connect to your modem.

AutoPlay: A feature in Windows that automatically searches for and launches a CD's AutoRun file when you insert a disc into a CD-ROM drive.

backup: A copy of the files on your computer that you can use to restore data in the event of a computer disaster.

banner: A form that accompanies each print job. The form displays the name of the user and prints ahead of the first page of each document so that multiple users of a printer can easily identify their documents. Also called a *separator page.*

barrel connector: A tube-shaped device that enables you to join two lengths of 10Base2 cable in a network. See *10Base2.*

BNC connector: A round device shaped like a fat ring, a BNC connector looks like a smaller version of the connector at each end of your cable television cable. Installed at each end of a length of coaxial cable (also called 10Base2 or thinnet), the BNC features a center pin (connected to the center conductor inside the cable) and a metal tube (connected to the outer cable shielding). A rotating ring on the metal tube turns to lock the male connector ends to any female connectors. See *10Base2.*

brownout: A drop in electrical voltage that can destroy a variety of computer components (hard drive, chips, and so on). You can prevent brownout damage by purchasing a voltage regulator. See *voltage regulator.*

bus: A slot on your computer's motherboard into which you insert cards, such as network interface cards. (Technically, the name of the slot is expansion slot, and the bus is the data path along which information flows to the card. However, the common computer jargon is bus.) See *network interface card.*

cable modem: A modem that connects to your cable television company's cable lines (but doesn't interfere with TV transmissions). Cable modems are significantly faster than standard modems but aren't yet available everywhere. Their speeds are measured in millions of bytes per second rather than in thousands of bytes per second like standard modem speeds. See *standard modem.*

client: A computer that uses hardware and services on another computer (called the host or server). Also called a *workstation.* See *host, client-server network.*

client/server network: A network scheme in which a main computer (called the host or server) supplies files and peripherals shared by all the other computers (called clients or workstations). Each user who works at a client computer can use the files and peripherals that are on his individual computer (called the local computer) or on the server. See *client, host, local computer.*

cluster: A unit of data storage on a hard or floppy disk.

coaxial cable: See *10Base2.*

computer name: A unique name assigned to a computer on a network to differentiate that computer from other computers on the network.

concentrator: The home base of a 10BaseT network to which all lengths of cable from the network computers are attached. (One end of each cable length attaches to the concentrator; the other end of each length attaches to a computer's network interface card.) Also called a *hub.* See *10BaseT, network interface card, star topology.*

defrag: To take fragments of files and put them together so that every file on a hard drive has all of its contents in one place. Defragging makes opening files a much faster process because the operating system doesn't have to look all over your hard drive for all the pieces of a file that you want to open.

Dial-Up Networking: A feature in Windows 98 and Windows 95 that enables your modem to dial out and connect to the Internet through an Internet service provider. See *Internet service provider.*

drivers: Software files that allow your operating system to communicate with hardware, such as network interface cards; or peripherals, such as printers.

EISA bus: EISA stands for Extended Industry Standard Architecture. Much less common than ISA and PCI buses, the EISA bus was developed as a 32-bit version (which means that it sends 32 bits of data at a time between the motherboard and the card and any device attached to the card) of the standard ISA bus. The EISA bus is faster than an ISA bus and was popular for several years. It isn't used in today's computers, but you may have EISA buses in older computers. See *bus, ISA bus, motherboard, PCI bus.*

embedded network card: A network card built into a computer's motherboard.

Ethernet: The most widely used of the several technologies available for cabling local area networks. See *local area network.*

evaluation software: A specially programmed version of commercial software. The software may stop working after a certain amount of time has elapsed or may be missing some features of the commercial version. See *freeware, shareware.*

expansion slot: A slot on your computer's motherboard into which you insert cards, such as network interface cards. See *motherboard, network interface card.*

FAT: FAT stands for File Allocation Table — an entry in the operating system that acts like an index or table of contents. The FAT keeps track of where all the fragments of a file are stored on a drive.

firewall: Software that protects a computer on the Internet from unauthorized, outside intrusion. Companies that have one or more servers exposed to the Internet use firewalls to allow only authorized employees access to the servers.

fish: Not a flounder, but a tool designed for fishing cable. A fish is used by electricians and is sold in hardware stores, but you can fashion a homemade version by untwisting a coat hanger and using the hook at the end of the hanger to grab the cable as you run it through your house.

freeware: Software that's free — use it as much as you like without paying anyone a dime. See *evaluation software, shareware.*

Home Phoneline Networking Alliance: An association working to ensure adoption of a single, unified home telephone line networking standard and to bring home telephone line networking technology to the market.

host: The main computer on a client/server network that supplies the files and peripherals shared by all the other computers. Also called a *server.* See *client/server network.*

hub: See *concentrator.*

I/O: Short for Input/Output. The process of transferring data to or from a computer. Some I/O devices only handle input (keyboards and mice); some handle only output (printers), and some handle both (disks).

install: To not only physically set up a device but to also set up the files (called drivers) that Windows needs to communicate with the device. See *drivers.*

Internet service provider (ISP): A company that provides Internet access to individuals and businesses.

IP: Short for Internet Protocol. The method by which data is sent from one computer to another computer on the Internet.

IP address: A number that identifies a computer's location on the Internet.

IRQ: Short for Interrupt Request. An assigned location in memory used by a computer device to send information about its operation. Because the location is unique, the computer knows which device is interrupting the ongoing process to send a message.

ISA bus: ISA (Industry Standard Architecture) is a standard bus that has been used for a number of years. It's a 16-bit card, which means that it sends 16 bits of data at a time between the motherboard and the card (and any device attached to the card). See *bus, EISA bus, motherboard, PCI bus.*

ISDN modem: A modem that offers faster transmission speeds than a standard modem. (ISDN stands for Integrated Services Digital Network, in case you were wondering.) The drawback is that an ISDN modem is generally more expensive than a standard modem and requires a special ISDN phone line (which is more expensive than a standard phone line).

jumper: A small piece of plastic in a network interface card that "jumps" across pins. Whether or not pins are "jumpered" determines IRQ and I/O settings for the NIC. See *I/O, IRQ, network interface card.*

LAN: See *local area network.*

Local area network: Two or more computers connected to one another so that they can share information and peripherals.

local computer: The computer you sit in front of when you access a remote computer. See *remote computer.*

local printer: A printer attached to the computer you're using.

mapping: To assign a drive letter to a shared resource on another computer to more easily access that shared resource. You can map another computer's drive, folder, or subfolder. The drive letter that you use becomes part of the local computer's set of drive letters. The drives you create are called *network drives.* See *local computer, network drive.*

Microsoft Backup: Backup software provided in Windows 98 and Windows 95. You can use it with floppy drives, network drives, removable drives, and tape drives.

modular duplex jack: A device that plugs into a telephone wall jack to convert that single telephone jack into two jacks so that you can plug in two phones, a phone and a modem, or — in the case of a telephone line network — a telephone and a telephone line network cable. Also called a *splitter.*

monochrome printer: A printer that prints in black and shades of gray (rather than a color printer, which prints in, well, colors). Some people call this a black and white printer, despite the fact that no white ink is involved.

motherboard: For a PC, a plane surface that holds all the basic circuitry.

multimedia PC: A PC that contains a CD-ROM drive, sound card, and speakers.

NetBIOS: Short for Network Basic Input/Output System. A software program that permits applications to communicate with other computers that are on the same cabled network.

network: Two or more computers connected to one another using network interface cards, cable, and networking software to communicate and exchange data. See *client/server network, local area network, network interface card, peer-to-peer network.*

network administrator: This is probably you if you're the one setting up your home PC network.

network drive: A drive that is located somewhere other than your local computer. See *local computer.*

network interface card: The primary hardware device for a network, a NIC attaches a computer to the network cable.

network printer: A printer attached to a remote computer on the network. (A printer attached to a local computer on the network is called a *local printer.*) See *local printer.*

network-ready computers: A new breed of computers that have telephone wiring adapters built into their motherboards for telephone line networking, eliminating the need to install telephone line networking NICs. See *motherboard, network interface card.*

network resource: A device located in a computer other than the local computer. See *local computer.*

NIC: See *network interface card.*

node: A connection point for distributing computer transmissions. Usually applied to computers that accept data from one computer and forward it to another computer.

packet: A chunk of information sent over a network.

parent-child relationship: If you share a hard drive, all the folders on that drive are shared. Folders are children of parent drives, and subfolders are children of parent folders. The most important thing to remember about this parent-child scheme is that all files are children (their folders are parents). When you configure folders as shares, you also configure the files contained in those folders as shares. You can interrupt this inheritance factor by changing the configuration of a child to be either more restrictive or less restrictive than its parent.

pathname: In DOS, a statement that indicates a filename on a local computer. When you use a pathname, you tell your computer that the target folder is on the local computer. Anyone working at another computer on the network must use a UNC statement to access that folder. See *local computer, UNC.*

PCI bus: PCI stands for Peripheral Component Interconnect. The PCI bus is built for speed and is found in most new computers. It comes in two configurations: 32-bit and 64-bit (32-bit means that the bus sends 32 bits of data at a time between the motherboard and the card; 64-bit means that the bus sends 64 bits of data at a time). Its technology is far more advanced — and complicated — than that of the ISA bus. See *bus, EISA bus, ISA bus.*

PCMCIA: A network interface card for a laptop computer. A PCMCIA is about the size of a credit card. See *network interface card.*

peer-to-peer network: A network in which all the computers communicate with each other — communication isn't limited to a client and a server. See *client, client/server network, network, server.*

peripheral: Any device connected to a computer: monitor, keyboard, removable drive, CD-ROM drive, scanner, speakers, and so on.

permission level: A setting that controls users' access to shared resources on a network. The person who creates a shared resource decides which type of permission level to grant, such as Read-Only, Full, or Depends on Password.

persistent connections: Mapped drives linked to a user (a logon name) rather than a computer. If multiple users share a computer, the mapped drives that appear are those created by the user who is currently logged on. See *mapping.*

Plug and Play: A software feature that reviews all the hardware in your computer during startup. When a new Plug and Play hardware component is detected, the software installation procedure begins automatically.

port: A connector located on the back of your computer into which you can plug a peripheral, such as a keyboard, mouse, printer, and so on.

print queue: The lineup of documents waiting to be printed.

print server: On a network, a computer to which a printer is attached.

print spooler: The place on your hard drive where printer jobs are lined up, waiting to be sent to the printer. See *print queue.*

profile: The computer environment that belongs to a particular user. A profile lets you personalize your Windows Desktop without risking ruin of your decorative efforts when the next person logs onto the computer.

protocol: Standardized rules for transmitting information. See *TCP/IP.*

proxy server: A server that acts in place of a client computer. For example, a proxy server performs all the functions of a Web browser for all the individual computers accessing the Internet. See *client.*

queue: The lineup of documents waiting to be processed — for example, the print queue is the lineup of documents waiting to go to the printer.

Registry: A database that keeps track of the configuration options for software, hardware, and other important elements of your Windows operating system.

remote computer: On a network, a computer other than the one you're working on.

remote user: A user who's accessing one computer but sitting in front of another computer.

RG-58 cable: The specific type of coaxial (10Base2) cable used in home networks. See *10Base2*.

RJ-11 connector: The connector at each end of a length of telephone cable for telephones and telephone line networking schemes.

RJ-45 connector: The connector at the end of 10BaseT cable — it looks like the connector at the end of your telephone cable, but it isn't the same thing. (Telephone connectors are called RJ-11 connectors.) See *10BaseT*.

root directory: A section of your hard drive that is not part of a directory (folder). It holds files needed for booting.

separator page: See *banner*.

server: See *host*.

shared resources: Files, folders, printers, and other peripherals attached to one computer on a network that have been configured for access by remote users on other computers on the network. See *remote user*.

shareware: Software that you use under an honor system — if you try it and like it, you should pay for it. See *evaluation software, freeware*.

shielded twisted pair cable: A type of 10BaseT cable. Metal encases the cable's wires, lessening the possibility of interference from other electrical devices, radar, radio waves, and so on. See *10BaseT*.

slot: See *expansion slot*.

sneakernet: The inconvenience you have when you don't bother setting up a network. With a sneakernet, information is exchanged between computers by copying files to a disk from one computer, walking to another computer (not necessarily wearing sneakers — you can wear your fuzzy pink bunny slippers and accomplish the task just as well), and then loading the files from the disk to the second computer.

splitter: See *modular duplex jack.*

standard modem: A modem whose speed is measured in thousands of bytes per second (Kbps) — 33.6 and 56 Kbps are common. See *ADSL modem, cable modem, ISDN modem.*

star topology: A 10BaseT network with multiple runs from the concentrator to each computer on the network, forming an arrangement that can resemble a star when several computers are used.

surge: A sudden spate of very high voltage that travels from the electrical lines to your house, and ultimately to your computer. A surge protector can help protect your computer equipment. See *surge protector.*

surge protector: A device that absorbs power surges so they don't travel to your computer. See *surge.*

system files: The files that Windows installs to make the operating system run.

T-connector: A T-shaped connector used to connect 10Base2 to a NIC on a network without interrupting the cable run. See *network interface card, 10Base2.*

TCP/IP: An acronym for Transmission Control Protocol/Internet Protocol, a set of standardized rules for transmitting information. TCP/IP enables Macintosh, IBM-compatible, UNIX, and other dissimilar computers to jump on the Internet and communicate with one another, as long as each computer uses TCP/IP.

terminator: A device with BNC connectors that lets you "cap off" the empty cross-bars of T-connectors at the beginning and end of a 10Base2 cable run. See *BNC connector, 10Base2, T-connector.*

thinnet: See *10Base2.*

topology: The way a network is laid out. See *star topology.*

twisted pair cable: See *10BaseT.*

UNC: Universal Naming Convention, a formatted style used to identify a particular shared resource on a particular remote computer. The format is \\computername\resourcename. See *pathname.*

uninterruptible power supply (UPS): A mega-battery that plugs into the wall outlet. You plug your computer and monitor into the UPS outlets. If power fails, your computer draws power from the battery to give you enough time to properly shut down your computer.

unshielded twisted pair: See *10BaseT.*

virtual drive: A drive that doesn't really exist — you add a new drive letter, but you don't add any new physical drives to a computer. See *mapping.*

voltage regulator: A device that constantly measures the voltage coming out of the wall and brings it to an acceptable minimum to protect against brownouts. See *brownout.*

Web interface: In Windows 98, or Windows 95 with Internet Explorer 4.0 installed, a graphical appearance that resembles the look of pages on the World Wide Web.

WinGate: A modem-sharing software application.

wizard: An interactive program that walks you through a software installation process.

workgroup: The group to which the computers on a network belong.

workstation: See *client.*

Y-connector: An adapter shaped like the letter Y that connects two devices to one input device. For example, you can use a Y-connector to connect both a modem and a telephone line NIC to a length of cable that's inserted in a wall jack for a telephone line network. The two ends at the top of the Y connect to the back of the computer (one end connects to the modem; the other connects to the NIC). The single end at the bottom of the Y connects the cable between the computer and the wall jack. See *NIC.*

Index

IDG Books Worldwide, Inc., End-User License Agreement

READ THIS. You should carefully read these terms and conditions before opening the software packet(s) included with this book ("Book"). This is a license agreement ("Agreement") between you and IDG Books Worldwide, Inc. ("IDGB"). By opening the accompanying software packet(s), you acknowledge that you have read and accept the following terms and conditions. If you do not agree and do not want to be bound by such terms and conditions, promptly return the Book and the unopened software packet(s) to the place you obtained them for a full refund.

1. **License Grant.** IDGB grants to you (either an individual or entity) a nonexclusive license to use one copy of the enclosed software program(s) (collectively, the "Software") solely for your own personal or business purposes on a single computer (whether a standard computer or a workstation component of a multiuser network). The Software is in use on a computer when it is loaded into temporary memory (RAM) or installed into permanent memory (hard disk, CD-ROM, or other storage device). IDGB reserves all rights not expressly granted herein.

2. **Ownership.** IDGB is the owner of all right, title, and interest, including copyright, in and to the compilation of the Software recorded on the disk(s) or CD-ROM ("Software Media"). Copyright to the individual programs recorded on the Software Media is owned by the author or other authorized copyright owner of each program. Ownership of the Software and all proprietary rights relating thereto remain with IDGB and its licensers.

3. **Restrictions on Use and Transfer.**

   (a) You may only (i) make one copy of the Software for backup or archival purposes, or (ii) transfer the Software to a single hard disk, provided that you keep the original for backup or archival purposes. You may not (i) rent or lease the Software, (ii) copy or reproduce the Software through a LAN or other network system or through any computer subscriber system or bulletin-board system, or (iii) modify, adapt, or create derivative works based on the Software.

   (b) You may not reverse engineer, decompile, or disassemble the Software. You may transfer the Software and user documentation on a permanent basis, provided that the transferee agrees to accept the terms and conditions of this Agreement and you retain no copies. If the Software is an update or has been updated, any transfer must include the most recent update and all prior versions.

4. **Restrictions on Use of Individual Programs.** You must follow the individual requirements and restrictions detailed for each individual program in Appendix B of this Book. These limitations are also contained in the individual license agreements recorded on the Software Media. These limitations may include a requirement that after using the program for a specified period of time, the user must pay a registration fee or discontinue use. By opening the Software packet(s), you will be agreeing to abide by the licenses and restrictions for these individual programs that are detailed in Appendix B and on the Software Media. None of the material on this Software Media or listed in this Book may ever be redistributed, in original or modified form, for commercial purposes.

5. **Limited Warranty.**

   (a) IDGB warrants that the Software and Software Media are free from defects in materials and workmanship under normal use for a period of sixty (60) days from the date of purchase of this Book. If IDGB receives notification within the warranty period of defects in materials or workmanship, IDGB will replace the defective Software Media.

   (b) **IDGB AND THE AUTHOR OF THE BOOK DISCLAIM ALL OTHER WARRANTIES, EXPRESS OR IMPLIED, INCLUDING WITHOUT LIMITATION IMPLIED WARRANTIES OF MER-CHANTABILITY AND FITNESS FOR A PARTICULAR PURPOSE, WITH RESPECT TO THE SOFTWARE, THE PROGRAMS, THE SOURCE CODE CONTAINED THEREIN, AND/OR THE TECHNIQUES DESCRIBED IN THIS BOOK. IDGB DOES NOT WARRANT THAT THE FUNCTIONS CONTAINED IN THE SOFTWARE WILL MEET YOUR REQUIREMENTS OR THAT THE OPERATION OF THE SOFTWARE WILL BE ERROR FREE.**

   (c) This limited warranty gives you specific legal rights, and you may have other rights that vary from jurisdiction to jurisdiction.

6. **Remedies.**

   (a) IDGB's entire liability and your exclusive remedy for defects in materials and workmanship shall be limited to replacement of the Software Media, which may be returned to IDGB with a copy of your receipt at the following address: Software Media Fulfillment Department, Attn.: *Networking Home PCs For Dummies,* IDG Books Worldwide, Inc., 7260 Shadeland Station, Ste. 100, Indianapolis, IN 46256, or call 800-762-2974. Please allow three to four weeks for delivery. This Limited Warranty is void if failure of the Software Media has resulted from accident, abuse, or misapplication. Any replacement Software Media will be warranted for the remainder of the original warranty period or thirty (30) days, whichever is longer.

   (b) In no event shall IDGB or the author be liable for any damages whatsoever (including without limitation damages for loss of business profits, business interruption, loss of business information, or any other pecuniary loss) arising from the use of or inability to use the Book or the Software, even if IDGB has been advised of the possibility of such damages.

   (c) Because some jurisdictions do not allow the exclusion or limitation of liability for conse-quential or incidental damages, the above limitation or exclusion may not apply to you.

7. **U.S. Government Restricted Rights.** Use, duplication, or disclosure of the Software by the U.S. Government is subject to restrictions stated in paragraph (c)(1)(ii) of the Rights in Technical Data and Computer Software clause of DFARS 252.227-7013, and in subparagraphs (a) through (d) of the Commercial Computer–Restricted Rights clause at FAR 52.227-19, and in similar clauses in the NASA FAR supplement, when applicable.

8. **General.** This Agreement constitutes the entire understanding of the parties and revokes and supersedes all prior agreements, oral or written, between them and may not be modified or amended except in a writing signed by both parties hereto that specifically refers to this Agreement. This Agreement shall take precedence over any other documents that may be in conflict herewith. If any one or more provisions contained in this Agreement are held by any court or tribunal to be invalid, illegal, or otherwise unenforceable, each and every other provision shall remain in full force and effect.

Installation Instructions

To install the items from the CD to your hard drive, follow these steps.

1. **Insert the CD into your computer's CD-ROM drive.**

2. **Choose Start⇨Run.**

3. **In the dialog box that appears, type** D:\SETUP.EXE.

   Replace *D* with the proper drive letter if your CD-ROM drive uses a different letter.

4. **Click OK.**

Now all you have to do is read the License Agreement, choose a software category that interests you, and then click the appropriate Install button for the software that you want to use.

For more information about using the CD, including detailed listings and descriptions of the software on the CD, see Appendix B.

YOUR ONLINE RESOURCE

WWW.DUMMIES.COM

Discover Dummies Online!

The Dummies Web Site is your fun and friendly online resource for the latest information about ...*For Dummies*® books and your favorite topics. The Web site is the place to communicate with us, exchange ideas with other ...*For Dummies* readers, chat with authors, and have fun!

Ten Fun and Useful Things You Can Do at www.dummies.com

1. Win free ...*For Dummies* books and more!
2. Register your book and be entered in a prize drawing.
3. Meet your favorite authors through the IDG Books Author Chat Series.
4. Exchange helpful information with other ...*For Dummies* readers.
5. Discover other great ...*For Dummies* books you must have!
6. Purchase Dummieswear™ exclusively from our Web site.
7. Buy ...*For Dummies* books online.
8. Talk to us. Make comments, ask questions, get answers!
9. Download free software.
10. Find additional useful resources from authors.

Link directly to these ten fun and useful things at **http://www.dummies.com/10useful**

SURF THE NET

WWW.DUMMIES.COM

For other technology titles from IDG Books Worldwide, go to **www.idgbooks.com**

Not on the Web yet? It's easy to get started with *Dummies 101*®: *The Internet For Windows*®*98* or *The Internet For Dummies*®*, 5th Edition,* at local retailers everywhere.

IDG BOOKS WORLDWIDE

Find other ...*For Dummies* books on these topics:

Business • Career • Databases • Food & Beverage • Games • Gardening • Graphics • Hardware
Health & Fitness • Internet and the World Wide Web • Networking • Office Suites
Operating Systems • Personal Finance • Pets • Programming • Recreation • Sports
Spreadsheets • Teacher Resources • Test Prep • Word Processing

IDG BOOKS WORLDWIDE
BOOK REGISTRATION

Register This Book and Win!

We want to hear from you!

Visit **http://my2cents.dummies.com** to register this book and tell us how you liked it!

✔ Get entered in our monthly prize giveaway.

✔ Give us feedback about this book — tell us what you like best, what you like least, or maybe what you'd like to ask the author and us to change!

✔ Let us know any other ...*For Dummies*® topics that interest you.

Your feedback helps us determine what books to publish, tells us what coverage to add as we revise our books, and lets us know whether we're meeting your needs as a ...*For Dummies* reader. You're our most valuable resource, and what you have to say is important to us!

Not on the Web yet? It's easy to get started with *Dummies 101*®: *The Internet For Windows*® *98* or *The Internet For Dummies*,® 5th Edition, at local retailers everywhere.

Or let us know what you think by sending us a letter at the following address:

...*For Dummies* Book Registration
Dummies Press
7260 Shadeland Station, Suite 100
Indianapolis, IN 46256-3945
Fax 317-596-5498

BESTSELLING BOOK SERIES FROM IDG